COME HERE OFTEN?

Published by Black Balloon Publishing
blackballoonpublishing.com

ISBN: 978-1-936787-22-7

Black Balloon Publishing titles are distributed to the trade by
Consortium Book Sales and Distribution
Phone: 800-283-3572 / SAN 631-760X

Library of Congress Control Number: 2014936999

Designed and composed by CDS | christopherdsalyers.com
Printed in Canada

9 8 7 6 5 4 3 2 1

COME HERE OFTEN?

53 WRITERS RAISE A GLASS TO THEIR FAVORITE BAR

EDITED *by* SEAN MANNING

FOREWORD *by* MALACHY MCCOURT

BLACK BALLOON PUBLISHING
NEW YORK

CONTENTS

Foreword
Malachy's (closed)
1076 Third Avenue
New York, New York 10065
Malachy McCourt

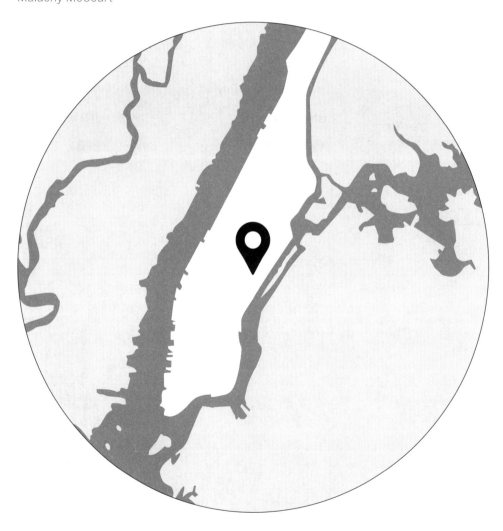

One friend said they are all shoeboxes varied in size. *They* being bars. Or sometimes called saloons, pubs, locals, drinking establishments, licensed premises, taverns, gin mills, grog shops, hosteleries, my office (wink, wink), joints, beer halls, etc. But all of them serve what is known as drink. Drink in this case means that which is alcoholic. This can be confusing to non-English-speaking folk as water is also a drink.

These shoeboxes have a door; and one wall usually covered by mirrors; and glass shelves holding a glistening array of bottles sporting multicolored labels announcing content; and usually a tabernacle-sized register and, protecting this sacred territory, a long counter called a bar with a serried line of barstools awaiting warm arses. All of which is presided over by usually a male but more lately a female who pours the drink, takes the money, makes the change, chats, wipes the bar top, bids farewell, greets arrivals, washes glasses, chops ice, answers the telephone, lies to various spouses seeking errant husbands.

Not all alcoholics are drunkards, and not all drunkards are alcoholics, but these folks generally speaking are not bar habitués. Economics play a large part in where one decides to drink. Usually the alcoholic beverage costs ten times more in a bar than if you buy a bottle and drink at home. So why drink in a bar? Because it's in the bar that you will find more misery than on your own ceiling, and false cheer is what you buy.

The Irish always used the pub as a sanctuary safe from female invasion. It was there that superior males held forth on the state of the world, the disrespect of the younger generation, the tyranny of women, the price of the pint. The decibel level was until recently a low murmur with no television, no jukebox, no radio to cause the raising of voices.

These days the man brings his mate and she is equally at home. Years ago women entered the pub at risk of losing their good name and were sequestered in a tiny, closed-off space called the snug. The snug is gone now. In England, head wardens would allow pubs inside British prisons and the more affluent prisoners could pop in for the refreshing draft. Conversely, some wardens who kept pubs were allowed to construct tiny prisons in the rear of their premises. Very civilized people the British.

In my native New York, I opened a saloon on 12 May 1959 that became the first so-called "singles bar" in New York if not in the USA. This was due to the proximity of the Barbizon Hotel for Women, whose denizens began wandering into Malachy's. And unlike at the old bastions of maleness along Third Avenue, these graceful young things were welcomed. It did not hurt business that Richard Harris, Richard Burton, Peter O'Toole, Alan Bates, and many more young actors from Ireland and the British Isles had made Malachy's their New York local. And like the hokey pokey, that's what it's all about.

If the joint is posing as a restaurant, food is of course important. If it's a pub then the alcohol plays a larger part. But the keeper of the bar and the wandering waitstaff are what counts. And above all, if you happen to be the owner you are perceived as a somewhat supreme being who bestows the blessing of recognition on those seeking refuge under your welcoming roof.

Keep perusing, dear reader, for further enlightenment. For it is here, in the following pages, that you will find out about things said, things done, things undone, and things unsaid.

Introduction
Sean Manning

I got the idea for this book in the summer of 2011, when within the span of a couple months, two of New York City's most iconic bars closed for good: Mars Bar and Elaine's. Opened in 1984, Mars Bar was legendary for its squalor; a graffiti-covered hovel in the East Village frequented by junkie punk rockers and surly old men, it got shuttered for endless health code violations, foremost a nasty fruit fly infestation. Located exactly 87 blocks north on Second Avenue, Elaine's—opened in 1963—was far more sophisticated. Its Upper East Side clientele were famous writers and actors, including Woody Allen, Norman Mailer, and George Plimpton. It closed for financial reasons, though coming just six months after the death of its 81-year-old proprietor and namesake, the boisterous Elaine Kaufman, it seemed as if the real cause was a broken heart, as if the bar was some elderly spouse that couldn't bear to go on after the passing of its betrothed.

I'd only been to Mars Bar once, unable to endure the potpourri of newly pissed jeans, cheap aftershave, and geriatric halitosis beyond a single beer. That still wasn't as putrid to me as the stench of pretension and old money that wafted from Elaine's, which is why I never even set foot in the joint. Yet their going out of business in such quick succession really bothered me. That summer also marked my ten-year anniversary of moving to New York and I was feeling awfully ruminative. I may not have cared for either bar, but they were a part of my New York, the city I'd fallen in love with, and way too much of that had been changing lately—the bars especially.

Everyone always talks about how Rudy Giuliani's "Quality of Life" crackdowns during his time as mayor devastated New York nightlife, particularly his enforcement of the long-ignored "cabaret law" left over from the Jazz Age, which requires bars to have a license if "three or more people are found dancing." (Still on the books, by the way.) But, in my opinion, Michael Bloomberg's City Hall tenure was just as disastrous to bars, if not more so. Yes, he got rid of smoking, and I admit I was a big fan of that move. Yet it was also thanks to Bloomberg that real estate prices got so ridiculously out of control. As a result, many bars shut down because they couldn't afford their skyrocketing rent, while others closed because their owners sold the building and made a bundle.

Several of these bars had been important to me.

Telephone Bar, in the East Village, was where I had my first beer in New York.

A&M Roadhouse, in TriBeCa, was right around the corner from the office and kitchen of the catering company where I worked for more than ten years. It was where we waiters would go drink after jobs, once we'd returned the coolers and rolling racks to the kitchen. We were all aspiring artists of some kind—writers, actors, filmmakers, musicians—and at some point we got the idea to make a low-budget movie together. When we needed a place to shoot a bar scene, we asked the owner of A&M. We'd never talked to him before, but he gave us the keys and let us open up early one Saturday and film there—no charge.

One of my most memorable nights in New York was drinking in the cocktail lounge of the Times Square Howard Johnson's, sitting in a booth and watching the jazz band of another catering buddy who was a saxophonist—the whole place flooded with orange light from the HoJo's neon sign outside.

Then there was the Cedar Tavern, a few blocks north of Washington Square Park. It was arguably the most famous bar in New York, for all the legendary writers and artists who drank there, Jack Kerouac and Jackson Pollack among them. But it was special to me because it's where some classmates and I from The New School graduate

fiction writing program—the reason I'd come to New York—would go after our weekly workshop. When we first started going there, we'd only talk about writing and books. But more and more we began talking about ourselves, our hometowns, and our families, until eventually we were discussing everything but literary matters. We'd become genuine friends, in some cases lovers. And, for at least one night, fighters: on the sidewalk outside the Cedar Tavern was where I got into my first and only fistfight. It wasn't much of one. The guy was completely shitfaced, and I got lucky—lucky to have clipped him square on the chin and lucky that he didn't hurt himself when he dropped to the pavement. But that's not what I remember most about that night. It was seeing one of my classmates—to this day one of my best friends—standing nearby, slinging off his backpack and readying himself to take on my foe's friend, even though this guy had a good four inches on my buddy and twice the reach. A few years later, a few of us from that workshop tromped to the Cedar Tavern from The New School writing building one last time. It was a weekday, early in the afternoon. We'd just attended a small memorial service of the most beloved member our group, who'd died of AIDS. I hadn't spoken to him since we'd graduated but he was a good man and had once been an important part of my life, and it meant a great deal returning to that place to share a drink and some stories with those old friends.

Those bars are gone. I cannot revisit them, never again push through their doors and bask in the memories, never be reminded of the person I'd once been and perhaps gain a little insight about the person I'd since become. I'm a sentimental bastard—I'll be the first to admit it. Some people go to bars to forget. I go to bars to remember.

Mars Bar and Elaine's wouldn't be the last casualties before Bloomberg left office: Lenox Lounge, Holiday Cocktail Lounge, Blarney Cove, Max Fish, Bill's Gay Nineties, The Rawhide. More than three centuries of combined history. . . Poof. Gone. Keyser Söze'd.

This being New York, the media capital of the world, most of these bars received lengthy eulogies in the press; Elaine's garnered remembrances in multiple print editions of *The New York Times* as well as at the Web sites of *Esquire*, *Vanity Fair*, and ESPN's *Grantland*. But what about bygone bars in other parts of the country—in other parts of the world, at that? Didn't they deserve similar homage? Wouldn't it be fun and moving to read about those places? And why limit it to defunct bars? Why not celebrate those still in business as well?

Because there damn sure are of a lot of them these days. Despite my grousing, the statistics argue that New York bars actually flourished under Mayor Bloomberg. For instance, in the month of September 2013, the city reported 106 applications submitted for liquor licenses—and that was only in the Brooklyn neighborhoods of Williamsburg and Greenpoint. It isn't just New York that's bar crazy, either; in fact, in a 2013 survey of bars per capita in U.S. cities, conducted by data collecting service Infogroup Targeting Solutions, New York didn't even make the top ten. (Pittsburgh ranked first.) The foodie culture that has run rampant in America for the last decade or so—spawning countless TV cooking competitions, gourmet food trucks, bestselling chef memoirs, and #foodporn Instagrams—has unequivocally extended to drinking. Gastropubs offering dozens of on-tap microbrews, faux-speakeasies featuring $12 bespoke cocktails over hand-cut ice, and European-derived beer gardens insisting on a special stein for each varietal of hefeweizen continue popping up around the country. As of September 2013, according to *USA Today*, there were more breweries operating in the United States—over 2,500—than at any time in history, and another 1,600-plus were in the planning stages. Meanwhile, the *Lexington Herald-Leader* reported in December 2013 that Kentucky's bourbon industry is, "in the middle of its biggest expansion since Prohibition, building $300 million in new distilleries, warehouses, and tourist centers, and filling a million barrels annually." Also last year, the Chinese government relaxed restrictions on the importing of higher-methanol alcohol in order to receive top-shelf tequila from

Mexico; China is expected to bring in more than 10 million liters of the stuff over five years.

If you ask me, the ongoing bar boom is owed in large part—perhaps even entirely—to social media; Netflix, Apple TV, and other streaming entertainment; and online shopping. Seriously, what the hell do you need to leave your house for anymore? The bar is one of the last bastions of genuine human interaction. "Public houses" they were once called; it's a moniker that seems more and more deserving to be revived.

But with so many bars these days, how do you choose? What makes a bar so great that you want to go back night after night until ultimately you're bestowed with that most honorific designation of *the regular?*

Each contributor in this collection offers a different opinion. For Neal Pollack, it's colorful staff and customers. For Andrew W.K., it's conscientious but not overbearing bartenders. For Bill Barich, it's standoffish bartenders ultimately won over. Same for Elissa Schappell—plus a kick-ass jukebox. For Paul Shirley, it's a chance at anonymity. For Duff McKagan, it's anonymity and great chili. For J. Maarten Troost, it's the view. For Hunter R. Slaton, it's the potential for mild danger after a long day's work. For Adam Ross, it's expertly mixed drinks. For Rosie Schaap, it's the challenge of better understanding an entire culture. For Robert Perišić, it has not a little to do with the bar stools. For Heather Havrilesky, it's all of these things combined: "Not the sweet hoppy nectars, not the décor, not the bartender's easy, rambling acceptance, but some strange blend of all of the above . . . they form a weird kind of poetry, a familiar landing spot for the senses."

Now New York has a new mayor, Bill de Blasio. As of this writing, he's only been on the job for a month. While I'm hopeful he'll deliver on his campaign platform of reducing the city's enormous wealth gap, that great financial divide that forced so many bars to take down their shingle, so far he isn't off to a great start. Just last week, another classic Manhattan bar, Milady's, closed its doors after seventy-odd years on the same Soho corner. A writer for *The New York Times* who was there the final night reported the following:

> Robert Orlando, 70, who grew up in the neighborhood, traveled down from Yonkers, as he has every Saturday night. "I was a regular as a kid," he said. "At 16, I had my first beer here. My friends would ask, 'Why do you come down there all the time?' It's just home. It's like coming home."

Exactly.

DIVES

THERE IS NOTHING WHICH HAS YET BEEN CONTRIVED BY MAN, BY WHICH SO MUCH HAPPINESS IS PRODUCED AS BY A GOOD TAVERN OR INN.

—SAMUEL JOHNSON

Spotty's (closed)
4141 Mayfield Road
South Euclid, Ohio 44121
Scott Raab

The name of the place was Spotty's. It sat in the middle of a block near the intersection of Mayfield Road and Warrensville Center Road in South Euclid, Ohio, a few miles east of Cleveland. Those weren't mean streets, except in the sense of undifferentiated middle-middle-class drab, and Spotty's wasn't truly a dive. By day, it was a small, slow neighborhood bar, mainly empty; at night, it picked up, thanks to John Carroll University students.

I was not one of them. I had left college behind in 1971, and, inspired by Charles Bukowski, decided to major in Bum Studies. I had a gift for it. I hitchhiked to Los Angeles, worked a few months as a general laborer chopping weeds in the yard of a jet-engine shop, panhandled for a week or two more, borrowed airfare from my mommy, and flew back to Cleveland, where I got a job selling men's shoes, on and off, at a store in Cleveland Heights that was turning from Jewish to black.

Mainly I drank—dollar wine, Jim Beam when I had a few more bucks—and smoked pot and took pills. I had a bedroom at a house a couple of blocks from the shoe store, with three other guys, one of whom was an old friend. They were two or three years older, college grads, guys with a plan, who drove decent cars and went out on dates with women. I had a salt-rotted '65 Bel Air that cost $150, no dates, no plan, and, after a few months and a screaming match with the owner of the shoe store over me demanding a Saturday off—by far the store's busiest day, which is exactly why I didn't want to be there—I also had no job.

The guys at the house were too kind to toss me out while I made a pretense each morning of looking at the *Plain Dealer* want ads. When the rent came due, I asked them to carry me, and they did, but as the months went by, of necessity they found someone able to pay rent, and kindly moved me to the sofa in the living room. The groceries I ate were theirs.

Fine by me. The fungal sofa, Vietnam, living off the other guys, Richard Nixon—it was all good. I simply did not care when I woke up, and in a matter of minutes after I woke up, I was too fucked up to care. I didn't read the paper or watch the news on TV; I wrote horrible poetry and blacked out. What cash I had I swiped from underneath the dining-room table pad at my grandmother's house a few minutes' away. She knew it was me—I had the house key and I knew which nights she worked at the bakery—so she kept it coming, ten and twenty bucks at a time.

After I turned 21, in August of '73, one of the guys in the house—he was in law school, paying his way by tending bar—set me up to talk with Spotty about a job; he had worked there before moving on to better joints, and he figured I could handle it. Spotty was old—at least as old as I am now, which would put him north of 60. His real name was Meyer Fleischer, and back in the '40s and '50s, he owned a joint in Cleveland proper, in the vicinity of East 105th Street and Euclid Avenue, which was then the commercial heart of a Jewish neighborhood. I know this much because when I came in to talk about the job and told him my name, he asked if I was any relation to Doc Raab, a physician whose office was at 105th and Euclid in those days, until he was arrested for performing abortions, convicted of income-tax evasion, and sent to prison. He was also my grandfather.

That was pedigree enough for Spotty. He wasn't worried about my lack of experience, because his customers didn't order mixed drinks more complex than a Screwdriver or Rusty Nail. He needed me three or four shifts a week and he paid me three or four bucks an hour. He called me The Boy Wonder, and not in a nice way. Spotty wasn't nice—he was big,

bald, rat-faced, and gruff. An old-school Jew, remnant of a vanished yore. I liked him a hell of a lot more than he liked me.

I liked his wife, too. Penny was a vintage broad, the kind of broad who referred to herself as a broad—a bottle-blond at least as old as Spotty, but still curvy, put and kept together by her makeup, her high heels, her skin-tight outfits, and a mouth more bawdy than foul. She didn't exactly flirt; she'd simply ask if I had yet encountered what she referred to as a *snapping pussy*. (I had not and have not.) Maybe Penny was mocking me and I was too slow to know it. I wasn't good with women. I didn't flirt; I yearned. In an era rife with easy sex, I'd never gotten laid. Oh, I'd gotten close enough to come in my pants, to be sure. A few times. But never laid.

I wasn't much good at bartending, either. I couldn't hide behind the bar, so I had to at least pretend to be friendly to every asshole I served. It was against the rules to drink at work, but I wasn't a social drinker anyway; I preferred to get hammered at home, alone on the cheap. I was a thief, thoroughly crooked—I stole from the till at the shoe store, and often cut side-deals with customers to undercharge them in exchange for a cash kickback—but there was squat to steal at Spotty's, no way to nip the register with him standing right at the end of the bar near the front door, and Penny on her stool at the far end, by the grill.

Truth to tell, I can't recall one moment at Spotty's when I didn't loathe the job and the joint. It was far worse than selling shoes. Selling shoes meant outsmarting a customer, convincing him that he looked pimp-slick in a pair of platform boots that would shame a blind hooker. Mixing another 5pm CC-and-soda for the tile-store salesman moaning over his wife's swollen cankles was no challenge; the challenge was not killing him, and myself, rather than listen to another soul-murdering word of it.

Even tougher were the nights—especially Friday and Saturday, when I always worked, hating every punk-ass college student who walked in for a greasy half-pound Spottyburger and a bottle of Stroh's. But the toughest part of the job was hearing "Benny and the Jets" played forty or fifty times night after night on Spotty's jukebox. Fuck Elton John. To this day, I can't listen to a goddamn note he's ever recorded.

And yet, so many years later—verily, unto this day—the same truths my time at Spotty's taught have served to guide and to gird me as a writer and as a man:

1. Poetry is where you find it.
2. It may not turn out to be poetry. Unless you're Beckett.
3. If you're going to marry a woman, try to marry one with good ankles.
4. Fuck Elton John.

For the life of me, I can't recall whether I quit after a few months or got fired. There was an issue about cleaning up on Sunday mornings: Spotty wanted me to come in and do it, while I preferred not to mop the floors or scrub Saturday night's caked vomitus off the bathroom thrones. To surrender my delicacy and my pride—to so disempower my inner bum—was a choice I refused to make.

There followed other, briefer jobs at other, less dingy bars—the Red Bull Inn, at Shaker Square; the James Tavern out on Chagrin Boulevard, whose Colonial Virginia theme required me to wear a get-up that included breeches, knee-high white hose, and a vest; and, at last, a single career-ending shift at another Chagrin Boulevard hothouse called, with no hint of irony, A Touch of Class, whose patrons' cocaine-and-gold-chain style and sensibility clashed with my own. After that, I got a job up the street at Sonitrol Security Systems, working the graveyard shift alone, monitoring sound-security alarms scattered across metro Cleveland until morning dawned or I passed out. It was, unlike Spotty's, a BYOB gig.

Dirty Franks
347 S 13th Street
Philadelphia, Pennsylvania 19107
Josh Emmons

What do Aretha Franklin, Frankie Avalon, Frankenstein, Frank Zappa, Frank Sinatra, St. Francis of Assisi, Frank Gehry, pre-euro French currency, and Major League Baseball Hall of Famer Frank Thomas all have in common? Their pictures are painted in a mural on the exterior of Dirty Franks, a bar at 13th and Pine streets in Center City Philadelphia. Does this mean that their music is played or their philosophy followed or their athleticism imitated or their monstrosity forgiven on the inside? No. It just means that Lou Silverman, who opened the place as "Franks" on November 8, 1933—27 days before Prohibition was repealed ("How did he know?" the bar's website asks)—sold it to a guy named Frank Vigderman, who didn't take showers. Is the bar dirty? Yes, but not because its floors are sticky or its beer mugs are crusty or its patrons have open sores on their mouths. It's dirty in a "the underwear flowing out of that woman's pants has alligators on it" and "one of those people is about to go down on the other" and "health inspectors must be shocked they never find anything here, like UN weapons inspectors looking for Iraqi weapons of mass destruction in 2002" kind of way. In other words, it's a good dirty that acknowledges and embraces the fact that human nature is messy and ruled by strong urges.

I've been going to Dirty Franks to drink cheap beer since 2007, when I moved from Portland, Oregon, to Philadelphia. My wife had just gotten a job in the area, and, having grown up on the West Coast and never lived in the East, I needed to find a comfort zone. An old college friend who'd coincidentally landed in the city a few months earlier took me there on a hot August night—our eight or nine pitchers made the heat bearable but destroyed me for days afterward—because it had a reputation as an authentic dive bar. That it was and still is both authentic and well-known is surprising, because when semi-professionals with down-market needs find out about such bars they often descend on them like locusts, displacing the native population and destroying the very quality that drew them there in the first place. Not so with Dirty Franks, which has kept its stripes because, like all real dive bars, it doesn't care what other people think. The ownership has changed hands a few times since Frank Vigderman died, but it hasn't forgotten that people take showers not to ward off disease, but because they want to impress others. And that this is bullshit.

Dirty Franks is classic Dive Deco. Booths line either side of the room, and in the middle there's a horseshoe-shaped bar that can seat fifteen. You walk in and see a jukebox on the right and a rarely-played *Sopranos*-themed pinball machine in a far corner. There's bric-a-brac on the walls: framed photographs of people no one knows anymore, bicycle wheel hubs, broken TV screens, curated exhibition paintings, sports pennants, Will Rogers quotations, a dartboard, Little League trophies, an American flag, and neon Yuengling signs. When things get seasonal, tinsel and paper snowflakes hang down from the ceiling, or shamrocks, or turkeys. There's space

I usually go to Dirty Franks with small groups of people—my friends are all writers, therapists, or healthcare workers these days—but sometimes I go by myself to talk to strangers about the things that preoccupy Philadelphia: its crime, its cultural renaissance, its disappointing sports teams, its rabid sports fans, its pollution, its rudeness, its honesty, its political corruption, its good restaurants, its thuggish unions, its racial disharmony, its bridges, its famously fucked-up New Jersey neighbor Camden, its pinched-nose accent, its track suits, the redneck stretch

YOU CAN YELL AND SPILL HALF A PITCHER OF BEER AND FALL ON THE FLOOR, AND THEY WON'T KICK YOU OUT.

for bands to play, but few do. Instead the music comes from the jukebox or a boombox behind the bar. This music can be sublime—the Fall followed by Lee Hazlewood followed by Bessie Smith—or it can be difficult. I was there once when "Doctor! Doctor!" by the Thompson Twins played all night. Over and over again, *Doctor, doctor! Can't you see I'm burning, burning?* It wasn't ironic. It was a cry of pain, and we all felt it. (A smartphone side note: none of the three members of the Thompson Twins was a twin or named Thompson.)

between it and Pittsburgh called Pennsyltucky. If someone's new to Philadelphia, they'll want to hear about the Mummers Parade, a kind of joyless Mardi Gras held on January 1 in which men dressed up in what look like killer clown outfits—these guys are called "fancies" and supposedly carry on an old Swedish tradition—march through the city dancing with umbrellas, some wearing blackface, some playing brass instruments, all creating a disturbing spectacle that, thank God, the rest of the country doesn't know about.

The bartenders at Dirty Franks are a mix of aloof tattooed South Philly gearheads and glue huffers, witches, redheads, professional alcoholics, and guest lecturers. They can be sour and humorless, but they never ignore you when you need a drink, and they tolerate a lot. You can yell and spill half a pitcher of beer and fall on the floor, and they won't kick you out. You can ask for endless quarters for the pinball machine—the bar is still cash only—and they'll give them to you. You can drunkenly say that the Kenzinger on tap, a popular, locally made beer, tastes like horse piss and they'll forgive you.

Is Dirty Franks a good citizen of the community? Yes. It sponsors softball, kickball, and two darts teams (both in the Olde English Dart League of Philadelphia). Whenever I'm there and hear about one of these teams' victories, I decide I'm going to join. That I don't later do this makes sense, because by that time I'll be at home or work, and like Hamlet I will have, wherefore I know not, lost all my mirth. After a couple of drinks at Dirty Franks, though, anything seems possible, and I feel good about my decision to remain in the city when lots of my peers have left for the suburbs or farms or small towns where housing is cheap and the air is clean and everyone has more in common than not. This is what I love about Dirty Franks, the way it validates your life by lifting your mood above the gray morass it was in before you walked into it. *Yes*, it says to

you, *you are 40 years old and softer than you used to be, and weaker and slower and less resilient and more reliant on comfort and quiet, and you might question your commitment to the expansive, low-carbon-footprint, architecturally invigorating, complicated matrix that is the American city today, because along with those things you get congestion and noise and danger and uncertainty, but you've made the right decision to live here. Resist the siren song of the Main Line's leafy neighborhoods. Say no to the isolation and paranoia of small towns out west. Embrace the dirt of here and now.*

Yet all this might change. Philadelphia isn't what it was in the 1980s, a prime example of the embattled and broken East Coast, which, to a native Californian like me, was frightening and fascinating. It is becoming a gentrified place where the mayor no longer bombs citizens (in 1981, a black nationalist organization in West Philly called MOVE was blown up, and one of its members, Mumia Abu Jamal, was thrown in jail for killing a cop), but instead wins federal development grants and presides over two booming industries (education and healthcare), and watches as Comcast builds the tallest building in America outside of New York City and Chicago. Dirty Franks' neighborhood used to be called Washington Square West, when it was rough enough to be part of the story of Philadelphia's insanely high murder rate, for which the city was dubbed "Killadelphia." But then, following a now-predictable cultural script, it cleaned itself up to become the "Gayborhood," and is now the sparkling and dynamic "Midtown Village."

To keep up, will Dirty Franks replace the kitschy Americana and eclectic art and battered beer taps with exposed piping and Twombly silk-screens and single-malt scotch stations? Will Lee Hazlewood and the Thompson Twins be jettisoned in favor of innovative elevator music? Will patrons have silkier hair and svelter bodies and more balanced politics? It's possible.

After all, in 1977 Woody Allen could ask a friend in *Annie Hall*: "Don't you see the rest of the country looks upon New York like we're left-wing, Communist, Jewish, homosexual pornographers?" Who in their right mind could say that now? I can imagine a future Dirty Franks that is as quiet, tasteful, and sexless as the mannequin ware-houses that call themselves bars in New York's Meatpacking District. But dystopias are always easier to picture than the more-likely reality. I suspect that Dirty Franks will soldier on and make small, almost imperceptible upgrades to make up for the natural wear and tear of life. Like the rest of us.

IF YOU MAKE YOUR PLEASURE DEPEND
ON DRINKING GOOD WINE, YOU CONDEMN
YOURSELF TO THE PAIN OF SOMETIMES
DRINKING BAD WINE. WE MUST HAVE A
LESS EXACTING AND FREER TASTE. TO BE
A GOOD DRINKER, ONE MUST NOT HAVE
SO DELICATE A PALATE.

—MICHEL DE MONTAIGNE

The Blarney Stone (closed)
795 Eighth Avenue
New York, New York 10019
Dan Fante

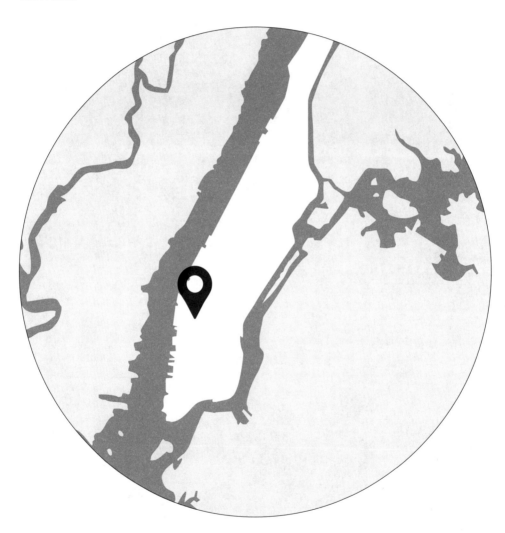

Driving a taxi in New York City is no cakewalk. I did the gig off and on for about seven years. The money was decent—a few hundred a week—but the shifts were ten to twelve hours, six days a week. That left little time for an aspiring writer/actor, so almost all of my creative interests were attended to at night—including my drinking.

It was the late '70s. I'd had a small success with a play I'd written and from that had come an acting group I called The Dante Theatre Group. I was the 29-year-old director even though my writing-acting resume consisted of only one college drama workshop and that one play after eight years.

The group rehearsed on Monday, Wednesday, and Friday nights at The Broadway Arts Studios on 56th Street. I had written a second play and was trying to get backing for it while my taxi gig paid for the rehearsal studio and the advertising and materials.

One night a few months after I'd formed the group and finished writing half the new play, I met a guy in the Broadway Arts lobby. His name was Bobby Wright and he called himself a music producer/songwriter. His day gig was managing a restaurant in Times Square. On weekends he was a disc jockey at WHBI, a radio station on the upper West Side. He'd been at the Broadway Arts rehearsing singers for a soul album he was producing and his rehearsal schedule overlapped mine three nights a week.

After bumping into each other for a month or so, and after he'd sat in on a couple of my rehearsals, and after we'd spent a few late nights around the corner at The Blarney Stone bar on Eighth Avenue pounding beers and shots, one night Bobby made me an offer: "I've got an hour a week of free airtime, and you've got an acting group. Why don't you do some live theatre on the air?"

Monday and Wednesday nights were two-for-one at The Stone and Bobby and I began to have our business/brainstorming sessions there while we drank. In those days The Stone catered to working class guys—serious drinkers mostly. It had a forty-foot long bar and half a dozen formica tables and chairs. There were old photographs of World War II generals and Fiorello LaGuardia and Babe Ruth hugging Lou Gehrig and large, dust-covered three-leaf clovers and an American flag tacked to the wall. You could almost never hear the jukebox. In truth the joint wasn't really a bar—it was a saloon.

It was north of Times Square but it still had its fair share of street people and Midtown hustlers because it was also near the seedy Eighth Avenue subway station. The place usually had three or four fights a week. The guy behind the bar most nights was named Mitch. Mitch was a big dude and went over two-fifty. He'd once been a minor league baseball catcher. His back-up was a sawed-off baseball bat that he kept under the bar, and when disagreements broke out big Mitch usually sided with his regulars. And soon enough Bobby and I had become regulars.

Bobby had a good gig that paid decently and most nights he picked up our tab. His airtime on WHBI was from midnight to four in the morning on Sunday. The Dante Theatre Group's first live radio show aired about a month later but immediately ran into a glitch: The station manager began to insist that I obtain written permission to broadcast copyrighted work. I had no time during the day to interrupt my driving schedule and park my cab and stop at publishing houses in Midtown to fill out a gazillion permission forms. Screw that! A week later, live theatre on Manhattan radio died a quick death.

But that didn't stop me. As a New York City cabbie and former street peddler, I could smell a good hustle. The new play I was writing was about a drug dealer in Brooklyn named The Swan. Seven of the actors I was rehearsing were black, so I decided, for convenience sake, that the show should feature an all-black cast.

A few nights later at The Stone I proposed another idea to Bobby: "How about a radio drama? Maybe a black kind-of James Bond character. I can write it on Monday nights and me and the cast can rehearse it during the week, then do it live on Sunday nights."

He looked me up and down and said, "Hey Danny, I'm a player. You think you can pull it off?"

I remember being well-fortified and fearless that night and without hesitation I told Bobby that I already had the first two episodes written but I'd forgotten to bring them with me. Two weeks later, Smoke was born: "He came from the festering volcano of humanity that is New York City. Crime was his target and trouble was his business. They called him Smoke but his game was fire!"

The show ran for six months on WHBI but the station was a small FM station with a limited audience. It was then picked up by WBLS, which at the time was the biggest black AM R&B radio station in America. At WHBI I'd already found two sponsors and was even taking home a few hundred a week as the writer/director/

announcer but soon my income from the gig would double.

Now my visits to The Stone became nightly. But because of my hangovers, at least once a week I began missing my ride to the taxi garage with Sid, another driver who lived in Williamsburg and drove to work across the Manhattan Bridge. Our deal was that he would pick me up if he saw me on my corner at 5:15 in the morning.

Then, a few weeks into the new show, the program director of WBLS left me a message on my home phone asking me to come down to the station and discuss the potential of a daily series. My ratty studio apartment was in the Alphabet City section of the East Village, and I remember pouring myself a fresh bourbon and Coke, then going to the window that looked out on First Avenue and yelling, "Holy shit, I've just hit the big time!"

A few days later a tentative deal was made: I'd write and produce the program and continue to be the announcer. The show would be aired five afternoons a week for ten minutes—just before the six o'clock news. That night Bobby and I hit The Stone and closed the place. Drinks all around from midnight on.

Three months later the name Smoke was written in graffiti on hundreds of New York City subway walls, and it was time for me and Bobby to re-negotiate our deal with WBLS.

The afternoon we met with the radio syndication team, Bobby and I had reserved the back room at The Blarney Stone. It was four o'clock and Mitch's shift had just started. I was well-oiled from a pre-meeting celebration with my partner and a couple of the show's cast members.

Half an hour into the meeting, after fish and chips, and hearing their excitement about the rebirth of radio drama in America and the network TV potential of *Smoke* and the fifty-station syndication, one of the guys in the suits pulled out a contract from his briefcase and low-balled me and Bobby. The offer was twice what we were currently being paid but less than ten percent of the nationwide projected revenue.

The loud conversation I had with one of the suits contained the use of the word fuck at least fifty times and, after hearing the breaking of glass and me yelling, Mitch appeared at the doorway with the baseball bat to recommend that I shut my goddamn mouth or he'd shut it for me.

Two days later I was back in my cab. I was no longer in the radio business and I was asked not to return to The Blarney Stone.

But that was just the beginning of the end.

The Pig's Ear Tavern
144 Brock Street
Peterborough, Ontario K9H 2P3, Canada
Craig Davidson

The Pig's Ear Tavern—also known as The Piggie, or simply The Pig—was your quintessential "warm-up bar." We all know the one, don't we? As an undergrad at Trent University, it was the bar that bridged the dormitory pre-gaming and the late-night clubbing. Like a can opener or a shovel, The Pig was built to do one thing, sell cheap suds, and it did so admirably. The Pig never aspired to be anything other than what it was. I appreciated that.

The bar sits on the corner of George and Brock streets in downtown Peterborough, Ontario, kitty-corner to the local YMCA and not far from a Catholic church, so you can always stop in for a quickie absolution before continuing on to the fleshpits downtown. The Pig is totally unspectacular—which, in a bizarro kind of way, makes it supremely spectacular. The façade is whitewashed brick covered in piss-yellow water stains. You enter through a black pressed-wood door with duct tape at every corner, the kind of backstage door you can imagine roadies shouldering through bearing amps and guitars. The high popcorn ceiling has the kind of checkerboard tile you'd find in a Legion Hall. The walls are covered in lacquered pine, giving the joint the look of your great-uncle's rec room. Pretty much all the tables are two-tops, but each is surrounded by four chairs. This works at the Pig, because nobody orders food. Aside from pickled eggs, pickled sausages, and bags of chips clipped to clothespins behind the bar, there ain't a damn thing to eat. Those two-tops do a dandy job of accommodating the pint glasses, the odd highball glass, and the omnipresent "trays" that the Pig is locally famous for—twenty eight-ounce beers for twenty bucks.

A pool table is jammed into one corner; there are a few warped cues you can use, as well as "Old Stumpy," a short-assed stick you'll need for tricky shots where the walls rule out the use of a regulation cue. The balls are so chipped from caroms across the floor that you can't trust the angles they'll play. It's generally best to avoid pool, anyway: gentlemanly billiard disagreements are the leading cause of fistfights at The Pig. Although if you have a mind to start trouble, you can be sure one of the middle-aged bartenders will encourage you to "take it outside"—which, Peterborough being northerly-situated, means that as often as not you'll be scrapping in the snow.

THE PIG'S EAR TAVERN, PETERBOROUGH, ONTARIO

To the right of the pool table are the shitters, and to the right of that is a bar rail with five or six padded stools. The liquor selection is miserly, but this is a college bar—ain't nobody ordering Tanqueray 10 or Lagavulin. When I went to school, The Pig had exactly one draft spigot. I couldn't tell you what beer it was; probably Labatt's Blue. To be honest, the brand hardly mattered. It was "tray" beer: dirt cheap, sorta sudsy, and eminently drinkable once you had a bellyful of it.

You couldn't run a tab at The Pig. That wasn't surprising at the time; as a 19-year-old, the idea of getting a short-term loan or being "good" for anything financially-related was an absurdity. I didn't expect the convenience store owner to run me a tab for a bag of chips, so why would I expect a bartender to do the same? The Pig remains a pay-as-you-go, cash n' carry joint. The staff is friendly and cool but they've suffered too many drink n' dashes to tender the civilities that prevail at your more upmarket establishments.

A compelling social experiment occurred just about every night at The Pig. Peterborough's a blue-collar town. After the shift whistle blew, the working Joes from Quaker Oats, General Electric, and the paper mill would stop in to, as they might say, "blow the foam off a few wobbly pops." They'd come in pairs or often alone, Caterpillar workboots clomping on the floor. They'd sit two to a table or take the stools along the bar and had the run of the joint until seven o'clock or so. Then the first students started trickling in. Like many towns, the locals and the students had an uneasy relationship. The locals saw us as haughty pissants slumming on our mommy and daddy's coin. And we generally viewed the townies as dead-enders whose lives were hemmed in by gray factory walls—an outlook that fairly branded us as haughty pissants.

As the night wore on, the student numbers skyrocketed. On a typical Friday night, the place would be a sea of (ironic) flannel come eight o'clock. The working Joes would clamp tight to their stools—*Steady on, boyos; we can't let these jumped-up jackholes push us out of our own goddamn bar!*—but it'd soon dawn that they'd lost the battle, for that night at least. Staring razorblades and mumbling curses, they'd abandon their perches and head off to bars like The Montreal House or The Tradewinds, where students wouldn't dare show their pimply faces.

Like I said, The Pig was a warm-up bar. Most nights began in the residence rooms—or in later years, the family room of a rented house—with beers, wine, maybe a few tequila poppers. In our sophomore year, my buddies and I discovered something called Bull Max, which was just about the closest thing to malt liquor you could get in Canada. It came in a 40-ounce bottle, with an alcohol content of 7-point-something. Two bottles led to corrosive intoxication, but one . . . one gave you a nice, swell buzz.

The night would get its legs. Inevitably one of us would flash a twenty, Mister Big Shot, and order The Pig's famous tray. The twenty beers would show up on that huge beaten-tin tray, sort of like you'd use to serve an enormous deep-dish pizza. The glasses clinked musically, those lovely eight-ouncers, perfect for boat racing. Yeah, there were boat races. Or just

THAT'S THE THING ABOUT A GREAT WARM-UP BAR: A LOT OF NIGHTS, YOU WANT TO STAY . . . RIGHT . . . THERE. THAT WAS WHERE THE NIGHT HIT ITS STRIDE, AND WHO WOULDN'T WANT TO STAY RIGHT THERE WITH IT, PERFECTLY IN STRIDE?

Fortified on Bull Max, we'd sally forth to The Pig. There we'd meet up with buddies from other dorms, play some pool if the table was free, cue up a little Hootie and the Blowfish on the jukebox. The girls would arrive sometime after that. Girls we'd known for a while by then, having shared the same coed residence. Cute girls who we liked, could talk to, and maybe, if the moon and stars were fortuitous in their alignment, take home to bed that very night—such were our foolish hopes.

chugging—funny how chugging a beer could be seen as a sign of manliness at nineteen, and later in life as a sign of morbid alcoholism. Inevitably someone would cue up "Friends in Low Places" and the entire bar would sing along. That's another sign of a primo bar: when the whole damn place sings along to the jukebox.

Round about eleven, someone would glance at their watch—usually one of the girls. They hadn't gotten glammed up to sit all night in the fucking Pig Pen, now had they? Soon everyone was slipping on their jackets and slipping into the night. Next stop: the finish-line bar. The throbby, bass-thumping dance bar. Joints with names like The Trasheteria, The Purple Rooster, and Copperfields (aka Shopperfields, aka The Meatmarket, aka The Butcher Shop). Once there, the vibe changed. Guys gave one another the feral eye, chins jutted as if daring you to punch. The girls you'd been pleasantly conversing with a few minutes ago were now looking over your shoulder, scoping the dance floor for Mr. Right Now. The game got real. Hell, sometimes that was just fine. I mean, damn, isn't that exactly where you'd want to be at that age: in a warm, sweaty, seething sea of flesh, bodies moving like oil in the black lights while the DJ hammered out a quicksilver beat?

But other times—man, why leave The Pig? That's the thing about a great warm-up bar: a lot of nights, you want to stay . . . right . . . *there*. That was where the night hit its stride, and who wouldn't want to stay right there with it, perfectly in stride? Who the hell breaks stride? Is that the act of a thinking, rational person? Hell no!

If I regret anything about those days, it was that we didn't trust that we'd hit the sweet spot of an evening right where we were. I regret that we didn't say, "Fuck Shopperfields.

Fuck all the dickhead DJs. Let's stay right here, order another tray, dial up the entire A-side of *Cracked Rear View* on the Rockola and spend these final hours of this night at the bar we all really, really like."

MUSHNIK: BRING ME WHISKY, RUM, WINE,
GIN, BOURBON . . .

WAITRESS: WHAT?

MUSHNIK: . . . SCOTCH, RYE, TEQUILA,
SAKE, MANISCHEWITZ . . .

WAITRESS: DID YOU BRING THE MONEY?

MUSHNIK: DON'T WORK ME ABOUT MONEY.
I'VE GOT TO GET DRUNK, NOW!

—*THE LITTLE SHOP OF HORRORS*

George's Buffet
312 E Market Street
Iowa City, Iowa 52245
Benjamin Hale

Moving to Iowa City for grad school was a culture shock for some of my colleagues—especially those with Ivy League pedigrees who hailed from the coasts—but it really wasn't for me, as I also grew up in the middle of the middle of the country, and was used to living in a pokey, snowbound place where Things That Happened happened on TV, always two hours ahead of or one hour behind our schedule. People who live in New York, L.A., and D.C. develop blasé attitudes about seeing the famous on the street, but it is an unusual event to see a famous person in the Midwest.

Iowa, however, which traditionally holds the hysterically-watched first caucuses in the presidential primaries, rightly or not believed a bellwether of the races to come, alone among the blobby-shaped corn-producing states of the upper Midwest can claim to be the center of national politics for about five months every four years, when famous men with famous voices and famous faces descend on the state in its frigid, windswept winter hoping to dazzle the natives like conquistadors stepping off the boat, and instead find flinty, sensible people admirably immune to starfuckery. (Watching Rudy Giuliani trying to act natural among farting dirt farmers in a roadside diner was a riot.) During caucus season it feels like you can't throw a rock in downtown Iowa City without hitting somebody who's running for President. People collect handshakes like baseball cards: I got Hillary, Bill (twice), Obama (three times), John Edwards, Joe Biden, Dennis Kucinich.

Fall, 2007. I pass a crowd gathered on the Ped Mall, see a friend at the edge of it, and ask, "Who's in there?"

"Chris Dowd, I think."

I look at my watch.

"Eh, fuck it," I say. "I'm going to George's."

There once may have been an actual buffet at George's Buffet (est. 1939), but now the only food available for purchase there are smallish cheeseburgers cooked in a grease-pit oven in the back, which come served with ketchup, mayo, limp pickles, and oleaginous onions, delivered wrapped in wax paper, and which taste an astonishing lot like McDonald's burgers ordered off the 99¢ menu two minutes before closing. These burgers are grotesque when sober and heaven after midnight when you realize you've been there since four o'clock and have long since drunk your way past dinner.

When I attended the Iowa Writers' Workshop in the mid-aughts, it had been handed down to us that there were generally two Workshop bars: There were many other satellites, of course, with less tradition and less charm than these two, but the pair that remained always in our orbit were the Foxhead and George's, located one block away from each other on Market Street. Both are dank, lovesomely vile places, and both, before the state of Iowa's relatively late adoption of the indoor smoking ban that is rapidly spreading across the developed world, had a bluish fog hanging at about head-level-up that kept out the health moralists and browned the ceilings the color of a hobo's teeth. These are the bars where grad students are unlikely to bump into the undergrads enrolled in their classes, who favor the cavernous Greek-System/meatmarket monsters farther downtown where Soulja Boy overpowers conversation (or did then, circa 2007) and frat boys wear blackface on Halloween (granted, it caused a short-lived local controversy, but it did happen), and from which a blacked-out 21-year-old might stagger home to mistakenly beat his neighbor to death (and that happened, too: had the wrong

apartment, apparently believed him to be an intruder). No, the Foxhead and George's are for more seasoned, mature, less violent and more politically aware alcoholics.

The Foxhead is contained in a single-room clapboard boxcar, often has Zappa or Charles Mingus playing on the jukebox (it's always the same dude who puts it on, and I'm sure he still hangs out there), and was then (and I hope still) by general agreement the fiction writers' bar. Down the street, George's, for whatever reason, is the poets' bar. We all spent a lot of time in both, but as I like hanging out with poets (they stay out later, their book recommendations are more interesting), George's was the one I gravitated to when my feet left my apartment on the odd weeknight in search of humans to talk to and drink with after my day in the cave, tracing shadows on the wall.

George's comprises the bottom floor of a squat, ugly, square brick building with few windows that stands as proudly as an overturned cardboard box in the middle of a parking lot. The bar's only window is in front, a plate-glass rectangle staring down the dark barrel of the place under a green and orange striped awning. Inside, the walls are covered in a gold on midnight blue floral-patterned wallpaper that gives one the impression of a

Mexican bordello in a spaghetti western. In my memory, red Christmas lights remain strung along the perimeter of the ceiling year-round. There's one of those chintzy pornographic photo hunt consoles toward the front, and a jukebox (Hank Williams heavily featured) in the back, but other than that, George's is free of any electronic bar-toys. If you order liquor, you'll get a beer back with your drink—a half-pint of beer gratis to wash down your whiskey. So if you're interested in financially efficient drinking, stick with the hard shit and you'll get 1.5 drinks with every order.

The afternoon/early evening clientele are truckers and machinists, members of a critically endangered species in the Midwest of proudly unionized workers who get off at four and were drinking Pabst Blue Ribbon by 4:10 decades before the young and knowing elected that brand of beer for cultural metamorphosis. The before-sunset drinkers gradually mesh with the poets and English lit grad students until about ten o'clock, when the two circles of the Venn diagram overlap, and you are as likely to be talking to someone who knows how to zero the x-axis of a metalworking mill with cigarette paper as someone who can quote Paul Celan in German.

The owner's wife (whose name I have spent this afternoon trying to recall, and am a little ashamed I can't) will often be behind the bar. She is a sweet old woman with gray hair in an unfashionable bouffant with Reba McEntire-in-the-'80s bangs, and on days when her glaucoma's acting up she'll be wearing her eye patch. Yes: the bartender at George's is an old lady who wears a black eye-patch, like a pirate. That eye-patched old lady was standing next to me when we met Bill Clinton: he had been eating breakfast at the nearby Hamburg Inn prior to stumping for Hillary; it was about 10:30 in the morning, and George's was of course already open. George's is the place where my friend T. Geronimo Johnson (as he goes in print; he's Nimo to everyone who knows him) bought me a lot of drinks the night that I broke up with my girlfriend of three years, and the same place where we watched Barack Obama win the Iowa caucuses on the night of January 3, 2008.

Nimo and I celebrated there direct from caucusing for Obama. An Iowa caucus, we found out, is an appallingly unscientific process. The rules are obscure and byzantine, but in the end, it is just a head count, primitive and nakedly vulnerable to human error. The whole thing feels about as democratic as the Salem witch trials. I remember that we were standing there for an interminably long time, because Nimo and I had both made the impulsive decision to volunteer to be delegates for Iowa at the convention. The room was emptying out, and the people running the caucus were getting frazzled and visibly exasperated with how long everything was taking. We were last in line in the row of ten or fifteen candidates (I think there were nine slots open), and I remember Nimo and I glancing at each other as one of the other delegate candidates was making her stump speech (democracy was the theme of the evening), and mutually agreeing to gracefully bow out of our respective campaigns because we wanted to go get drunk at George's.

I thank our mutual enabling we left when we did, because if we'd stuck around to be elected delegates, we probably would have missed Obama's victory speech, which I seem to recall happened only a few minutes after we got there. The mood in George's that night—and all across Iowa City, and the state of Iowa, which got to feel like the most important place in America that night—was exuberant elation, of having participated in something far greater than ourselves. We, the registered Democrats of Iowa, had changed the world.

Like many people my age, I would feel on that night, as I also would ten months later on the night of Obama's election—also spent at George's, naturally—the way Wordsworth felt about the French Revolution: "Bliss was it in that dawn to be alive, / But to be young was very heaven!" And like the French Revolution, its actual results were—well, mixed. Ultimately, however, I'm still a qualified supporter of both, as I will always and with ardent approval raise my glass to the beheading of monarchs and the tentative, disappointing, disillusioning crawl toward a more just earth.

THE MEANEST BEGGAR DARES TO SPEND ALL
HE HATH AT THE ALEHOUSE . . . FOR THE
POORE MAN DRINKS STIFFLY TO DRIVE CARE
AWAY, AND HATH NOTHING TO LOSE.

—JOHN TAYLOR,
A LATE WEARY, MERRY VOYAGE AND JOURNEY

Milano's
51 E Houston Street
New York, New York 10012
Madison Smartt Bell

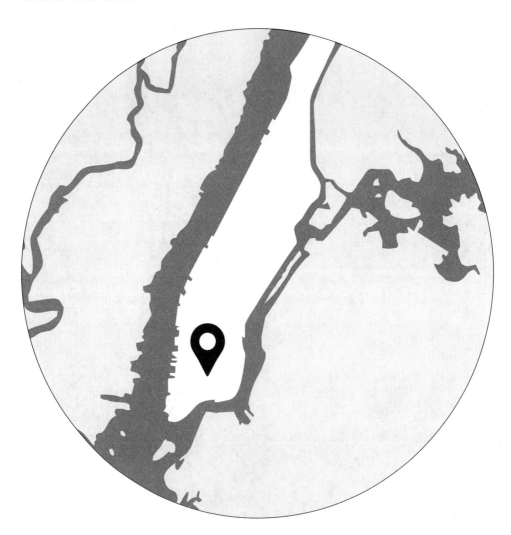

Où sont les bars d'antan? The line worms its way between my ears when I walk the New York streets these days, although I have forgotten the rest of Villon's poem, or even that it was a poem by Villon. *Where are the bars of the good old days?* Those being, for me, the late '70s and early '80s, bad and dangerous days for New York in fact. But I was young, what should I care?

In the winter of 1977, I was young and foolish enough to go to New York City with a twenty-dollar bill to see me through a week. After a quick assessment of the local economy I bought a jumbo jar of peanut butter. Eighteen bucks left. I was sleeping on a couch in Chelsea. That night it snowed three feet. Next morning my host pointed me in the general direction of the West Village. I set forth, wading through the hip-deep snow. The shops were closed, and no one else was crazy enough to be out. New York was absorbed in a thick cushioned silence I would never in my whole life hear again.

A sign reading "Bleecker Street" evoked the iconic image of Bob Dylan and Suze Rotolo strolling the neighborhood in shallower snow. I turned east and walked till the street ran out, leaving me standing in front of CBGB, also iconic, also closed. A dogleg maneuver brought me to the corner of Bowery and Houston, where stood the first enterprise I'd so far found open: a bar. If it had a name I never knew it. Impossible, but I remember it standing all by itself in the midst of a snow-covered plain, like a woodcutter's hut in Siberia.

Inside were winos, as they were then called, some stacked along the walls like firewood, some hunched over the bar or the tiny tables, some shooting pool for a dollar a game. I wasn't much good, but at school I had played on a regulation table and this one was the size of a bathtub. In a couple of hours I'd run up my stake and warmed myself with a few shots of bourbon. I was dry, too, when I hit the street, though that part didn't last long.

Milano's would have been just a block or so away. But never mind, we'll get there.

Where are the snows *of the ancient days?* is Villon's real line—*Où sont les neiges d'antan?*—and the only line anyone is likely to remember. Still, not bad considering that the author vanished, without a trace, an epitaph, or even a cadaver, sometime in the middle-fifteenth century.

He used to worry about being hanged, but nobody knows for sure if he was. The rest of the poem, if you look it up, is an ode to heroines already bygone then, from Joan of Arc to Abelard's Heloise, and singable, if you like, to the tune of Zachary Richard's "La Ballade de DL 8-153."

Weather permitting—I'm too old to slog through blizzards now—I stroll with a chaplet of the old bars running in my head: The Marlin (boneless chicken dinner); Murphy's (a kindly Head; McCarthy's; Al's; and the other used-to-be-countless Bowery bars—all gone with scarcely a sigh. The once-ubiquitous Blarney Stones, exhaling under their green canopies a reek of stale beer and three-day-old cabbage dehydrating in the steam table. The cascade down Second Avenue, from Dan Lynch where they had astounding live R&B shows for free, to Eileen's with its ceiling of brown plastic ivy, to Nightbirds and the other, hipper joints around the mouth of Saint Mark's Place. The

THE BARMAIDS PLAY MUSIC I DON'T KNOW BUT LIKE, AND HIGH IN THE COBWEBBED EAVES ABOVE THE DOORWAY A LONE TUBE TELEVISION PLAYS OLD MOVIES, NORMALLY WITH THE SOUND OFF.

aging Doberman at the door); Spring Lounge (still exists, by cracky); Milady's (vanished between two drafts of this document); Mare Chiaro (closest thing to a social club you could enter without being a member of the Mob, now gone forever with the wind and the rain); Three Roses (barmaid with foot-long fingernails twined round her hand like a DNA molecule); The Rum-Runner; Sheehan's (Irish-American detectives ran it); the cop bar across from the Tombs on Bayard Street; The Lion's Chinatown gang bars that just barely tolerated round-eyes if we kept reasonably quiet in a corner, one gone in a blaze of automatic weapons fire, the other become a movable feast, last seen facing Columbus Park, then never seen again.

There are still some good places here and there, unruined by flat-screen TVs as easy to hang as a cheap mirror. Even some new ones, or new to me, a few I have more recently found. But one can't give them all away in one go. One is recommended to be discreet, in the interest of historic preservation, of having a refuge in time of need.

Suffice it to say that Milano's is an easy walk from my ur-Bowery bar which no longer stands on the corner of Houston—if it ever stood there at all, if it wasn't some figment of my imagination. How long has Milano's been there? I don't know. An archaeological indication: behind the bar, flanked by a framed, signed photo of Humphrey Bogart and a caged fan of a vintage to resemble a propeller on a small plane, hangs a *John F. Kennedy for President* button, at an angle beneath another button of the same generous, gardenia size, depicting Ol' Blue Eyes young enough his face was still lean, still wearing the mob-style fedora, captioned, *It's Sinatra's World, We Just Live In It*. So it's been there at least that long.

From the street it's easy to miss. The sign's real small, obscured by larger signs all around hawking trendier establishments, newer, snazz-ier bars and restaurants, and now, in the fallen world we must inhabit, overpriced clothing shops, too. It would be too much to call the interior space a shotgun; it's more like a .22-caliber rifling to the back, where there's a bit more breathing room to accommodate the blue glow of the jukebox, green glow of the ATM, and saloon doors swinging into the toilets. In the front there's just room to squeak along the row of barstools, rubbing your shoulder over the dense layers of good-time photos and ancient posters coating the east wall as you apologize your way to an empty seat.

The little daylight allowed by the small plate-glass window in front is unlikely to penetrate as far as your seat. Rather, it spills on the rumpled tabloids on the corner of the bar, the nook where the daytime barmaid will tuck herself to read a swollen paperback when business is slow. Patrons slip in and out the door to smoke in a pocket in front of the window, featuring a plywood partition as a windbreak. Painted on the partition, in black and white and gray tones, are a short-haired woman—elegant in a car coat, white collar, white stockings, and a hint of black garter—who faces the street, and behind her a man looks into the bar, while behind them both are a few others, indistinct. Though I don't know, it very well could be the work of Milano's semi-resident painter, a tall, craggy individual who wears a sort of gaucho hat with enough confidence it doesn't look stupid. Often he's to be found there in the morning, when the light by the window is pale and a little bleak, reading day-old papers, mixing paint, sliding in and out for a smoke. An old school boho, he gives the place a slight flavor of Hemingway's Paris.

The barmaids play music I don't know but like, and high in the cobwebbed eaves above the doorway a lone tube television plays old movies, normally with the sound off. I study the layers on the bar-back wall, which rises a long, long way in the shaft-like space to the shadows of the stamped-tin ceiling, thinking maybe the artifacts get older the higher they go, hurled ever upward and out of the way. There's a World War II swabby's cap tossed onto a dusty set of mounted bull's horns; once white, the round cap is no color now. Higher still is something I used to think was a photo of some freak show monstrosity in a pickle jar, which made me reluctant to look close, but when I finally did it turned about to be a gag poster of a contented infant who's . . . well, let's just say the caption reads, *Times ain't so hard, I'm holding my own.* Even higher up, on half-invisible protrusions, hang metallic loops of Mardi Gras beads, which I imagine being slung up there on one or another festive occasion, such as the Saint Patrick's Day I dared to look in and found, among other phenomena, a patron with his hair and beard dyed green.

There's a dog sometimes but not always—an amiable old barhopping mongrel. I'm not sure if maybe he's the painter's dog.

You can talk to strangers if you want to at Milano's. Some strangers have come from a long way off and simply lucked into the place, and other strangers are there every day, and so are not strangers, except to me. If you don't want to talk, the strangers are happy to let you alone. I've never seen anyone act like a jerk, though I did once see a young guy apologize to a barmaid, at some considerable length, for acting like a jerk on a previous occasion—the sort of apology that looked like it might morph into a repeat of the original offense if he let it run on long enough.

But I'll be out the door by then, when the blood-orange late afternoon light is gilding the windowpanes across Houston Street. Around the corner it's not far to the Basilica of Saint Patrick's Old Cathedral, with its ancient brick wall turning rosy in the sunset. If I look in on the mounded sleepers under the stout old trees of that graveyard, I can fancy a few of them might have popped in for a nip at Milano's, after Mass.

Oh, and of course the computer knows: Milano's has been running since the 1880s, with a brief hiatus for Prohibition. Not quite long enough for Francois Villon to have stopped in, although I'm pretty sure he would have liked it.

DEAR MOTHER, DEAR MOTHER, THE
    CHURCH IS COLD,
BUT THE ALE-HOUSE IS HEALTHY &
    PLEASANT & WARM

—WILLIAM BLAKE

UPSCALE
JOINTS

THE FLOORS WERE OF BRIGHTLY COLORED TILES, THE WALLS A COMPOSITION OF RICH, DARK, POLISHED WOOD, WHICH REFLECTED THE LIGHT, AND COLORED STUCCO-WORK, WHICH GAVE THE PLACE A VERY SUMPTUOUS APPEARANCE. THE LONG BAR WAS A BLAZE OF LIGHTS, POLISHED WOODWORK, COLORED AND CUT GLASSWARE, AND MANY FANCY BOTTLES. IT WAS A TRULY SWELL SALOON, WITH RICH SCREENS, FANCY WINES, AND A LINE OF BAR GOODS UNSURPASSED IN THE COUNTRY.

—THEODORE DREISER,
SISTER CARRIE

The Patterson House
1711 Division Street
Nashville, Tennessee 37203
Adam Ross

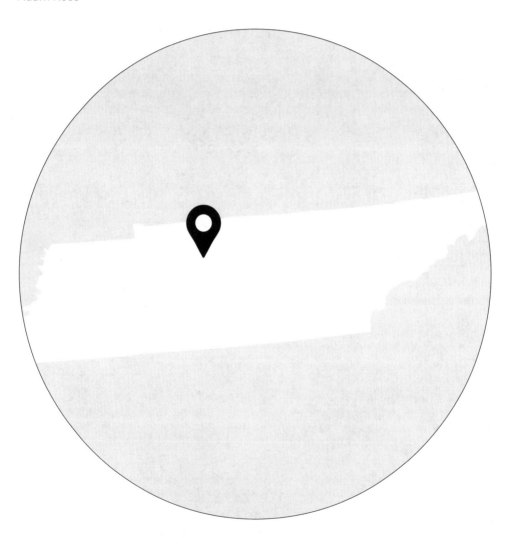

Like any great city, Nashville has her share of legendary bars. The unapologetically divey Bobby's Idle Hour on Music Row is a must-visit venue for aspiring songwriters who want to pound beers, have a game of pool, and play at the Thursday evening songwriter's night in the same hallowed space as former regulars Rodney Crowell, Kris Kristofferson, and Emmylou Harris. Meanwhile, any visit to the honky tonks on Lower Broadway demands a stop at Robert's Western World for some two-stepping and PBRs. Crossing the Cumberland River to East Nashville requires a visit to both 3 Crow Bar (a great place to watch football) and Family Wash—the suds at this former laundromat are no longer soap— especially on Tuesdays, for the ever popular $10 Pint & Pie night. The number of universities within our city limits has also earned us the designation of The Athens of the South, and any authentic Nashville bar crawl merits a few rounds at the college hangouts in Hillsboro Village, including the smoky Villager Tavern for ice-cold drafts and a game or two of darts. (See if you can find any of your friends getting loose on one of the billions of snapshots decorating its walls.) I nearly wrote about the Hermitage Hotel's Oak Bar since it's the Tennessee legislature's hangout when it's in session and a nexus of political gossip and intrigue. It also boasts Nashville's (and some say America's) most beautiful bathroom: a green and black Art Deco design with toilets that look as if they were made in the Emerald City. It's designated for men but unisex visitors are welcome to take a peek.

But ever since its opening in 2009, The Patterson House has become my go-to place to start the night or bring out-of-town visitors. It's the brainchild of thirty-somethings Benjamin Goldberg and his younger brother, Max, arguably the city's most influential restaurateurs, the pair responsible for bringing some of the finest and coolest dining establishments to a city whose Achilles' heel was long its culinary and bar scene. Since opening Bar 23 back in 2003 in the then-emergent Gulch neighborhood, the Goldbergs have launched the already nationally-recognized Catbird Seat restaurant, as well as Paradise Park, the live-music venue City Hall, the beautifully refurbished Merchant's, and Ariel, not to mention their most recent venture, the wildly buzzed about Pinewood Social, a multi-functional space that's part coffee house, part restaurant/bar, part bowling alley and—I'm serious—part swimming pool.

It was here that the elder Goldberg and I sat down to talk about Patterson House's five-year anniversary, which most reporters and critics covering the Nashville restaurant and bar scene no doubt considered unlikely when it opened. Modeled after New York's Milk & Honey and Chicago's The Violet Hour, The Patterson House was, in Goldberg's words, "a place where we could bring the processes and thoughtfulness of a great kitchen into a bar." Because it was also the first place in Nashville to charge $11 for a cocktail, "no one," Goldberg

I'm a big fan of the bar's rules, which I'll go through one by one, albeit not in order, since they give the best idea of the place.

1. Please refrain from using your cell phone for anything other than texting in the bar area.

This doesn't mean you can't talk on your cell phone *outside* the bar area, a large foyer lined with book-filled shelves and enough seating and standing room to comfortably accommodate twenty. The far wall is dominated by a mantel,

NO STANDING, NO FIGHTING, NO PLAY-FIGHTING, NO TALKING ABOUT FIGHTING, NO STAR F*CKING, NO NAME DROPPING, NO ONE UNDERAGE.

said, "thought that was a good idea at the time." But facts are facts: when Nashville made the cover of *The New York Times* last year, it was as a national hot spot for food and culture. Yet half a decade ago it was The Patterson House that was on the tip of the city's culinary spear. That it's thrived is a testament to the Goldbergs' vision of what kind of culinary city Nashville could become, or the kinds of places to which Nashvillians would come if you built them.

atop which sits the framed portrait of the man from whom the bar derives its namesake, and reads as follows:

From 1907 to 1911, Malcolm R. Patterson was elected to the governorship of Tennessee. During his second term, Patterson vetoed the return of statewide Prohibition, arguing that the issue should be decided at the local level rather than by the state. In a rare instance for the era, his veto was overridden by the state legislature. "For a state . . . to attempt to control what the people shall eat and drink and wear. . . is tyranny and not liberty."

Liberty may be celebrated here, but management is tyrannical. You're greeted by a hostess, who takes your name along with the size of your party. Patterson House unwaveringly abides by the first come, first served policy. It doesn't matter if you're Keith Urban, Nicole Kidman or *Gone Girl* author Gillian Flynn when I took her this past October. There are *no* exceptions and no reservations. In my experience, the wait usually runs somewhere between fifteen minutes to an hour, Monday through Sunday, unless you show up near closing time, which is three a.m.

The bar area is curtained off by ceiling-high gray velvet, its color matching the patterned tin ceiling. Its effect is the same as the one that separates first class from coach. You can't help but glance through the opening whenever it's parted. Life seems richer and certainly more comfortable on the other side. Also, it makes you want to stick around. Once you're led to your seat, you find the cell phone rule isn't hard to abide by: Why would you want your attention focused elsewhere, now that you've finally arrived?

2. No standing, no fighting, no play-fighting, no talking about fighting, no star f*cking, no name dropping, no one underage.

The emphasis at Patterson House is on *not crowded*, on *not rowdy*. No looking over meatheads to spot your posse. No date-distracting array of flat-screen TVs flickering from the walls. The room seats only seventy-eight patrons at a time—its several tables surrounding the four-sided bar. You don't go flag the bartender or server. He or she comes to you. The emphasis is on service. Thus:

3. You must be seated to order a drink. No seat . . . no drink. This is to ensure our servers can get your drinks in a timely manner.

The Patterson House's mood, then, is decidedly mellow and intimate. It was designed by Landy Gardner, who does residential interiors, and he's imparted to the place a hushed, becalmed feel. It's your rich aunt's library or coolest cousin's old-fashioned study. Hanging between the tables are delicate chandeliers that look like inverted wedding cakes made of icicles. Bar to tabletop, the woodwork's tones are the darkest chestnut interrupted by ivory and silver wallpaper, modern floral patterns that add an Art Deco touch to the space. The bar's chairs, covered in black leather, are large and comfortable. Because the bar sits so high and entirely dominates the room's center, Patterson House doesn't lend itself to people watching. From the tables, you can't see across the room, nor can you really be seen, which brings me to the next rule:

4. Enjoy the company that you keep. Men must refrain from introducing themselves to women, unless invited or introduced by a friendly party.

You leave The Patterson House with the person who brought you and the place is designed so that *nothing* interferes with that, although every time I've gone alone and sat at the bar I've always fallen into friendly conversations with the people adjacent to me.

5. Please be patient, each cocktail is hand-crafted, and quality takes time.

At the bar's center, tiered like a ziggurat, are the several hundred arrayed spirits. Lining its base are the brown-glass eyedropper bottles of various handcrafted bitters and syrups that put you in mind of a turn-of-the-century apothecary.

The menu is long but not vast, comprehensive but not overwhelming. It's organized by spirit: gin, rum, vodka, potable bitters, whiskey, agave, and brandy—all $12. (Ah, inflation. It's as constant as death and taxes.) As well, there's a limited wine and beer selection and an assortment of classic cocktails. But it's the mixologists' concoctions that make drinking here special, the menu tweaked quarterly in the

bartenders' lab—yes, they really have a lab—and subsequently refined during their weekly Mixology Monday meeting.

When I was recently there on a very cold December night, I ordered one of their new menu's hot drinks, The Forest Fire: Old Forester bourbon, Falernum, maple syrup, and Laphroaig scotch. The lemon slice with which it was garnished was speared with cloves. The best way I can describe the concoction is that it tasted like I'd just French-kissed a dragon.

Not that you can't get something cold. My Boulevardier, made with Russell's Reserve six-year rye, Carpano Antica sweet vermouth, and Cynar (the Cristal of Camparis) was poured over an ice sphere the size of a cue ball. Patterson House makes its own ice daily, using a Japanese manufactured Taison ice mold at the rate of only one every four minutes. They go through 250 of these a day, so you do the math. Water content being essential to a great cocktail, the bartenders require ice with a larger, slower-melting surface area. True, it's not efficient, and I'd hate to be the server responsible for the side work, but the difference in the drinks' undiluted flavors is inarguable. Attention to detail like this is what makes The Patterson House truly great.

(And don't even get me started on the food. The sage and rosemary pork rinds are made so fresh they continue to crackle and pop until you're finished with them. The deviled eggs are the best I've had in the city, and we are on the buckle of the Deviled Egg Belt. The mini burgers' short rib patties are served with Benton's bacon, smoked cheddar cheese, bibb lettuce, and house aioli.)

"With Patterson House," Benjamin Goldberg told me, "we wanted to be as good as possible at this one thing: making drinks."

I couldn't help but think of this the last time I was there, listening to local band The Kings of Leon play over the sound system, followed by our equally famous transplant, Jack White. Like Nashville's music scene, The Patterson House is not only great at one thing but much, much more.

Café Crème
4 rue Dupetit Thouars
75003 Paris, France
Rosecrans Baldwin

Bars don't really exist in Paris. Of course, the city is home to a thousand white-leather cocktail lounges, a hundred Irish pubs, a handful of beery way stations for New Zealanders who just want to watch some rugby. But a *bar* bar is a rare bird in Paris, a type unseen, like peanut butter, or bagels, or decent customer service.

Most often, a bar is simply just that: a zinc or linoleum counter where a man or woman stands in a white shirt, serving coffee or wine or a glass of Aperol to people who don't have the time to sit down.

In other words, in Paris a bar is a thing found inside a café.

My wife and I moved to Paris in the spring of 2007 for an advertising job. We came from New York City, where we'd been regulars at several bars, all wonderful, some gone, some thriving—Grange Hall in Greenwich Village, Rain Lounge in Williamsburg, Frank's Cocktail Lounge in Fort Greene.

Our first night in Paris, we tried to find someplace near our new apartment where we could start to make a home, to have a drink, unwind, and celebrate the fact that none of our luggage had gotten lost.

But the apartment was located behind the Place de la République, a big traffic circle in the 3rd *arrondissement* ringed by retail. The exercise was a bit like looking for a drink in a shopping mall. Around us were chain restaurants, chain stores, chain hotels. The McDonald's a block away did sell beer, but who wants a beer in a McDonald's?

We ended up in an Australian pub and split a carafe of pretty awful red wine.

It took us a week to find Café Crème. Back in the States, our friend John had said it was his favorite café in Paris. Two blocks behind our apartment, in the opposite direction of Place de la République, down a quiet old street named after a composer (Pierre-Jean de Béranger), hooking right on an even smaller street named for a writer and politician (Eugène Spuller), there's a quiet little square. The neighborhood's considered the Marais Nord, or Haut Marais, the north end of the quarter. Quiet, residential, almost commonplace. In the center is an old covered market. On the sides are restaurants, furniture shops, an art gallery; massive old trees providing shade; a store that mostly sells hard-to-find art books; a store that mostly sells athletic trophies for little kids. And on the corner, looking over it all, Café Crème.

For the next eighteen months, we'd be there at least once a week, more than that if the weather was nice. But still there at least once a week when it was cold, for a *café*, a *citron pressé*, or something harder, maybe a

Service was always slow, but that's just Paris. The scene bustled all day. Old people drank there, young people drank there. Workmen stood at the bar for a restorative pinkie glass of white wine. Young mothers met for lunch with their strollers in tow. Yuppies arrived after work on their scooters, in suits and dresses, blue jeans and nice shoes, and they'd always set down their helmets and tousle their hair before kissing their friends.

A *BAR* BAR IS A RARE BIRD IN PARIS, A TYPE UNSEEN, LIKE PEANUT BUTTER, OR BAGELS, OR DECENT CUSTOMER SERVICE.

whiskey, or some wine with friends. The French don't really do cocktails the way Americans and Brits do. They're starting to, but the emphasis is still on wine—better, cheaper, and consumed from hearty-sized carafes. The café also served excellent cheeseburgers, and a good chicken plate with salad. Inside, the rough wooden tables were crammed together, though intimately, with a sense of home. Same for tables outside, with a great view of all the passersby.

Women wore scarves year-round. Men wore scarves year-round. For a while, everybody smoked, then the ban came into play, and then everybody simply smoked outside.

Being a regular is a special commodity. It must be earned, can't be traded. It barely can be bought. Our favorite waitress took a few months to acknowledge us. After that we were familiars, old friends. She was too short to be a dancer but she looked like one—slender, pretty, with curly black hair tied up and bright blue eyes.

She seemed somehow to flirt with both of us separately, at the same time. We learned her name but didn't write it down. Afterward I never got up the courage to ask again. She liked us. Another customer would say something obnoxious, or break a glass, and she'd roll her eyes at us from across the room. She knew our orders. She knew we were both still learning how to speak French and always encouraged us to practice, rather than automatically switching to English. She was lovely.

The other two servers we saw regularly, a young man and woman, could have been models. Tall, beautiful, always sullen. We never really knew them. I got the impression that, despite their beauty, despite living in Paris, they considered themselves punished and were resigned to their fate.

I got this impression from lots of Parisians.

Café Crème was our place. We were possessive about it. We never got to know the other regulars, and we didn't really want to. Sunday afternoons were the best time to go, to do nothing but sit outside and talk, eat, drink wine, order dinner. Or it would be a rainy Tuesday lunch in the winter, if I could sneak away from the office. Then we'd spend an hour over something warm. Our friend the waitress would say hello, flirt a little, take our order, occasionally check to see if we had what we needed, but otherwise she'd leave us alone. We could stay for hours. We wanted little else.

Kir (closed)
22 NE Seventh Avenue
Portland, Oregon 97214
Emily Chenoweth

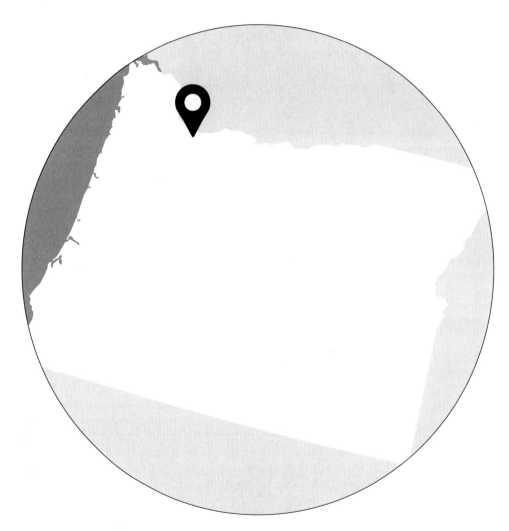

"You have to try this one—it tastes like the tears of Jesus."

Holly pushes the glass of wine toward me, its rim smeared with bright red lipstick. We were supposed to meet at seven, but as usual, she got here early. She's on red number two and she's been reading a book about the theory of time, which later, after glass number four or five, I know she will try to explain to me.

"Here" is Kir: a tiny wine bar just east of the Willamette River, on a quiet side street with a wide view of the western sky, the lights of downtown Portland, and—just across the street—the stark white façade of the Oregon Artificial Limb Company.

I take a sip and agree with Holly that the wine is delicious. Transcendent. Holy.

Still, I order what I always do: the rosé cava, at six bucks a glass. Our waiter, Russell, doesn't look down on me for failing to spring for one of the Son of God's bodily fluids. It's a subtle magnanimousness fueled by his knowledge that Holly throws down for the premium stuff. Plus she tips thirty-five percent.

Kir can seat a couple dozen people, give or take. The décor is simple, even minimalist. White walls contrast with dark wood. A few candles flicker before the enormous chalkboard listing the day's wine selections. The minuscule kitchen, which has two tabletop gas burners, serves beautiful small-plates: smoked trout with fennel and sweet pea slaw on spelt bread; summer squash and leek soup with crème fraiche and dill flower; mussels in green garlic broth; adorable little sugar-flecked tarts.

But Christ, that's not a bar, is what I'm thinking as I write that. It's a *boutique*.

•

I first tended bar in college—as in, I slopped terrible beer into plastic cups in the basement of an old stone house that, at our studious, socially handicapped institution in the Philadelphia suburbs, passed as an actual rock club. It stank down there in a way that I liked back then—like stale Budweiser and sweat and crotch. I got work-study money and a mild but undeniable rush of power for being the girl in charge of the tap.

Three years later, when I was teaching high school in rural West Branch, Iowa, I took a second job as a bartender at a grill-your-own steak house. The restaurant was lively enough—people hanging around the enormous grill in the center of the room, flipping thick cuts of the various fleshes they'd selected from the coolers—but the backroom bar never had more than four bodies in it, mine included. A glass of beer was seventy-five cents, and rare was the farmer who left me the quarter for my trouble. The truckers tipped only marginally better: bananas and watermelons from their loads.

•

"This is a really funky wine," Russell says, setting a new glass in front of Holly. "It's not for everyone, but I love it. Kind of has that barnyard thing going on."

Holly raises her eyebrows. "Oh, *barnyard*," she says. "I like the sound of that. Do you want to serve it to me in a trough?"

"You wish, honey," Russell says, gliding away.

Kir's filling up now. There are two or three people at almost every table and a handful at the bar, and, as usual, the vast majority of

them are women. They're deep in conversation with each other. They're sipping tasteful, biodynamic wines. Their laughter is low and melodious.

I'm on my second glass of cava when it occurs to me that we Kir patrons don't look like we're out on the town on a Friday night. We look like we're in a General Foods International Coffee commercial.

The wine flows. The candles dance. We are, as the commercial instructed us, celebrating the moments of our lives.

The question is: Why am I doing it here?

•

The first bar I ever went to as a Portland resident gave me a panic attack. My boyfriend, Jon, whom I knew from college but began dating in New York City, had finally succeeded in dragging me back to his hometown. A few days after we arrived, we had plans to meet another couple for drinks. But the bar turned out to be packed with people Jon knew. They all stood up eagerly, telling me their names and holding out their hands for me to shake, and in the dim light I could see only their white, flashing teeth. Suddenly I couldn't breathe—and I just *bolted*.

Outside in the parking lot, I proceeded to sob and hyperventilate as my vision darkened and my face and hands went numb.

I wasn't having a stroke, as I'd first thought; I was only terrified. Somehow walking into that bar had caused me to understand that I was stuck in this slow, damp, earnest town, possibly forever. We'd already bought a house, which, too late, I realized I hated. We didn't have jobs. I'd sold a book I didn't think I could write. I missed New York and I was always cold. That's when I thought, with the logic of the desperate: *the only thing can salvage this miserable situation is a baby*.

Not that I said that to Jon, who'd followed me outside. I said, "Let's have a drink somewhere else." Then I said, "God, does it always rain like this?"

·

"The thing about *time*," Holly says, sniffing a Sicilian frappato, "is that it's a subjective experience. Like, we feel it moving forward."

I nod. Cava number three appears on the table unbidden, and so far the science makes sense to me.

"But that's totally super weird, actually," she says, "because Einstein said the distinction between past, present, and future is only an illusion."

The sun is setting through the big plate-glass window, turning the sky a thousand shades of pink. It's a quirk of the weather here: even if it's rained all day, the sky often clears at dusk. For half an hour, the sun casts a silvery, horizontal, dazzling light—and then it sinks down behind the West Hills.

I tell Holly that I slept through high school physics.

·

When Jon and I went back to New York to visit, we stopped in to what had once been our neighborhood Carroll Gardens bar. Like Kir, Brooklyn Social had white walls and dark wood, antiqued mirrors, and a whiff (a subtle one, anyway) of decorum.

But it had more men in it, and a pool table, and in the back garden you could hear the screech of the subway. Maybe that was why it still felt like a real *bar*—the kind of place where you ordered the drink you didn't need, where you peed squatting eight inches above the toilet seat, where you became fast friends with someone you'd never see again.

That night, after many cocktails, we walked by our old apartment, past the white brick wall we used to see out our bedroom window. Jon took out a ballpoint pen. *Will you marry me?* he wrote on it.

•

"According to Newtonian physics," Holly says, "the future is determined by the past and so, in a way, the future already exists. Isn't that crazy?"

Fed up with my cava, she's ordered me a red that smells like mushrooms.

"In the very near future, I'm going to bed," I tell her. It's 10 p.m., and I'm tired.

Part of me misses group-drinking in dives: the Commonwealth in Park Slope, Spain in the West Village, and even the Space Room here in Portland, a black-lit, windowless cesspool a half-mile from my house that serves a drink called the Fresh Underpants.

I don't even love wine—I'd much rather drink an IPA. But I do love Holly, and this is her place. We've been coming here for years now.

Holly says that when she first met me, she thought I was a hippie. Well, when I first met her,

I thought she was a lunatic. We became friends anyway. She used to host parties on Saturday nights that would begin with red wine and reasonable conversation and end with drunken dancing and the kind of Polaroids you could start a blackmail career with.

"When I think of your and Jon's baby, I think of it as *our* baby," Holly once told me. That baby—nonexistent when she said that—is now five. Her little sister is three. These days, Holly babysits them almost every Saturday.

Russell comes over and places a single, perfect profiterole between us. "Just a little something," he says. "On the house."

Holly is delighted. "God," she says, pouncing on it immediately, "this is *amazing*."

"Celebrate the moments of your life," I sing.

Holly's mouth is full. "What?"

"Nothing," I say. I swirl the mushrooms around in my glass. "Never mind."

I realize I don't want to ruin the moment. It *is* amazing. *Life's* amazing. And no matter what Einstein says, time fucking *passes*.

Because I wrote the book and moved out of the house I hated. Because, although Jon and I have yet to get married, we have two kids. Because, according to my eternal fiancé, the yuppies have finally ruined Portland with their eco-brewpubs, DIY coffee roasters, and faux-modernist condo towers with horizontal slat wood cladding.

Because I used to be young and now I'm not, and that's why I dig, wholeheartedly, this middle-aged ladies' wine bar.

But still, I like the idea of past and present and future all lying together in a giant heap. If that's true, then everyone I know and love has been with me forever, and they always will be. No matter what.

"Seriously," Holly says, "you have got to try this. It tastes like a fairy dipped in Belgian chocolate." She shoves the plate in front of me. I take a bite. It's delicious.

•

Kir closed down at the end of last summer. The owner wants to open a place on a main drag somewhere, so she can get a bigger crowd. Maybe a crowd with a few Y chromosomes. "I want people coming in after work," she tells us. "I want foot traffic *and* tourists *and* oenophiles."

Of course Holly and I—along with a bunch of our other friends—went to Kir on its final night. The tab was enormous, and Holly picked it up.

But she and I haven't been to a bar since. Instead, I walk to the wine store a few blocks from my new house and I buy a bottle or two. They've got a fantastic bargain table.

By the time I come home, she's waiting for me on the porch.

Le Sirenuse
via Cristoforo Colombo, 30
84017 Positano, Salerno, Italy
Jim Shepard

When I used to ask my father why he didn't tend to make small talk with strangers in bars, he would always answer, "I'm not there to make friends; I'm there to relax," by which he meant that he saw his time in bars as a quiet time for himself, a time to people watch, and/or to think. When chatted up, he was more than friendly enough, but he almost never initiated conversation, except occasionally with the bartender. The reader probably won't be floored to learn that I'm the same way in the presence of strangers in almost all locations, and so when I think about my favorite bars, I tend to conceive of two categories: either A) those that give great pours—and there is a bar in my town whose bartenders have been cheerfully incompetent in that regard for years, so that when I order my standard Jameson's on the rocks, I unfailingly get a portion that's three sizes too large—or B) those that feature amazing settings. Given that category A is a little prosaic, and might also suggest that I have a problem, I'll here choose category B.

In that category, I *could* have chosen my first runner-up, which is the rooftop bar of the Hotel Raphael, located one piazza west of Piazza Navona in Rome. Although loudmouths like me are now blowing its cover, it used to be a pretty well-kept secret. It's not marked in any way on the ground floor, or on the outside of the hotel—which means that even at this point in time it's still not usually mobbed. And it should be, because its split-level seating area is not only a beautiful patio garden in the sky, with all the expected box hedges and myrtle and umbrellas and stucco and tile, etc., but it also features, right over the railings and in all directions, staggering views of Rome, especially at sunset, or at night. To the northwest there's St. Peter's. To the southeast, the Pantheon and the Vittorio Emmanuele monument. Right alongside, to the southwest, the great bell of the dome and the transept of Santa Maria della Pace, rising a couple of stories higher than the bar. Off to the northeast, the obelisk in Piazza del Popolo with its promise of the two amazing Caravaggios in yet another Santa Maria on the other side of the city's center.

In terms of views, it's one of my favorite places on earth. And it doesn't even qualify for my favorite bar. First, because it's not even my favorite place in *Rome*; at any given moment, wherever I am, I'd rather be sitting in front of the Pantheon. And second, because while, like my father, I'm not necessarily looking to make friends, the service at the Hotel Raphael is, um, brisk—or maybe even a little dismissive, even by Italian standards. Who wants to feel even slightly as though you're putting out somebody when you're just trying to relax and have a drink?

Which brings us to the bar I *have* chosen: the bar in Le Sirenuse hotel in Positano, Italy. I first visited Positano thirty years ago and passed right by Le Sirenuse, intuiting, correctly, that I couldn't afford it. I still can't, but I've been going to that bar and staying in that hotel for five years now, thanks to the Sirenland Writers' Conference, held every late March or early April. The Sirenland Conference is a wonderful conference as conferences go, and one of its highlights, I'm happy to report, is its cocktail hour: every evening at around 5 or so my family and I wander down to the bar level—the entire hotel is terraced into the steep hillside—where Lucy, who's now 11, gets a pear juice, and Emmett, who's now 16, gets a prosecco, and Aidan, who's now 21, gets a Peroni, and Karen, my wife, gets a martini, and Robert or Roberto (you wouldn't confuse the two, believe me) or Antonio, rotating bartenders and all-around endlessly appealing guys, ask me a question that I never tire of fielding: Would I prefer the Macallan or the Dalwhinnie?

In other words, I love single-malts, and in my own defense can only offer that I got into them

long before all of those people that most of us find appalling jumped onto that particular bandwagon.

The inside of the bar is an L-shaped living room of a southern Italian palazzo, which is to say it's full of light and air, and which, by way of furnishings—since it *is* part of a world-class five-star hotel run by people who have wonderful taste and are not at all screwed-up by their ongoing intimate interactions with the super-wealthy—manages to seem both more effortlessly elegant than anything *I'm* used to and a place where you can put up your feet and completely relax.

If *that's* not enough for you and/or you want to get outside into the Italian sun, the bar opens out onto a patio with a pool, as well as tables that overlook the whole panorama of Positano and the Mediterranean.

But wait: it gets better. I'm also one of those guys who believes that the occasional bar food, offered gratis, just makes a whole place seem warmer and more inviting. Even if it's just a bowl of peanuts. At the bar in Le Sirenuse, you're provided with a small ceramic bowl of Marcona almonds, as well as a small ceramic bowl of the best green olives on the planet, each refilled as soon as it's near-empty. You can imagine how those go over with the kids.

To get back to the subject of Roberto and Robert and Antonio: if the service at the Hotel Raphael is a good example of how one can be made to feel that not everyone wants you around all the time, the service in Le Sirenuse is a reminder that the toxicity of the class-based distinctions that we maintain in America is not inevitable. Without making a huge deal about it, the staff members at Le Sirenuse are just really *good* at what they do, and proud of that, and most of them have been doing it for decades and have parents who held the same job. No one in Positano thinks *Jeez, he's still a bartender*, mostly because they're way better paid, and way better treated, than their counterparts in America.

The result is a bar you'd want to go to every day even if you *didn't* want to drink. I'm not sure I can think of a higher recommendation than that.

Even so, I don't want to overdo it here. At this point I should in the interest of full disclosure point out something that's always been anomalous about my visits to Le Sirenuse. The conference always takes place the week before the hotel officially opens, which means that the hotel and the town are each much less crowded than they usually are. So the crowd—at least in the bar—is a little unusual: I'm surrounded mostly by avid readers and writers, rather than whoever might possess the fathomless amounts of wealth that would be

necessary to book the place in the high season. So, a caution: what I'm describing as such an amazing experience in late March or early April might not have precisely the same contours in late July, or early August.

Which means that my favorite bar on earth, all things considered, is the bar in Le Sirenuse in the off- (or just about off-) season. Would I love it equally in the high season? I have no way of knowing. And given what it costs to stay there, I'll almost certainly never find out.

The Tonga Room
950 Mason Street
San Francisco, California 94108
Katy St. Clair

The seven-mile by seven-mile patch of civilization that is San Francisco is a giant pinball machine. As a local bar columnist here for over a decade, I like to imagine myself as that round silver ball being shot out of the gate by a 1977 stoner in a Blue Öyster Cult t-shirt. In a day's time I can bounce from The Mission, to The Castro, down the zigzag of Lombard to North Beach, then Chinatown, each bumper I bang against draining my wallet of at least $80, naturally. This is one of the most expensive cities on earth. If, heaven forbid, I find myself rolling down the machine and toward the game's gutter—better known to snooty locals as "Oakland"—I have to think fast with that flipper and catapult myself back up into The Haight.

Covering bars in this patchwork of freaky America has been a blast. *SF Weekly* originally hired me as a "clubs columnist," knowing full well that I hated to go out at night and had no idea what reggaeton or dubstep were. But the editors saw something in me, something lazy yet cerebral that liked to sit in dive bars and get drunk. Something that wasn't afraid to go up to random strangers and make an ass of myself and then write about it. My first assignment wasn't even in a bar. It was at some ranch way up on the coast, at a "tribal gathering" of trance geeks who had rented a yurt and formed the dreaded drum circle. They were all on acid. The story wrote itself, though I ended up hanging out with the pygmy goats on the property for most of the night anyway. I filed my piece the next day, the farthest thing from a nightlife column you could get. My column, "Bouncer," was born.

I've always thought of this city as a carnival, maybe even a gigantic Disneyland ride. Therefore my favorite bars here have always been a bit over the top. The Owl Tree was a gem: a corner bar in the Tenderloin full to the brim with owl figurines and run by the Town Curmudgeon, Bobby, God rest his embittered soul. The Gold Dust Lounge at Union Square was a deep red, velveteen and brass watering hole that sadly relocated to the tacky Fisherman's Wharf recently, causing hipsters to take up arms, pitchforks, and the keys attached to the chains on their skinny jeans in revolt. And we can't leave out The Condor, a titty bar in North Beach that witnessed the horrible '83 death-by-hydraulic-piano-gone-awry of bouncer Jimmy Ferrozzo and his moll Teresa Hill. The pair was wrapped in carnal embrace on top of the ivories when the lift was accidently tripped, pressing them into the ceiling and asphyxiating Jimmy. *"Yeah, but he died doing what he loved most."*

For a town that is so cosmopolitan, we fiercely hold on to tradition, and every time an old-school cornball bar changes owners or even worse, shuts down, we have a collective freak-out. We seem to be losing these treasures more and more. So, in 2009, when the owners of The Tonga Room at the bottom of the luxurious Fairmont Hotel announced that they were planning on gutting the legendary tiki bar and turning the whole building into condos, well-regulated militias were immediately formed to combat the tyranny. Historic preservationists, rabid tiki culturalists, and the San Francisco Planning Commission all weighed in on whether to put the hammer down on the evil developers. "Happy Hour protests" were organized, where locals crowded the Tonga and ordered a ton of drinks to boost the bar's reportedly flagging revenues. They won, and to this day the Fairmont still stands. Better yet, The Tonga Room still, well, *tongas*. The owners nickel and dime you, don't get me wrong—there's a cover charge, a band charge, a drink minimum, etc. But I gladly pay it. A world without Tonga ain't a place I want to be in.

The lounge sits at the bottom of the fancy-schmantzy Fairmont in Nob Hill, complete with brocade sitting areas, marble accents, and golden filigree. Hop into the elevator and travel down to the basement, however, and you will find something entirely different. Owners in 1945 decided to turn the swimming and rec area into a bar, so they transformed the pool into a "lagoon" and created a gigantic Polynesian-themed saloon with *Gilligan's Island* touches like thatched-hut seating, bamboo gimcrack, and exotic palms. It's dark and lovely, something Aunt Angela from Jersey City would call *bee-u-dee-ful!* The main attraction is the water, which takes up much of the room and has a covered lanai/stage in the center. The Island Groove Band plays nightly, and periodic "rain showers" fall from sprinklers above.

The Tonga Room blew my mind the first time I went there, way back in the early '90s. We didn't have stuff like that back in East Central Illinois where I came from. The closest I ever got to Polynesia back there was Spam. Now I go to the Tonga periodically to relax and get away from everything. When you cover bars for a living, it can get old going out. When I go to the Tonga, though, I feel like I am in an entirely different country. It's a busman's holiday for me, sure, but with a tropical breeze. Hotel bars are like going on a mini vacation. You can surround yourself with fellow travelers and rarely worry about running into anyone you know—the same reason most locals go to these places, to hide an affair or to meet a call girl. All that combined with rich people and tourists makes for some prime people watching. Some of my best columns come from spending time in these transient home-away-from-home fishbowls, overhearing arguments, confessions, and declarations of love.

On a recent night I saddled up to the bar and ordered a mai tai—the house drink, natch. There are many imperfections in the Tonga Room that add to its mystique, and one of them is the fact that the servers and bartenders are all way too busy to crack a smile or give a shit. There is something soothing in that. They remind me of those ants that farm aphids and caterpillars for their sweet "milk": they have a job to do and they methodically do it, delivering what the other bugs need so that they will in turn get what they want. My bartender put a napkin in front of me and gave me a cold stare.

"Mai tai," I said, and he was turning on his heel before I even finished saying "mai."

Once you actually get the drink there it never tastes very good, but that's OK because if you are there at happy hour you can put even worse flavors in your mouth from the hot buffet. It costs ten bucks and requires a one-drink minimum, but trust me you will be requiring more than that once you pop one of the carbohydrate masterpieces into your mouth. It's the general pupu fare, with sesame chicken

wings, king prawn cracker thingies, and Asian noodles. The food is heavy as hell and seems to crawl down your throat and set up a man cave in your stomach.

On that night, the usual suspects were lined up with their tiny plates. There is a universal look to the kinds of people who like all-you-can-eat buffets. Like the Polynesian Samoans, they are a large, proud people, only our American version includes women who pocket Sweet & Low packets and men who double-dip.

Right on cue, the rain shower hit, a steady stream of water that made a pleasant white noise whoosh for about five minutes as the droplets landed in the pool below. The diners in line paused and looked up and then at each other, marveling at the display . . . and then jumped back into piling more chicken wings onto their Jenga plate of trans fats. *YOLO! I'm on vacation, dammit!*

Even though I swore I would take a pass, after a few drinks it became necessary to pay the buffet charge and convince myself that this time it would be different. Yes, I am in an unhealthy relationship with The Tonga Room and I just can't break free.

Sadly, the management had apparently nixed the crab Rangoon and replaced it with plain old egg rolls, but they were deep fat fried at least.

I ate them and then of course immediately felt regret.

Fittingly, nausea plays a big role in Tongan folklore. There is the myth of 'Aho'eitu, the first Tu'I Tonga. As the story goes, a lone Polynesian maiden was hanging out on the beach when a god decided to swoop down and have sex with her. He split soon after she got pregnant, because he "already had a family in the sky," according to *Tonga on the 'Net,* a site about

back up into a bowl. He covered the bowl and rechecked it hourly for signs of his dead son, like some supernatural sourdough starter. By morning his son had reformed from the puke. As penance for their deed, all the descendants on earth of the evil brothers were meant to be the slave caste, and all the descendants of 'Aho'eitu were to become royalty. So what I'm telling you is, whenever you go to the Tonga Room and the buffet slowly reincarnates itself up your esophagus,

THERE IS A UNIVERSAL LOOK TO THE KINDS OF PEOPLE WHO LIKE ALL-YOU-CAN-EAT BUFFETS . . . WOMEN WHO POCKET SWEET & LOW PACKETS AND MEN WHO DOUBLE-DIP.

the region's folklore. It's comforting to know that even divine beings can be douchebags. Anyway, her son, 'Aho'eitu, grew up and wanted to meet his dad, so his mom explained how to get to the heavens to see the no-count bum. The son went there and met his father and also his half brothers, who were jealous of his good looks and their dad's divided attention. They chopped off 'Aho'eitu's head and then roasted and ate his body. Their dad was not happy and he forced them all to vomit their brother's flesh

you are taking communion with the original Tongan, 'Aho'eitu.

As good as it feels to walk into the Tonga Room, it feels just as majestic to leave it, back up on the elevator and then out to the massive hotel atrium. Nob Hill is in the part of the city that houses much of the old-money society; it's the "high on a hill . . ." line from "I Left My Heart In San Francisco." It's a downhill walk to the subway, and I usually pass cable cars and the well-heeled. Until recently, if you were lucky, you could run into famous residents of the neighborhood known as the "San Francisco Twins," Marian and Vivian Brown. Vivian died last year at the age of 85, but when the two were together they were adorable. Each standing at about five feet and wearing bright red lipstick and matching outfits, they would walk arm-in-arm and wave at people on their nightly jaunts. I happened to pass them once. I came around a corner and all of a sudden there they were, tiny and identical in their cheetah-print vintage jackets and matching hats, their red skirts a canopy over shiny black boots.

(Twins play a role in Tongan creation folklore as well. Several pairs of twins were created by the spirits and lay together incestually to populate the earth.)

Slowly but surely, as the city changes and the old haunts shutter, all of this will be looked upon like old artifacts in a museum, just as we look at San Francisco's gold rush and 49er history through sepia tones. I have a record of all my travels out here, a weekly diary of my life as I bounced from bar to bar in the Barbary Coast pinball machine called San Francisco. No matter what happens to these places, they will live on in my writing. I remember this every time I go to the Fairmont, and I give thanks to 'Aho'eitu for sparing our lovely maiden, The Tonga Room.

Sonny's
83 Exchange Street
Portland, Maine 04101
Kate Christensen

There are few things more cheering than walking into a familiar bar to meet a good friend. Nothing (except maybe a good chicken soup) has ever been more effective at warming both bones and cockles of the heart, at banishing the deep chill and the early dark of winter, than that anticipation of a few rounds of drinks, a good conversation, warmth and conviviality.

During the twenty years I lived in New York City, I had a handful of favorite bars, among which were a hipster bar (Pete's Candy Store), a hotel bar (Bemelmans), a secret bar (Angel Share), a neighborhood hangout (Irene's), and a faraway bar (Ruby's at Coney Island). Like most people I knew, I felt passionate about and possessive of and proud of knowing these places.

I felt the same about my friends in New York, who were just as carefully selected and highly cherished. Instead of a group of them, I had individual close friends. I preferred to see them all alone, on "dates," so we could hunker down face to face and really *talk*.

So, for many years, drinking in bars was a nighttime, one-on-one thing for me, in a favorite place with a favorite person.

Then, in November 2011, I moved to Portland, Maine with my boyfriend of almost three years, on a sort of wild but solid hunch that it was the right place for us. The year before, we'd been using his family's farmhouse in the White Mountains as a home base for our frequent travels and had often flown in and out of Portland's little jetport. We found ourselves falling in love with the old brick buildings in the small downtown; the seagull-bustling wharf; the long gorgeous views over Casco Bay on the East End; and the tree-lined streets of the West End.

So it came to pass that, on an updraft of optimism and faith, we bought a 19th-century brick house in the West End. We moved in as soon as the deed was in our hands, having never spent a night in that town before, knowing no one. On our first night in our old, drafty "new" house, we ate Vietnamese delivery amid stacks of unpacked boxes, sleet beating at the windows.

That first winter, we spent a lot of time alone together in a bar around the corner from us called Local 188. It's big and airy but cozy, full of couches and comfortable tables, with an open kitchen in the back and a full menu. It was comforting to have other people around us, thronging the couches and tables, greeting one another, but we had yet to find a tribe of our own, or even a friend. Luckily, we love each other's company, because that's all we had for months.

When spring came, I signed up for twice-weekly Pilates classes and started volunteering at a women's soup kitchen. Brendan started going off to write at a café, and every morning, we walked our dog on the trails along Casco Bay, on the East End. We were working hard, writing, keeping our heads down, our noses clean and to the grindstone, elbows to the wheel, etc. All of that was well and good, but every night, it was just the two of us. We kept up frequent correspondences with our old friends, all of whom lived elsewhere, while making a new life for ourselves. But we still had no friends in town.

Finally, in early May, our friend Jami, a Brooklyn novelist who was temporarily homeless, came to live with us for a few weeks. She took stock of our sorry lack of a social life and intervened.

"You need friends," she said. "I'll introduce you to my writer friend Ron and his girlfriend, Lisa."

I've always been slightly leery of other writers, as well as friends of friends. I'm afraid they'll be competitive and/or standoffish, and that I won't like them as much as I should. But I couldn't

afford to be leery of meeting anyone right now. In fact, I leapt at Jami's offer like a hungry dog catching a thrown tidbit.

The next night, while Brendan was out of town, Jami and I met Ron and Lisa at Local 188. I liked them instantly. Ron was a novelist and Lisa worked in local politics; they both grew up in a small town north of Portland called Waterville. They were friendly, charming, low-key, smart, and (it must be said) extremely good-looking. The four of us chattered the night away.

Happy as I was to meet them, they were Jami's friends, not mine. And then, after Jami went back to Brooklyn, Brendan and I spent most of the summer in the White Mountains, writing in his family's farmhouse, while contractors banged and sanded away in our Portland house.

So that might have been that. But in September, when we were back in town, we got an email from Ron, inviting us to come and meet some of Portland's other writers at a bar called Sonny's. Improbably, this was to take place on a Wednesday at the astonishingly early hour of 5:00 pm.

When I lived in New York, I rarely met anyone for a drink earlier than 7:30 (except, of course, for brunch dates.) Dinnertime was generally around 10, so to me, 5 was arguably still lunchtime.

Nonetheless, we accepted Ron's invitation with gladness in our hearts.

When Wednesday came around, I closed my laptop at 4:30 and walked downtown to Brendan's café and picked him up from "work." We walked together around the corner to Sonny's, which is housed in the former Portland Savings Bank, a high-ceilinged antebellum building on Exchange Street in the Old Port, tucked into a corner of Tommy's Pocket Park, a tiny European-feeling square where street musicians congregate on benches under the old trees.

It was still light out. Tree leaves rustled in an ocean-scented wind. Seagulls shrieked on updrafts above mansard roofs. The brick of downtown glowed in the sunlight. It felt far too early, too nice out, to duck into a dark bar.

Then we caught sight of Ron with some other people at a big table in the plate glass window in the front. He saw us, too, and waved. In we went, feeling half shy.

We entered through red velvet curtains into a foyer that wouldn't have been out of place in a Victorian bordello, which I mean in a good way: brocade fainting couch, low-hanging fringed lamps. When the new owner, Jay Villani (who also, coincidentally, owns Local 188), bought the place in 2000, he took great pains to preserve the old details—exposed brick, vaulted ceilings, tile floors, stained glass windows. The booths and tables were clearly designed to blend in and look as if they'd been there forever. There's an old bank-vault door high over the bar.

The menu features two of my favorite things, a tamale of the day and an intriguing assortment of original tequila cocktails. The tamales are very good and wholly authentic and only $5 each. For my new favorite cocktail, the Jaycito, house-infused chile tequila (the bar wizard, Christina Klein, also infuses vodka and gin) is shaken with cilantro-infused simple syrup and fresh lime juice, then finished with seltzer. I never order anything besides these two items, even though both the food menu, which is South American- and Mexican-inflected, and the drink menu, which features many great-looking cocktails as well as new world wines and craft beers, are extensive and imaginative. Why branch out when you hit on the perfect thing?

The same goes for a bar. The same goes for friends.

That first Sonny's night, in addition to Ron, there were Monica and Jessica, both novelists, and Bill and Chris, who run Longfellow, the local indie bookstore, all of whom live in Portland, as well as an old friend of Ron's from Waterville. We sat around that table until after 8:30. (We would come to appreciate that in Portland, this is late, just as we'd come to appreciate getting home by 9:00 after a big night out on the town.)

Throughout the fall and following winter, Wednesday night at Sonny's turned into a semi-regular thing. More writers and their spouses were folded in. One night, so many of us showed up that we took over the long table in the back room.

Two years later, Sonny's nights have become a social regularity. The point is not to get drunk. We all generally have two or maybe even three drinks over the course of an evening, enough to relax us but not enough to send us off our rockers. We're a warm, convivial, cheery bunch. We laugh a lot and have much to discuss. And this is Maine: We create zero psychodrama— no contentious spats or pissing contests, no factions, backbiting, or bitchiness. We talk shop, commiserate over hardships and setbacks and struggles, congratulate one another on books begun, finished, published, or good reviews, prizes won, and plum assignments.

The thing about Sonny's itself, and our group of friends in Portland, is that we didn't choose them. They happened to us, just as we happened to them. But we couldn't have chosen a better bar or better people. Sometimes life is just lucky.

Our meetings have expanded to cocktail parties at our various houses, smaller dinner parties, individual friendships, and—gasp—occasional meetings at other bars in town. But Sonny's is still the writers' bar of Portland, Maine. And it's always a Sonny's night in my mind when we all get together, wherever we are.

THERE WAS A KINDLINESS ABOUT
INTOXICATION—THERE WAS THAT
INDESCRIBABLE GLOSS AND GLAMOUR IT
GAVE, LIKE THE MEMORIES OF EPHEMERAL
AND FADED EVENINGS.

—F. SCOTT FITZGERALD,
THE BEAUTIFUL AND DAMNED

FAR-FLUNG

MAJOR STRASSER: WHAT IS YOUR
NATIONALITY?

RICK: I'M A DRUNKARD.

CAPTAIN RENAULT: AND THAT MAKES
RICK A CITIZEN OF THE WORLD.

—*CASABLANCA*

Southern Exposure
107 Main Street
McMurdo Station 96599 Antarctica
Hunter R. Slaton

Even more than most bars, Southern Exposure—a joint that in the space of six short months I found, loved, and then crashed and burned in—has to be reconstructed from memory alone, because I will never be able to go back. Not because I'm banned for life, or the place burned down—for all I know, it still does a brisk business, six days a week. No, the reason why I probably won't ever again darken the double-door vestibule of Southern Exposure is because, well, it's on Antarctica.

In the late spring of 2004, I accepted a contract to wash dishes (or be a "dining attendant," in the corporate parlance) for Raytheon Polar Services Company at McMurdo Station, the largest of the United States' four permanent research stations on "the Ice." I'd always been fascinated by stories of the old Antarctic explorers, and—not having $15,000 on hand for an Antarctic cruise—working for Raytheon Polar Services, a branch of the infamous munitions manufacturer, was my best way to get down to the seventh continent. So in early August of that year, I flew commercial air from New York to L.A. to Christchurch, New Zealand—and thence by a ski-equipped U.S. military C-130 south to McMurdo Station.

McMurdo is situated on Ross Island, at the edge of the New Zealand "side" of the continent, and is the site of many famous Antarctic expeditions: Shackleton wintered here, as did the doomed Capt. Robert Falcon Scott, who in 1912 missed being the first man to reach the South Pole by five weeks (losing the race to a Norwegian team led by Roald Amundsen) and then perished with his men on the long march back to their base. Today McMurdo is the largest of the U.S. bases, but that's not saying much. During the summer season its population swells to 1,200 souls, and in the winter shrinks to a skeleton crew of approximately 200.

In many ways McMurdo resembled a small mining town. There was a galley, various "dorms," a carpenter's shop, a heavy mechanic shop, a general store, various scientific research facilities, a coffee shop, and a post office. There was once a bowling alley but it has since been ripped up. But even before the bowling alley was gone, it never was the most popular recreation option on station. Those were the bars.

There were three of them; they were the hubs of social life on the station; and which one you frequented said a lot about you. The first was the coffee shop, which at night turned into the "wine bar." People went there to drink pretty bad red wine, play board games, and listen to the occasional singer-songwriter or band play. I only went there once or twice.

Gallagher's was known as "the non-smoking bar." It was where you could get a burger a couple nights of the week, when volunteer shift-workers were on hand to fire up the grills, and where they also had karaoke. It didn't reek of smoke and no fights ever broke out—and thus the place was too much good, clean fun for me.

Southern Exposure was "the smoking bar," and it was where most of the cooks and the dishwashers went after our ten-hour work days. It also was where the hard-drinking heavy equipment operators and machinists and carpenters from Alaska and Wyoming who couldn't give two shits about being on Antarctica—to them it was just a job—would come and get lit up on a nightly basis.

You walked in through the double-doored vestibule (to keep out the cold), entering what looked like a badly neglected Elks Lodge. The ceiling had exposed wood beams. The tables were six-sided card tables. The chairs were worn armchairs that leaned back just far enough so that you would think they were about to tip over on you but obstinately kept upright. There was a shuffleboard table, a pool table, and two dart boards. The blond wood bar was in decent condition, while the barstools were topped by swivel chairs. It was dark, smoky, bedecked with scraggly Christmas lights, and everybody was either drinking canned beer from New Zealand or Jack and Cokes and smoking Marlboro Reds like they had an endorsement deal. Even if I hadn't been a smoker at the time, it would've been the place for me.

(Ironically, during the station's U.S. Navy days, "Southern"—as everyone called it—had once been the officers' club, whereas the relatively spit-shined Gallagher's had been the lower-ranking noncommissioned officers' club.)

There weren't any professional bartenders on the Ice. (Or, should I say, there weren't any bartenders who were hired specifically to tend bar on the Ice; there were quite a few bartenders there on sabbatical.) Rather, it was all done on an ad hoc basis—you got a nominal wage, and you got tips, but it was essentially picking up an extra part-time job for a few hours a week outside of your full-time, sixty-hour-a-week gig. (On the Ice you only got one day off: Sunday.)

There's that fizzed feeling when you first walk into a place where you just know you're going to have fun. Your chest sort of expands, you toss your shoulders back, stand up a little straighter, and suppress a grin. *This shit is going to be good.*

It's a feeling I associate with imminently feeling like my best self: confident, able to make friends, talk to girls, drink all night and not lose my head, be funny, throw darts, talk shit, smoke half a pack, get buybacks, hear great songs, and feel cool doing it. Southern was that kind of place for me.

Most nights after work (except for Monday, when the bar was closed, in a token Raytheon nod to preventing alcoholism—ha!) I would head back to my room, shower off the accumulated sweat and grime of ten hours scrubbing pots and pans in a hot kitchen, throw on a clean blue polo (our regulation dishwashing shirt, but mine fit so well that I wore them even on off hours) and my denim jacket, and head over to Southern with whoever was coming from Building 155, the station's nerve center where I started out living, or later "Hotel California," the first-year dorm I moved to after a few weeks on the Ice.

Mostly I drank Speight's, the best of the canned New Zealand beers. We would also do lots of shots of Jagermeister, ordered by various members of the kitchen or dishwashing staff in absurd quantities. "I'll take thirty-two shots of Jager!"—for, like, nine guys. Invariably at the end of the night, in a closing-time panic—11pm work nights and midnight Saturday—we would order beers to go in order to keep the party going back at the dorm. "Can I get eighteen Speight's to go?" We'd stuff the beers in every available pocket of our massive "Big Red" parkas and tramp out—flushed, drunk, and happy—into the frigid, shockingly bright Antarctic night.

Most nights I'd be in the corner with the darts, which was kind of the galley crew's thing. I wasn't much good, but no one hassled me for it.

Then one night in mid-September I met her.

I'm at the bar, surrounded by people, and in my memory her luminous pale face, icy blue eyes, slightly upturned red mouth, and white-blond hair are somehow in shadow, as if in a dream where the shadows and light don't correspond to where they ought to be.

She says something to me but I can't hear her. It's Saturday night and loud in the bar.

I lean in: "What?"

"I didn't think there would be hipsters down here," she says again.

I don't remember what else happened that night, or how much we talked—but from that point onward I was a goner. She'd walk past my dish window in the galley and my gaze would involuntarily tractor-beam onto her. She was from Boise—went to school some 300 miles away in Moscow—and though I'd never been to

Idaho, the vision I have in my head of her driving across the state to college, listening to Modest Mouse's album *This Is a Long Drive for Someone with Nothing to Think About* on repeat in her CD player, remains my indelible and iconic image of that place.

She was there for the same reason I was—an adventure—and over the next few weeks I fell hopelessly under her spell . . . which was a

supposed to be exclusively for night-shift workers—and got so shit-cocked that one of them slugged another hard in the jaw as part of a *Fight Club*–esque dare, knocking him out. Violence of any kind was the biggest no-no on station, one that would instantly get you put on the next flight back to New Zealand. That particular incident got hushed up and the guy, a friend of mine, didn't get fired.

THERE'S THAT FIZZED FEELING WHEN YOU FIRST WALK INTO A PLACE WHERE YOU JUST KNOW YOU'RE GOING TO HAVE FUN. YOUR CHEST SORT OF EXPANDS, YOU TOSS YOUR SHOULDERS BACK, STAND UP A LITTLE STRAIGHTER, AND SUPPRESS A GRIN. *THIS SHIT IS GOING TO BE GOOD.*

big problem because I had a girlfriend back home. It was all a mess. I ended up winning her, and for a time it was glorious, but it cost me a lot.

I mentioned fights earlier. There were a few at Southern, especially toward the end of the season, as people began to crack up a bit. Once, some day-shift workers went to Southern during "day bar" hours—which were

But I did. Even though things ended badly for me, I remember Southern Exposure and the Ice in golden-hued tones. I was angry at my far-too-corporate bosses and wracked by guilt and obsession surrounding the girl; I drank too much, both at Southern and in my dorm room; I overslept, waking in a panic and rushing in late to work one too many times; and because of that I got fired toward the end of January, after about half a year on station, unceremoniously dumped on a plane back to fragrant, green New Zealand.

I knew my pink slip was coming, though, and so on the last Saturday before the hammer dropped, everybody came out for my last night in Southern. The dining staff made me a card, and bought me about a million drinks—and I felt that sweet, last-night-in-town pang, when all the old grudges and troubles are forgotten. I felt somehow weightless.

Yet that wasn't how my last day on the Ice was. I went in to work and immediately got accosted by the executive chef. "Well, they finally decided to fire you," she said, in her dismissive way, as she marched me into the HR office. That morning was a blur. I hadn't packed at all. I threw all of my clothing and accumulated detritus into the orange duffels I'd been issued back in August and tried to find the girl, who was out in the field that day, miles from station. I briefly considered temporarily going on the lam—hiding out in various friendly dorm rooms and other spaces in town until the girl could get back—but I lost my nerve.

She found me, eventually, out on the ice runway, waiting to board the plane. Someone had radioed her that I'd been fired and would be gone in a matter of hours. A truck pulled up and she got out of it. We embraced on the runway and said goodbye, her crying and me—I don't remember.

The Otintaii Bar
P.O. Box 270, Bikenibeu
Tarawa, Republic of Kiribati
J. Maarten Troost

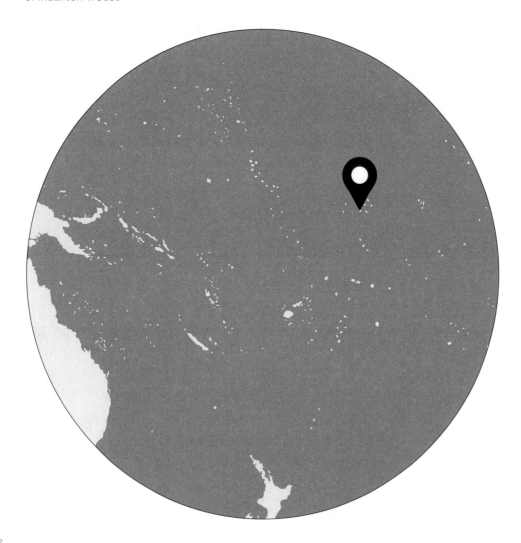

When I lived on Tarawa, a sun-blasted atoll in the equatorial Pacific, I quickly learned the three words that would come to define my time on the far side of the world: *Mauri, I-Matang,* and *Akia.* In I-Kiribati, the local language, they are but three simple words, but when translated into English they conveyed a kind of challenge, a trial even. How one responded determined whether you were doomed to a long slide into Kurtzian madness, or whether you had the fortitude, the character, and the disposition to live on a sandbar in the middle of nowhere. The words? Greetings (*Mauri*); one who comes from the land of the gods (*I-Matang*); we do not have what you are looking for (*Akia*). Said together, *Mauri I-Matang Akia* formed a kind of holy trinity for the expat on Tarawa, a summons to cheerful deprivation.

I had followed my girlfriend to Tarawa, a lonely outpost some 2,500 miles southwest of Honolulu. I was twenty-six, a semi-professional student/temp/waiter, and didn't really have anything better to do. My girlfriend worked for an NGO, and when the Country Director for Kiribati suffered some kind of mental breakdown, she had volunteered herself as an emergency replacement. Also, she said she was married. That's where I came in, the supportive spouse.

And so I found myself living on the slender ridge of an undersea volcano a gazillion miles from anywhere.

Mauri was an easy enough word to get used to. It's friendly-sounding. Enunciate *Mauri.* Breathe deep. You will feel peaceful, serene. It's a verbal corpse-pose. *I-Matang* is kind of jarring, a ceaseless reminder that even after a couple of years on the island, during which you will have forsaken pants for the comfort of a lava-lava, you are still—and always will be—an outsider, a foreigner, something other. But it is *Akia*—and your response to its constant refrain—that determined whether you had the mettle to live on an island not more than two hundred yards wide, just a notch above the equator, and about as distant as one can be on this planet without quite leaving it.

Akia was the refrain from the fishmongers on the side of Tarawa's lone road should you enquire about the possibility of purchasing something other than rotten shark. *Akia* was the response when you'd stop by Tarawa's power station, tucked inside a tin-roofed shed, and ask whether there might be any electricity forthcoming this week. *Akia* was the rejoinder at the hospital should you have a pressing need for anesthesia, seeing as your appendix picked a most inopportune time to burst. Rumors would circulate around the island that the ship—it was always "The Ship"—that called on Tarawa every month or two was laden with oranges, and for a few desperate hours, you'd roam the island, your mouth watering at the prospect of fresh fruit, only to be told time and again—*Akia*. No matter, you thought, as you resigned yourself to another day of grim island fare. The parasites inhabiting your intestines weren't particularly picky, and eventually, neither were you.

Fortunately, there was one outpost—an oasis, if you will—where you could escape the torrent of *Akias*. The Otintaii Hotel was built by the Japanese back in the 1980s. It was a gift from the fine people of Japan, a little *something something* to show their appreciation to the government of Kiribati for granting licenses to the Japanese fishing fleet, which swept through nearby waters from time to time, hauling in tuna, and leaving behind nothing more than a few sharks and the lagoon fish we considered too dodgy to eat, on account of the lagoon being polluted (toilets too were *Akia* on Tarawa). It was a two-story building, a rare sight on Tarawa, and it had a bar/dining area that opened to the lagoon. Only itinerant consultants and aid professionals ate inside. The rest of us— the twenty or so expats who called Tarawa

home—gathered outside every Friday, where we sat on plastic chairs around folding tables on a seawall that jutted into the lagoon. If the tide was in, this was quite likely the loveliest drinking establishment on Earth. As the sun set in crimson grandeur, the fairy terns would flutter and dance above water so blue that it made your soul melt. Across the way, you could see the northern part of the atoll, a serpentine cascade of palm trees languorously stretching toward a horizon where ocean, lagoon, and sky converged and the whole scene was one of such calm and tranquil prettiness that you couldn't help but sputter about the glory of existence and that this right here was what it was all about. When the tide was out, it smelled like shit and we just drank a little faster.

We were all beer drinkers. Perhaps elsewhere we'd drink wine or spirits, but on Tarawa . . . well, you know, *Akia*. Sometimes you'd be able to find gin at the Otintaii. At others times, there'd be tonic water. But the two would never make a joint appearance on the island. We contented ourselves with prodigious amounts of Victoria Bitter. Most of the expats were involved in "international development," a high-falutin', kind of condescending term used to describe work that involves doing what you can to ensure that people don't die unnecessarily. You wouldn't think that an island in the South Seas would attract the adrenaline junkies of the aid world, but you'd be wrong. I've read about the special bond soldiers feel when they're in combat—brothers in arms and all that—and something similar existed on Tarawa. True, it wasn't Afghanistan— no one was shooting at us. That would be where they sent the Seal Team Six of international aid; Tarawa was where Seal Team One washed ashore. It was hardcore, but the view was great.

It was a decidedly Anglo crowd at the Otintaii— English, Aussie, Kiwi, Scot, Canadian, a sprinkling of Americans and Germans. This was where we all gathered to share our experiences and laugh our way to sanity. Stripped of the pretensions of the continental world, the conversation was raw and ribald, as if the mask of civilization no longer applied.

"I had the shits so bad that I just laid down on the beach for a couple of hours and shat myself until there was nothing left of me but . . ." And so began an anecdote by an Aussie specialist in bacterial infections.

"Got a fax from New Zealand," said a volunteer from Auckland (the internet too was *akia*). "That police trainer who was here last month tested positive for cholera and leptospirosis."

"Well, he was a bit of a wanker." Here followed a lengthy discussion on the susceptibility of wankers to cholera.

"Any news about Gavin?"

"Still marooned on Onoatoa."

"Six months now?"

"Seven."

"His wife really misses him."

"I'm sure he has a new one by now. He'll be fine."

Then we'd drink to Gavin while the pilot of Air Kiribati's lone plane, a cherubic Aussie who'd crashed the nation's pride and joy into a coconut tree—thereby marooning dozens on the outer islands—sheepishly raised his glass.

In other latitudes, sunsets tend to be languorous and deliberate, a slow-moving denouement to the day. On the equator, they are, frankly, orgasmic, a lush climax of color flaming across the sky. They don't last long. We'd stare at the scene in rapturous wonder, and with a gathering beer buzz, the night would pass under the white-hot glare of a million stars, each a reminder of our good fortune—because it was good to be here on an island that had fallen off the map.

Then, one day, our world crashed. It was a typical Friday. The sun hovering above the lagoon, the sky aflame, a sailing canoe near shore, drifting on water so still that the fins of porpoises seemed ominous. We'd gathered at the Otintaii like dutiful lemmings—the microbiologist, the surgeon, the teacher, the nurse, the pilot, the NGO Country Director, the supportive spouse. Same-o same-o, happy hour in the forgotten world. The usual requests: "VB." "VB." "VB." "VB." "VB." "Do you have gin and tonic?" (So hopeful, this NGO Country Director.)

Akia was the response. Inexplicably, the island's shipment of ale had been sent to Christmas Island, some 2,000 miles away. The Great Beer Crisis had begun. It was, in retrospect, the greatest challenge yet. Perhaps some of us even asked, how much, really, did alcohol contribute to our ability to cope?

The answer, it turned out, was a lot. The days suddenly felt long and bleak. A dreary resignation beset the atoll. Without our beer goggles on, life on Tarawa seemed glum, wretched even, as every *akia*, every hardship, stung as if a personal affront. True, these were peaceful times. No beer, no brawls. The road, typically a surreal obstacle course of passed out bodies and drunk drivers, was now safe, or safe-ish. There were still errant dogs and pigs to contend with. But in no way did this make up for the gloom of a beer-less evening.

Yet we still gathered at the Otintaii, noting now the rats that foraged in the dining room and the stench of the shit simmering on the beach in the equatorial heat. At least we had the view, the finest vista on this earth, a riot of color that spread toward the horizon, where every evening our eyes would gaze, searching for The Ship and its promise of happiness, cases and cases of happiness.

GOOD LIQUOR NEEDS NO SIGNBOARD.

—JAPANESE PROVERB

Yuki's
1-1-10, Ogaitocho
Hirakata-shi, Osaka, Japan 573-0027
Buzz Poole

Like all college-aged Deadheads who had only gotten to see the Grateful Dead in the '90s, I'd checked out Phish. I liked the funk, but the jamming and lyrical eccentricity struck me as too derivative of the Dead and Frank Zappa. But one humid August afternoon in 1999, standing in Hirakata in Osaka prefecture in Japan, those Phish t-shirts hanging in the window grabbed my attention.

It was the early days of my semester abroad. I'd been to Japan a couple of years before, just shy of cherry blossom season. As my friend and I had wandered around Yoshino, in Nara prefecture, a little yippy dog with dyed pink hair (presumably for the cherry blossoms) bit her. What had struck me most about Japan on that trip, and what drew me to it enough to finagle spending my final semester of college there, was how thousands of years of tradition garishly rubbed up against the now: pink dogs and the national reverence for a longstanding tradition; ancient Buddhist rituals and jazz; geishas and neon. These vivid snippets stuck with me, so I returned to further explore the country, on my own terms. That's why I'd decided to stay in the dorms and not do a home-stay. Sure, my language skills would have improved much

faster but I still hadn't honed in on the critical difference between being an observer and a participant.

I'd been pedaling around my new neighborhood on the used bicycle I'd just purchased. After the first week or so of adjusting to the Kansai Gadaii campus and its immediate surroundings, I was ready to feel out Hirakata, a commuter city about midway between Osaka and Kyoto. Standing out on this street just a block away from an entrance to a subterranean mall that connected to the train station, I had no idea what kind of storefront I was looking at, but my resourceful mind was already at work: maybe I could get a lead on some pot. So I entered.

Low-ceilinged and narrow, wedged in close enough to the train tracks to cause the cluttered racks of vintage American jeans and sweaters to vibrate regularly, the place turned out to be a clothing store. But as Yuki, the owner, conveyed to me through pantomime and his limited English, which was far superior to my essentially nonexistent Japanese, at night he moved the clothes aside and converted the place into a bar. I should come.

I'd been working on a hunch after seeing those Phish shirts, but my first night drinking at Yuki's, the copies of *High Times* and the fake pot plant on the bar told me all I needed to know. Better than I understood the language, though, I understood that American brashness would get me nowhere. So I made no mention of the blatant paraphernalia, and instead signaled at a Steal Your Face sticker stuck on the surface of the bar. This was the game changer. I didn't just like the band. I'd seen them. To Yuki, that was beyond the pale. I might as well have told him that I was Jerry Garcia's illegitimate son and we'd been scuba diving together in Hawaii.

The more time I spent at Yuki's the more comfortable I became. I'd ride my bike down after dinner, sometimes with one or two American friends, often alone. The bar's customers were Yuki's buddies, along with the stray salaryman who'd missed a train or was stalling before heading home. It was never crowded and I really took pleasure in returning time and again. I'd been going to bars since well before I was legal, thanks to a fake Florida license, but never with any meaningful regularity, even after I'd turned 21. But at Yuki's I settled in to the routine of being a barfly, learning to favor neat Johnnie Walker Red over the Kirin from the tap. And by tap I mean the keg Yuki kept on the floor behind the bar, adding to the vibe that this was more rec room than bar. The racks of clothes were pushed against the walls, revealing a small wooden L-shaped bar—a snug seven-seater— behind which stood a shelf holding assorted booze.

Yuki got his inventory from twice-yearly raids on thrift stores in Washington, Oregon, and California, buying clothes by the garbage bag. Yet he wasn't much of a clotheshorse himself: he always wore some variation of a non-sports related ball-cap, cargo pants, and flannel shirt. His wiry facial hair was more free range than groomed. I guessed he was a few years older than me, though I was never sure. Our friendship wasn't built on these sorts of details. Rather, music was our common ground. I'd brought with me to Japan some choice bootlegs burned onto CDs, which I shared with Yuki, who would DJ the night's soundtrack on a stereo. Or we'd watch VHS tapes of concert films: various Miles Davis electric bands, Bob Marley, Talking Heads, and, yes, lots of Grateful Dead.

As the semester progressed, Yuki's English shaped up and my Japanese improved. Although I spent more and more time at the bar, I was getting plenty of other tastes of local flavor. I'd been invited over for dinner at people's homes. I frequented the neighborhood *sento* for baths. Most of my interactions with Japanese people, from students in class to the cashiers in the grocery store and the family sitting around the *kotatsu*—a low heated table draped in a blanket—were choreographed by formality. But it was Yuki's that let me feel like I was starting to penetrate Japan. People were not putting on a show for me because I was not from there; the folks at Yuki's were really and truly being themselves.

It took a few weeks of drinking at Yuki's before I felt loose enough to bring up the fake pot plant on the bar. He seemed surprised that I knew what it was.

"Can you get the real stuff?" I asked.

Yuki was a master of eye contact. He was like this with everyone, but I think he paid special attention to me since linguistic navigation was a choppy affair for us, especially at first. But he understood my question this time, probably because of some bloodshot gleam in my eyes. Maybe he'd just been waiting for me to ask.

"Yes," he said.

The logistics of the operation surprised me, involving a friend of a friend rendezvousing with some Iraqis in a park in central Osaka. Arrangements were made, money exchanged hands, and then I waited, for a few weeks.

In the meantime, summer wound down and Yuki would bring in furry edamame pods freshly picked from his mother's garden, which he steamed in the microwave he used to heat up sake. I'll never forget the lip-smacking saltiness of the pods and sucking out the candy-sweet beans.

Then one night I arrived and two commuters were having a drink. Yuki poured my Johnnie Walker and we chatted. I had another. When the commuters left, Yuki put up the closed sign on the door and cracked a huge shit-eating grin. Not only had the delivery come through but Yuki had also procured a bong. As he filled it with water I said something about locking the door.

"If someone come in," he said, still smiling, "they will think it's incense. Japanese don't know what marijuana smell like."

It was now autumn—an amazing time of year in this part of Japan. Temples stay open at night, illuminating the trees and leaves; the redolence of baked sweet-bean cakes and roasted chestnuts toasts the brisk air; wood smoke rises off the hills from harvest festival fires. Yuki's had likewise become more cozy, the floor lamps tucked into the room's corners casting warm and welcoming light the color of scotch. I leaned into that bong like I was back home, though at the time "home" was not easily defined. I'm from Philadelphia, but had been crashing with friends in Palo Alto just weeks before the Japan opportunity was finalized. It's fair to say that in the big picture, I was feeling out of sorts. So that, along with not having smoked since leaving the States a couple months earlier and the drinks I'd already consumed, resulted in the first hit flooring me. As I drew in my breath the smoke gathered in the plastic tube, a thickening swirl, until I sucked it all into me. It went right to my

watching, I was working overtime trying to make it seem like I was watching. The movie is shot in black and white and as behind-the-scenes making-of-albums documentaries go, this one is exceptionally self-indulgent. So by the time Anthony Kiedis is doing a nighttime monologue about the band's "bass humping your face" sexual freedom, leaning against the hood of some classic convertible in an empty Tower Records parking lot in Los Angeles—I just

MY FIRST NIGHT DRINKING AT YUKI'S, THE COPIES OF *HIGH TIMES* AND THE FAKE POT PLANT ON THE BAR TOLD ME ALL I NEEDED TO KNOW. BETTER THAN I UNDERSTOOD THE LANGUAGE, THOUGH, I UNDERSTOOD THAT AMERICAN BRASHNESS WOULD GET ME NOWHERE.

head, feeling like a muted gong had just been struck in my skull, leaving me feeling like I could feel the feeling of my brain feeling itself. Yeah, I was that high. Yuki gave me a knowing nod. Of course, I took another hit.

Our session complete, Yuki reopened the bar and we sat there watching *Funky Monks*, the documentary about the Red Hot Chili Peppers making *Blood Sugar Sex Magik*. Well, Yuki was

lost my shit. It was acutely American, in a way that reminded me of everything I didn't miss about home, while simultaneously making me paranoid about being such an utter outsider in Japan. What to do? I went into the bathroom. I don't know how long I was in there, but when I came out, the movie was over.

I smoked pot with Yuki one other time, right before I left Japan. It was December, almost

Christmas. By now, my Japanese had become passable, to the point where I could hold decent conversations. I like to think that Yuki was proud of me. The Japanese love giving gifts to show gratitude—another formality— and with my departure just days away, he and his friends surprised me with a trip into Osaka to see a Grateful Dead cover band. The band was horrible, but the night was great. One of the guys had a car—I think it was the first time I'd been in one since being picked up from the airport back in August—and after warming up at Yuki's, we piled in and drove to the city. By then, I'd re-acclimated to getting high and was able to keep my cool, and even talk to girls.

Yuki's was typically a male-dominated environment, but girlfriends did show up from time to time, and with them, other women, like Sana. She was very un-Japanese: loud and in your face. She had her own apartment and grew pot there. My dream woman. We shared a kiss, just a kiss, but one of those kisses that imparts the wonderment of what might have been. Or maybe I was just drunk and high. Either way, in that too brief catch-and-release of lips, I imagined a whole parallel Japanese existence, lazing around Sana's apartment, having sex and getting high. It would have been great. I might have fallen in love and lived there for the rest of my life.

That didn't happen, but Yuki's did, and while I experienced much more of the country beyond a single bar, for me, that place *was* Japan.

Limb
Plitvička ulica 16,
10000 Zagreb, Croatia
Robert Perišić

When my former wife and I separated, she demanded I leave Limb to her.

"Please don't go there anymore. It's my only anchor. I have to carry on and forget all this."

I was to blame for *all that*, and I agreed to anything to minimize the damage.

But Limb was actually my bar. Located on the edge of the inner city, on the first floor of a smallish, old apartment block, it served average-priced drinks—two or three bucks for a pint of beer—to rock and jazzy sounds. On the wall opposite the bar was a mural of buxom women by the ironic, female pop artist Nikolina Ivezić. I'd been a regular there for eight years—just a bit less than my wife and I had been together. I met the owner, Selma, in the '90s, through my buddy Kokanović—her husband at the time. Since then, I'd hardly gone out anywhere else. If I wasn't writing, you knew where to find me—where the bar juts out, in the throng or, on a quiet evening, searching for something to connect home, freedom, and the mass of little worlds full of unexpected possibilities.

Yet, as agreed, I decamped and wandered the city in search of a great bar like Limb.

A great bar has to have a certain density. I've found this in its purest form in Tokyo's Golden Gai: two-hundred tiny bars crammed together in a small area—a sub-neighborhood—where a dozen people make a crowd. The night simmers and smells of hot sake. That's concentrated, condensed Japan for you.

A great bar also has to have great bar chairs. Bar chairs raise you up and free you of the table and its obligations. Of course, there are ordinary chairs in bars. But the essence of a bar resides in the bar chair—and also in standing, which is in fact a radical version of sitting on a bar chair, the total abandonment of the table. A table is a centralized world; there is always a father figure enthroned—"We have to talk"—but with bar chairs there is neither table nor father. Sure, you can sit on bar chairs with your father, but then he's no longer a father; he surrenders his role. If you sit down at an ordinary table he starts all over again. A father means structure, and structure disintegrates in a great bar.

Every great bar is unique like a work of art: it has its own code, its own narrative context, its own tone and style that distinguish it from others. They're places of both reality and fiction. But a great bar avoids the epic of the novel, its grand gestures and long renderings—it has the rhythm of the short story, the smokiness of the poem, the luster of the one-liner. Its language is scattered and messy like free verse.

and that these places were empty apart from our lonely love. Why didn't these people communicate, why couldn't you make friends with someone here, just like that, without the intention of making friends, and why did I never burst out laughing here, swing and sway to a spot where I could shake a leg, just like that, and do a funny dance? I realized that I just couldn't conjure that persona any more, outside of Limb. I couldn't reconstruct that me that could be fun even in the midst of melancholy,

A GREAT BAR AVOIDS THE EPIC OF THE NOVEL, ITS GRAND GESTURES AND LONG RENDERINGS— IT HAS THE RHYTHM OF THE SHORT STORY, THE SMOKINESS OF THE POEM, THE LUSTER OF THE ONE-LINER. ITS LANGUAGE IS SCATTERED AND MESSY LIKE FREE VERSE.

These are some of the many thoughts I had as I sat in bar after bar looking for a replacement for Limb. Yet I had to keep these thoughts to myself. Because my new love was usually there with me, and she considered any mention of Limb to be nostalgia for the life I'd put behind me.

I was pretty forlorn in that new life, cut off from everything, and I felt we were sitting so horribly alone there at these other bars, me and my love,

from which, with the help of others and with self-irony and pessimistic humor, I could glide out into feeling good. Where had that persona gone? I realized it had existed at Limb like a character exists in a book, together with other characters; but transplant it to a different book, to a different bar, and the character doesn't exist because neither do the others it's linked with in a specific, unwritten code of place.

There were certainly plenty of characters at Limb. Filip Šovagović might have played one of the main roles in *No Man's Land*, which won an Oscar in 2001 for Best Foreign Language Film, but at Limb he was best known for his morose, whining ways. Everyone teased him by calling him "Swine," and he went along with it. You could never be taken terribly seriously there. If some lout came in and started causing trouble, he was at a loss with Selma, who just loved to laugh, even when she was in a pickle. The troublemaker would quickly leave once he realized there was no one to lock horns with.

When I met some of these characters elsewhere, however, after I stopped going to Limb, I noticed we no longer had a common framework. There are chance friends from some bar or other who you never made a point of calling or seeing outside of the bar. If you stop going there—or they do—and you meet somewhere else, you both say a warm hello and want to talk about everything, but it feels like your communication has got lost somewhere along the way, in a different atmosphere and key, and it's awkward for you that you now seem like superfluous acquaintances, and nothing more. You chat for a bit as if trying to reassemble a broken vase. For a minute it feels like you're reliving some old party, but the very next instant you know it's not going to happen, and you say goodbye a trifle too

quickly and with the aftertaste of words unsaid, as if you'd reached into a void.

Alternately, if you've stopped going and have lost touch with the place, and then go back a long time later and see different people there, a kind of antagonism arises inside you. You feel the newcomers are usurpers, and if you wait long enough for someone old to come in who you know at least by sight, you view that person as an ally, a guarantor of continuity, a hand waving from the past.

Sometimes whole cliques remain like that in some island of the past, and you go there and see a flashback of your former life, or a shadow of a generation. Time and again you expect all those people to come in through the door, but they don't, so you drink your drink and glance around like an archaeologist. All those evenings are still inscribed somewhere under the first layer of paint, and you can sense them in the air.

A fata morgana from the bar.

That's what I felt when I started going back to Limb after several years' break. Different people were there, a different generation with its stories, a different atmosphere.

The first time I went back, I didn't know a single soul. I was a random stranger, haggard and graying, and the waitress wanted me to pay straight away.

"Where's Selma?" I asked her.

"Selma got married again," she said. "She's pregnant and doesn't come in."

I asked about my ex. She didn't recognize the name or my description of her.

There was at least one reminder of my past. In a little alcove where the waitresses and regulars store things, I came across the old Complaint Book that Selma kept. Many of the entries were from Šovagović:

> The place is so fucking full of kids getting high and pretending to be wizened artists, the Stella is warm, expensive, and awful.

> Jeezus, that waitress who's just come from the Cure concert and hasn't washed for 240 hours doesn't even know which way up to stand the Natreen. This has got to be the worst dump in the hemisphere. You can't come here without running into some actor constantly navel-gazing and talking to himself about what he has to do.

> This joint is absolutely the pits and no black hole in the universe can compare.

Birthday of that idiot Perišić. What a vile crowd.

The date of that last entry was actually a month away from my birthday, but the Complaints Book, and the memory of Šovagović scribbling away at it in his chair at the bar, brought back my laughter from Limb in those years—that irretrievable laughter, laughter from the edge of the abyss.

—*Translated from the Croatian by Will Firth*

DRINK! FOR YOU KNOW NOT WHENCE
    YOU CAME, NOR WHY:
DRINK! FOR YOU KNOW NOT WHY YOU
    GO, NOR WHERE.

—OMAR KHAYYÁM

The John Hewitt
51 Donegall Street
Belfast BT1 2FH Northern Ireland
Rosie Schaap

The bars I love best are never the ones I've read about in travel books or magazines, and rarely the ones someone or other tells me I ought to check out. They're the ones I come across instinctively, or am led to by a stranger, with no expectations. This is the way it should be. Sometimes one bar leads to the next, and even maybe to a third, in a great chain of pints and tumblers of whiskey, a chain of the people who drink them, and of the stories they tell, until you arrive at the one where you're supposed to be.

So let's start in The Spaniard, my favorite bar in Belfast, before we get to the John Hewitt, which is my second-favorite bar in Belfast, but the one I really need to tell you about.

It was October, 2010, a cold and damp night, and I was not well. I squeezed into a space near the front corner of The Spaniard, and as soon as the barman heard me try to speak—the fluey thing I had made me croaky—he didn't wait for me to order. He nodded and said thoughtfully, "Right. Hot whiskey for you." Prescriptive, perfect.

Still, something was off. There was a rotten smell in the place (many subsequent visits to The Spaniard have assured me that this was a fluke) and I must have twisted up my face. The woman to my right noticed.

"Awful," she said. "*Awful.* Some plumbing problem. Lucky your drink smells so good." We both laughed.

"What brings you to Belfast?" she asked.

With that question, I flashed back nearly twenty years to the summer of 1991, the only time I'd been to the Northern Irish capital before.

That summer, I lived in Dublin, where I was enrolled in an Irish Studies summer program for American students. In a grave *in loco parentis* spirit, one of the faculty members warned his charges not to go to Northern Ireland. He suggested that not only was it dangerous, but also, with palpable condescension, that there was nothing to see there anyway. I hadn't considered a Belfast excursion until I was told not to take one. I did some perfunctory research before catching a bus north. I would have a look around, visit two famous old pubs, and return to Dublin not long after I'd downed a pint in each.

I felt uncharacteristically shy there, and disoriented. And scrutinized—like a stranger blowing into a saloon in a Western. Normally, pubs are where I feel most at ease, most welcome, most open to strangers. But the professor's admonition had gotten to me. A Belfast pub was no place to make small talk, I told myself. Maybe I'd say the wrong thing, whatever that was. I kept my head down and avoided eye contact. Was it really hostile, or had merely being told it was hostile been enough to make it so? In retrospect, the latter is likely—but I was relieved to return to Dublin, and especially to Grogan's, the pub that had become my local there.

I would not encounter the poetry and prose of one of Belfast's greatest writers, Ciarán Carson, until years after that first visit. His poem "Last Orders"—its title a fine, grim double entendre—is set in a bar where "you never know for sure who's who, /or what/ you're walking into." The poem ends, so to speak, with a bang:

> . . . how simple it would be for someone
> Like ourselves to walk in and blow the whole
>   place, and ourselves, to Kingdom Come.

The tension I felt in the pubs on that 1991 visit didn't compare to this, but at its core the anxiety was the same: How was I to tell who was who? How could I know what to say, what to withhold?

I had little idea how to read the city, how to read its bars, how to read the signs and signifiers, layers of them built up like coats of paint. The weight borne by signifiers of many kinds, I would gradually come to discern on further visits to the city, was heavier in Belfast than anywhere I'd ever been.

But by 2010, things had changed. The Good Friday Agreement was more than a decade old. Tensions still flared up from time to time, certainly, but the city felt so much more open, calmer, happier.

Ciarán Carson, I told the woman next to me at The Spaniard that October night in 2010, was in fact my reason for being in Belfast, or at least the reason that made it possible for me to justify the cost of the visit. I was there to interview him, and to build an essay around that interview for The Poetry Foundation website.

"Well, since you're a writer, you should follow us. We're going to the Hewitt. That's where writers drink. We can't stay here another minute."

Her name was Kerry, and, as it happened, she was an off-duty Belfast constable. I followed her and her friends to the John Hewitt, only a few blocks away. Uncertain as to whether I'd been invited to drink with them, or if they were only leading the way, and not wishing to crash their party if the latter was the case, I thanked them for bringing me there, and stood at the bar.

I'd only just ordered my first pint when the guy to my right struck up a conversation. The first thing he told me (really, the very first thing) was that he was a Catholic and went to mass daily. I doubted this was something anyone would've announced to a stranger in a Belfast pub even just a decade earlier. Then he leaned in closer.

"So what are you?" he asked. "Catholic or Protestant?"

I thought about how that question might've made me feel in 1991. Terrified, no doubt.

"Neither," I said. "I'm Jewish."

Under the circumstances, my answer, and it was an honest one, felt pretty safe (even if it might also be true that announcing one's Jewishness seldom feels *totally* safe, outside of New York, anyway, but that's a whole other story). He didn't seem sure what to make of this, and neither commented nor turned away. I thought of another Carson poem, perhaps his best known, "Belfast Confetti." This is how it concludes—

What is
My name? Where am I coming from?
Where am I going?
A fusillade of question marks.

—testifying to a time when the answers to any of these questions might have put a person in very real danger, when questions themselves were, in their way, acts of war. The questions in "Belfast Confetti" are only marginally less direct than "What are you? Catholic or Protestant?" Anyone who really knew Belfast, really inhabited it, would have been able to tell from a name, from a neighborhood, what it was that you were.

And there I was, in Belfast in 2010, in a cozy, busy pub that rightly prided itself on its excellent variety of craft beers and real ales, from Ireland and England and elsewhere; where young, sweet-faced musicians played old traditional airs and reels on a small stage just beside the front door; where a soft fire burned in a small hearth; in a pub, I learned from reading a brochure tucked inconspicuously into a corner, that was owned and operated by a local nonprofit agency, The Belfast Unemployed Resource Centre, which was founded by the bar's namesake, a Belfast poet and outspoken Socialist named John Hewitt (whom I've also heard, in a small comic irony, was a teetotaler). There I was, in this warm, welcoming place that existed largely to benefit programs and services for unemployed citizens of Belfast, being asked directly: *What was I?* Even though I felt unmenaced by the inquiry, it was a shock to have been asked. I wondered what it meant to the asker. My sense was that he was luxuriating in the freedom to declare who and what he was, which, as my contemporary, I figured he hadn't always been able to exercise, and wanted to extend the same to me. Even if my answer threw him a little, he was open, and curious.

The Hewitt felt like a very safe space, and a brilliant model, too: Why didn't more nonprofits run pubs, instead of writing one little grant after another? It didn't seem to shout its agenda at anyone; but then, I was less equipped to read the signs than locals were.

The daily communicant—I regret that I cannot now recall his name—and I stepped outside for a smoke. It was raining less now but late, and Donegall Street was dark. An older man approached, brandishing a copy of that day's *Belfast Telegraph,* the major local newspaper. He walked right up to my new drinking buddy; they knew one another.

"Did you see the news?" the older man asked the younger.

The news wasn't about a bombing, or a plot, or politics at all. The news was that, in a poll,

readers had chosen The Undertones' punk anthem "Teenage Kicks" as their favorite song.

"It's one of my favorites, too," I said.

The older man looked at me skeptically. "Oh, you know it?"

"Of course I know it." I probably rolled my eyes. "It was John Peel's favorite."

"Oh, you know who John Peel was, do you?" He seemed even more doubtful.

I was exasperated. Did any music lover not know who John Peel—the great English DJ, the champion of many of the best bands of my youth, and before, and after—was? I'd encountered this strain of condescension before, in Ireland, and elsewhere in Europe: the ready assumption that Americans know nothing. Much as I'd often rather let it go, it pissed me off, and still does. The older guy and I had a brief, terse argument, and as he stepped inside the Hewitt, I'd written him off as prick.

My smoking companion told me that the man's name was Terri, and that he was known as the godfather of Northern Irish punk rock, that he ran an indie record store in the city, and that it was he, in fact, who had sent the demo of "Teenage Kicks" to John Peel. Well, I was impressed, but I still didn't like him.

The following day, as I walked around the city, I happened upon Terri's record shop, Good Vibrations. Of course he recognized me.

"Last night at the Hewitt," he said, narrowing his eyes.

Within an hour, we were laughing and talking about music in the back of the store. I bought a copy of his memoir, *Hooleygan*, which had recently been published, and in which he inscribed his name and drew a flower. The next day on Facebook, he proposed. It was only later I'd learn that Terri addresses most every woman he meets as "the future Mrs. Hooley"— a running joke around Belfast, at least among those who know him, and most people seem to know him. Still, I knew it meant we'd reconciled.

The impulse to scrutinize is hardwired in the people of Belfast. They want to know what each of your tattoos means (even if they mean nothing, and are mostly just sailor flash you like the looks of). They want to know who you are. Where you're from. Where you're going. They want to test you. They want to figure you out. Let them try. I learned this from Terri, who has been kind and generous and great

fun in my subsequent visits. Sometimes true friendships start in skirmishes outside bars.

•

So here's a bar—a great bar—named for a poet, to which I was led by a policewoman, where I met a punk hero, and where, I like to think, one drinks with greater purpose than usual, as every drink consumed helps the unemployed people of Belfast. It's like a pub out of a dream.

Well, to me it is. But not to everyone.

On my next trip to Belfast, in 2012, I'd had a great session at the Hewitt. If there's anything I want most from a bar, any single thing that I believe makes a bar special, it's a mix of people. On a spring evening at the Hewitt, I got into a rambling, ranging conversation with two old gents who'd grown up in the Cathedral Quarter long before it became a nightlife destination with posh hotels and tapas bars, and a young lesbian couple. One of the women was raised in the Antrim countryside. Her partner was a tough, funny Belfast native. We quickly coalesced into a happy party of five, told stories for hours, and treated each other to round after round. It was one of those bar nights that reminded me, as if I needed reminding, why bars matter so much to me.

On my way back to my hotel, I stopped into The Spaniard for a nightcap, still floating on the fun I'd had at the Hewitt, and got to talking to two history graduate students. When they heard that, for my living, I mostly write about drinking, they cracked up, as people often do.

"You've found a great bar here," one said, gesturing at the tiny front room of The Spaniard, kitted out like a fanciful pirate's grotto, full of pictures and posters and maritime tchotchkes, oozing low-lit, low-ceilinged charm. I agreed with him.

I sipped my daiquiri (The Spaniard has a way with rum drinks) and thought about what the student had said. There are bars in Belfast that announce their allegiances clearly. Nothing at the Hewitt ever struck me as sectarian. I heard no talk there that I would call Republican. As an outsider, I felt at home. In my visits to the bar, politics never even came up.

I was troubled by what he'd said, and embarrassed by the possibility that I'd misread the place. But the more I talked to

THE BARS I LOVE BEST ARE NEVER THE ONES I'VE READ ABOUT IN TRAVEL BOOKS OR MAGAZINES . . . THEY'RE THE ONES I COME ACROSS INSTINCTIVELY, OR AM LED TO BY A STRANGER, WITH NO EXPECTATIONS.

He asked where else I liked to drink in the city.

"I've just come from The Hewitt," I told him.

He got very quiet and paused before speaking again. "I never go there," he said. "It's a Republican bar."

He and his friend finished their pints. He wished me luck, said it had been nice talking, and left.

other people in the city about it, the more I asked questions, the more I listened, I was not persuaded by his assessment, even as I do not doubt his own conviction. To me, it didn't make sense. John Hewitt, for whom the pub was named, was raised a Methodist. His politics were, above all, Socialist. His cause, poetry aside, was economic justice.

Belfast isn't easy. There are some, I was told, for whom the Left (particularly those involved with labor politics, as Hewitt was) and Republicanism are completely bound together. To others, this is emphatically not the case. Signifiers that mean one thing to the history student don't mean the same to others. There are places, and people, that can't be read simply as Catholic or Protestant, Loyalist or Republican, one or the other.

Nearly four years after I first stepped foot in the Hewitt, I still have not written that story about Ciarán Carson, and the editor who acquired it has long since left The Poetry Foundation. It is a source of burning shame, for which I have devised a multitude of excuses: I had been ill when Carson and I met and could not read my notes, written while I was feverish (true); when I returned home to New York, my mother was gravely ill and my attention turned toward her and away from work (also true).

But after all this time, what's really kept me from my task is rooted in the same thing that keeps bringing me back to Belfast, every year now: My suspicion that I'll never get it right. Maybe no one gets it right. But the city, the poems, the pubs—especially the Hewitt—they're under my skin now. The city is worth the difficulty. Even if I never get it right, I want to keep trying, one pint, one stranger, one pub, one conversation after another.

Mao Mao Chong
12 Ban Chang Hutong, Dong Cheng
Beijing, China
Mitch Moxley

The doughy Chinese cops at the station across the alley never bothered us. Even in the summer, when we drank outside the bar under orange street lamps, smoking cigarettes, talking and laughing at volumes that surely bothered the neighbors. The cops—with their messed up hair, baggy uniforms, and Double Happiness cigarettes dangling from their lips—never cared. That's the way it was in Beijing: anything went.

The bar was called Mao Mao Chong, which means "caterpillar" in Chinese. It was in one of Beijing's *hutong* alleyways, those featured in countless newspaper and magazine articles about "Old Beijing"—courtyard homes, reeking public toilets, laughing old grannies giving each other back massages with their fists. It was inside the Second Ring Road, a short bike ride from the Drum and Bell Towers and the Lama Temple (bicycles being the preferred mode of transportation among the young hipsters, both Chinese and foreign, that increasingly populated the *hutongs*). It was best known for its specialty cocktails, the Mala Mule, for example, infused with Sichuan numbing spice—*mala*. It was a small bar with only a handful of stools and tables; it averaged about a dozen customers on a weeknight, and forty people was a squeeze. Even though it was modern and, in many ways, Western, it was very much a Beijing bar. It could only have existed in Beijing, at that time.

I started hanging out at Mao Mao Chong toward the end of the sweet spot of the six years I lived in Beijing—between 2009 and 2011, when China had fully grabbed hold of me, as it does if you stay long enough. Mao Mao Chong was one of the dots on the map of my Beijing life. I went there with big groups of friends. I went there on dates, and by myself to drink alone. I went there on those sweltering hot Beijing summer nights when you just *knew* something good would happen if you stuck it out long enough, and I went there on winter nights when the cold and pollution clawed at your lungs and all we did was talk about *getting the fuck out of China*. I went there for birthday parties and for going away parties. People were always coming and going in Beijing, and I often wondered what my last day in China would be like, whenever it came. I sketched out a rough outline in my mind: Chinese class; coffee at my favorite café, where I spent most days working on whatever freelance assignment was keeping me busy; maybe a big dinner at a greasy Sichuan restaurant. All I knew for sure was that in the evening, I would be drinking at Mao Mao Chong.

The bar was owned by a petite Chinese woman who went by the English name Stephanie, in her mid-thirties with an enormous smile, and her Australian husband, Stephen, a quiet man around the same age with a shaved head and boyish face. Stephen spent most nights making pizza in the closet-sized kitchen hidden to the side of the bar. He was an artist and his work hung on the bar's walls. Stephanie was Stephen's opposite. She came from Guangdong province, in southern China, and was opinionated and gregarious. She knew all the regulars by name and often won "Best Personality" in the various expat listings magazines' bar and club awards. Stephanie didn't drink, but her cocktails were among the best in the city, and she had competed in bartending competitions as far away as Mexico.

Beijing was a boomtown, and it had a lot of great bars, but Mao Mao Chong was, to me, the best. Because it was both Chinese and Western, old and modern, it reflected the city that Beijing was becoming. It was also impermanent—one day, probably sooner rather than later, Stephanie and Stephen would move to Australia; they had a young boy, and Beijing's air and the long hours running a bar were wearing them down. A landlord dispute, or falling on the wrong side

of one of Beijing's endless urban development schemes, could see the bar shuttered even before that. Those kinds of things happened all the time. In that way, Mao Mao Chong represented the city Beijing already was. Nothing ever lasted—even if sometimes it felt as if things might go on forever.

•

Drinking was a big part of the expat life in the Chinese capital. When I first moved to Beijing, in 2007, to work as a reporter and copy editor at *China Daily*, a government-owned English-language newspaper, I became acquainted with some of the most accomplished boozers the world has ever known. It was an easy job, and *China Daily* attracted an oddball cohort of foreigners. Some were young and looking to live out the build-up to the Olympics; some were runaways from Western society; some had spent decades hopping from one English-language paper to another, all over Asia. There was a group of Indian editors; a quiet fellow who was a member of the Scottish Communist party; and a few mystery men who showed up at work smelling of liquor and then disappeared into the night as soon as their shifts ended. The common denominator was a modest talent for editing in the English language and a great fondness for drink.

During those early days in Beijing, when I worked the late shift at the paper, from 3 to 11 p.m., copy editing (or "polishing," as the task was known around the office) the business section, the foreign editors often gathered after work at a dingy restaurant across the street from *China Daily*, which was simply known as "The Noodle Shop." (It had a name, written in Chinese characters above the front entrance, but nobody ever bothered to learn it.)

"It's owned by gangsters, The Noodle Shop. Whole block is," a pale, bespectacled British editor told me the first time I went, on a warm evening in late April.

"Is that true?" I asked.

"No clue, mate," he said, "but sounds good, doesn't it?"

We sat around outdoor tables, on cheap plastic chairs, drinking beer and eating peanuts and soybeans, tossing shells and pods on the ground. We drank for hours, sometimes until the sun came up. We talked about our jobs, about stories we would like to freelance elsewhere, about trips in China we hoped to take. People got roaring drunk at The Noodle Shop and I saw a number of fistfights, including one in which two Chinese men went at each other's skulls with empty Yanjing beer bottles. Both men ended up lying in the fetal position in pools of their own blood before ambulances came to haul them away.

It was during that time, and in the following years, that Beijing became a true party city. Chinese were getting richer and foreigners were pouring into the city in swelling numbers, especially after the 2008 financial crisis, when China offered opportunity to unemployable university graduates everywhere. The bar scene began to reflect these changes. In the years before I arrived, a night out meant heading to one of the city's upscale hotel bars, or congregating at a tiny hole-in-the-wall on one of the city's "bar streets," most of which were demolished before the 2008 Olympics to make room for office buildings and apartments.

By the time the Games arrived, Beijing was a city in which you could buy 50 cent bottles of beer from a corner store (or The Noodle Shop, for that matter) and drink them in a taxi on the way to a massive nightclub with an international DJ, or to watch a soccer match on live TV at a British sports bar, or to drink $10 cocktails in Sanlitun, the most popular nightlife area. Old bars closed, new bars opened, then the new bars closed and re-opened in a different location, only to close and re-open again with a new name and interior. The Noodle Shop eventually became a 7-11.

A few years after my time at *China Daily*, when I was working as a freelance journalist, my life gravitated almost entirely to the area of *hutongs* at the north end of the Second Ring Road. I eventually moved into a huge apartment in a *hutong* not far from the Lama Temple, and most of my friends and favorite hangouts were within a few blocks. I went to Mao Mao Chong for the first time one night in the early fall of 2010, with a friend who liked to drink whiskey and had heard they had a great selection. We sat in the bar sipping Scotch and I looked around the place—the dim lights, the Chinese hipsters, bottles lined neatly behind the bar, Stephen's artwork, the A-frame roof and wooden fixtures—and thought, *this bar is perfect.*

•

One night, a little over a year later, I noticed a hand-written sign taped inside Mao Mao Chong's door: "Bartenders needed. Experience Necessary." This was after the sweet spot of my time in Beijing. I had been in China almost five years and so many friends had come and gone it was hard to care anymore. I had no vision of what I would do when I left, even though I knew I would, eventually. For all the highs of living abroad—and there are many—it is never easy to live in a place where nothing ever lasts.

Simply looking for things to occupy me, I peeled off the sign, slowly, to not rip the tape,

and walked back in toward the bar to talk to Stephanie. I weaved through a crowd; it was a Saturday night and Mao Mao Chong was packed. When I got to the bar, I held up the sign above my head and tapped it with my index finger to get Stephanie's attention as she made a drink.

"Do you have experience?" she asked.

"None," I said.

But Stephanie and I got along well, and she appreciated her regulars, and so she decided to give me a shot.

I thought being a bartender would be something like Sam Malone in *Cheers*—sliding foamy mugs of beer down the bar, merrymaking with regulars, getting eyes from pretty girls. Not so. Did you know, for example, how many ingredients it takes to make a good cocktail? Did you know that there are different sizes of "jiggers"? I didn't even know what a jigger was.

On my first shift, Stephanie handed me a thick binder of drink recipes and said I needed to learn them all. They were paying me in pizzas, and homework wasn't what I had in mind.

"I sort of thought I'd be opening beers and delivering pizzas to the customers, that kind of thing," I said.

"This is a cocktail bar," she said. "You have to make cocktails if you want to be a bartender."

Throughout the night, I struggled to make Old Fashioneds, Dark and Stormies, and Mala Mules. I used the wrong ingredients in incorrect proportions. I sweated through the Mao Mao Chong T-shirt they'd made me wear. I forgot to place pizza orders and I had to re-make several drinks.

Later, after the bar quieted, I made some practice drinks and chatted with Stephanie and Stephen. They were both drained, and I got the impression they took very little joy from running Mao Mao Chong anymore. Their son was with Stephanie's parents in Southern China, and this weighed on them. Stephen was especially ready to leave China.

"Can't wait," he said.

He had that look on his face—a look you saw sometimes in foreigners who stayed too long—that said, *I don't know if I can take another day*. I wondered if I had the same look on mine.

I worked two more shifts at Mao Mao Chong then went back to the other side of the bar.

•

I left China just over a year after that. There were a lot of reasons, the biggest of which was that it was simply time. I still adored the country, and it broke my heart to leave it, but it needed to happen. When I told Stephen I was leaving, he didn't even ask why. He didn't need to.

I went to Mao Mao Chong even more often during those magical months at the very end. But I didn't go on my last night in China—I didn't go to any bars that night. I spent the day running around the city saying goodbye to friends, and at night came back to my apartment near the Lama Temple to finish packing. There's nothing celebratory about leaving a place you love after six years. I could have gone for one last drink at Mao Mao Chong—a Mala Mule, maybe—but if I did, all I would do was wish I was back living at a time when I still foolishly entertained the idea that something that could never last forever possibly would.

THE
MANAGEMENT

THE CHEAPEST AND EASIEST WAY TO
BECOME AN INFLUENTIAL MAN AND BE
LOOKED UP TO BY THE COMMUNITY AT
LARGE, WAS TO STAND BEHIND A BAR,
WEAR A CLUSTER-DIAMOND PIN, AND
SELL WHISKY . . . YOUTHFUL AMBITION
HARDLY ASPIRED SO MUCH TO THE
HONORS OF THE LAW, OR THE ARMY
AND NAVY AS TO THE DIGNITY OF
PROPRIETORSHIP IN A SALOON.

—MARK TWAIN,
ROUGHING IT

Big John's Tavern
251 E Bay Street
Charleston, South Carolina 29401
Jack Hitt

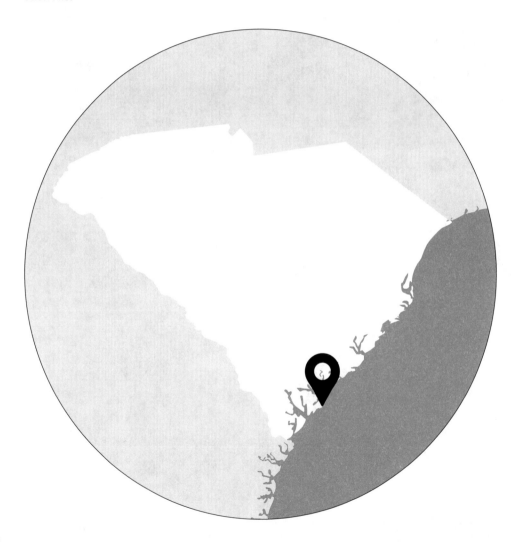

The first story I remember hearing about my local bar, Big John's, involved the long ago night that some guy came in waving a pistol and commanded the bar owner, whom everyone knew as Big John, to empty his register. Now, Big John came by his nickname honestly. As a few old photographs and a framed bubble gum trading card on the wall proved, Big John Cannady had been a fullback for the New York Giants before he retired to open a bar in Charleston, South Carolina, in 1954.

Big John was friendly, almost all of the time, even with a gun pointed at him. So, Big John explained to the agitated man that a terrible mistake was being made, and he offered the man a deal. Big John would permit him to surrender his gun and in exchange, Big John would not beat him into a bloody pulp. The guy declined the offer and shot Big John in the stomach. As regulars at the bar told it, the bullet had about the same effect as, say, one of the confetti'd sticks, a *banderilla*, has on a raging bull in Spain. Snorting with fury, Big John wrenched the gun from the guy's hand and pounded him until the guy slumped to the floor unconscious. Eventually, the cops came and took him off to the hospital and then, only as an afterthought, took Big John there, too.

I was 15 years old when I first heard that old story—it was the mid-1970s—and I had just learned how to order a beer. In those days, everyone went to Big John's to practice drinking at a bar. The open secret about the place was that Big John would serve a teenager. It was a local ritual that had the tacit approval of most parents. For one brief shining moment, getting your first Pabst in Charleston was handled with this sort of Gallic wink. The parents knew it would happen, expected it to happen, and didn't even mind it happening, as long as it happened at Big John's, where mom and dad knew that their dopey teenager would be safe, even from a half-wit waving a pistol.

Physically Big John's looked like any hard-worked pub. There was a not-quite-level pool table at the end of the long bar. The few booths were cozy and redolent of a certain tobacco and beer funkiness—what professional perfumers might call "frat-house sofa cushion." The bathrooms were an endurance test in holding one's breath. The floors had a spelunktacular dampness that defied the primal laws of evaporation. In short, it was a bar.

But it was also a bar where teenagers went to explore a new frontier, the one between drinking and stupid. Downing beers at Big John's meant mastering this distinction, in part because we all knew that Big John might, quite discriminately, card any boy or girl he felt couldn't handle the challenge of behaving older than they were. Most picked up on all this right away and learned how to be garrulous without becoming an ass. But some did not. I knew more than one guy who embarrassed himself so thoroughly that he realized afterward: *Shit, I can never go back to Big John's again.*

The man with the pistol, that was probably his first thought when he came to.

Another guy, whom I will call Gary because that was in fact his name, got totally hosed one night. Somewhere in the evening, he started shouting filthy obscenities at some girls. There was just so much wrong with that, Big John-wise. He did not like loud shouting or foul language, or hollering sex words—especially hollering them at girls. All wrong. His friends hustled him out of there, and I remember thinking, *Gary's going to wake up tomorrow engulfed with self-loathing. And not just with the usual hangover remorse but one made worse by the realization: Shit, I can never go back to Big John's again.*

The paradox of Big John's was that, eventually, everybody had Gary's epiphany, just without the humiliation. At some point, you graduated Big John's and matriculated to other bars. It happened somewhere toward the end of high school. You just woke up one late afternoon and realized that Big John's was less a place you drank in than one you reminisced about.

Bars get romanced for all kinds of reasons. They have some smoky allure for those who love to drink during the golden hour. Or maybe a group of like-minded souls temporarily become regulars, rediscovering the pleasure of gathering around the age-old gravitas of a large chunk of dark wood.

The romance of Big John's was altogether different, though, because it was a kind of bar that might not exist anymore. Big John's was a generational bar where the eponymous barkeep not only knew your name, but in my case, knew my brother's name and each of my three sisters' names. They had all preceded me there. When I first worked up the nerve to walk illegally through that notorious white door and belly up to the bar, Big John leaned in to ask, "Are you a Hitt?" He just knew—from my hair, my face, my laugh. He then went on to tell me stories about my brother, each one of my sisters, and about a certain day long ago, when my father—not a beer drinker—stopped in to have a draft to make sure Big John's would be okay for his kids. Big John knew everyone in my family. He knew who my *cousins* were.

My first encounter with Big John was friendly enough, although I immediately caught a whiff of a melancholy side. He asked me how come he never saw my sisters anymore and why it had been a decade since he'd seen my brother. Big John's easy demeanor was streaked by an undercurrent of sorrow—that gradual bitterness one sees in some college professors saddened by the fact that students seem to get younger, then they just move away, and tempus just keeps on fugiting. Apparently Big John was the last to comprehend that his joint was not just a beer hall, but a practice field.

These days, my big brother Bobby is the Commerce Secretary for the state of South Carolina, the second most prestigious job of his career. The first? During one storied summer, Bobby was Big John's bouncer, standing sentinel at the corner of East Bay and Pinckney streets, outside the barn-red bar's bright white door. Although Bobby was definitely someone you'd want on your side if trouble started, he didn't work at being the tough guy. It didn't matter. For this job, he could have been the skinny guy in a Charles Atlas ad who gambled a stamp. Bobby told cantankerous people twice his size to get lost. They might start to push past

but then, almost immediately, Big John would communicate whole paragraphs of meaning by shooting a look clear across the bar and out the door like a poisoned dart: "You're messing with my bouncer? Seriously? You haven't heard about the guy waving the pistol?"

I don't want to give the impression that Big John's was merely teenage day-care because the underage crowd was only part of the scene. Big John's was (and still is) a straight-up regular bar and boasted a motley assortment of established characters and curious cohorts. There was that small crew that always sat at the bar, a few middle-aged men with ruined faces and a slowly encroaching disdain for razor blades. A few older women sat at the far end, too—sinewy from too much gin and with stoved-in cheeks and each retaining a gravelly patter with just enough charm to comfortably bum a cigarette off a kid.

Serious working men stopped in, too, just off the clock from the wharves a few blocks away, sporting massive biceps and in work clothes smeared by actual labor. Cadets from the local military college, The Citadel, came to drink there—never in their blue and whites, always dressed down, but easily recognizable because their "knob" haircuts made them stand out in any crowd. There were girls and young women there too, learning the crucial skill of drinking in a room full of potentially belligerent men. There were a few rednecks learning to be chill in a place that wasn't dominated by rednecks, and there were a few adventurous black guys enjoying those first years after the successes of the civil rights movement—social swashbucklers, really, drinking alongside their new long-haired white friends. For that time, Big John's was the city in miniature, and that was the reason, as much as any, that parents let their teenagers drink there. This world had to be met, and if you were learning how to drink like a man (without turning into a leering boor) or if you were learning how to drink like a woman (without earning a reputation as an easy lush), then you could ask for no better Virgil than Big John.

At that age, for a boy, the most sought-after emblem of adulthood was a car. But there were lots of smaller appliances one had to master. A cigarette, for example. Some of us were already proficient at the ash-launching thumb flick or the proper Dean-like dangle of a Lucky while, say, changing a tire. But a lot of people did not smoke.

Beer, on the other hand, knew no conscientious objectors. All of us would have to master the easy-going style of clutching a long neck at the top and letting it dangle beside one's thigh like a weapon of mass cool. Or maybe you drank from a can and had to decide whether you were going to wrap the base in a couple of paper napkins, balancing the usefulness of that move (it kept the beer colder) against the fact that it seemed a bit preppy louche. Back then, these were crippling fucking decisions. Did you sip your beer, toss back a solid swig, or guzzle it audibly? (The answer is swig.) For young men in particular, learning to drink a beer was a rite of passage, and for us, Big John's was our coming-of-age ball.

While we knew we were there illegally, we also knew it was with unwritten permission, and that awareness haunted our every action, afraid of the ultimate humiliation. Big John might actually toss you, sure—or he might threaten to call your parents. Which was worse: Earning a beat-down like the pistol guy, or having Big John bellow in front of your friends that he was phoning your mom? Tough call.

One late afternoon, I was there drinking beer with my friend Dickie. We were playing pool in the back with a couple of Citadel cadets, knobs who seemed a little itchier than usual. Cadets often got touchy back then because this was an era of long hair and they didn't get to have any. I can't quite remember how I crossed the line, but I did. I said something slightly incoherent, like, "Do you cadets eat your dead in the winter?" It was some kind of allusion to a big story then about a plane-load of rugby players crashing in the Andes and resorting to cannibalism. But in some tangential way, the insult conveyed the idea that the cadets were more, say, *feral* than the rest of us. One might debate that point, but here was one indisputable fact: those four cadets could definitely beat my ass.

At some point, hollering began and Big John got angry and suddenly Dickie and I were sprinting up East Bay Street to his Datsun parked a block away. We slammed the doors just as four cadets descended on the car like a pack of wild animals, pounding on the hood and trunk with their bare fists. "I believe I have made my point," I said as Dickie squealed up the street. Being right never felt so terrifying.

We left the bellowing cadets standing in the street, and a few blocks later, Dickie pulled over to appraise his car. If you remember those Datsuns—the last of the Datsuns—the bodies were made from what appeared to be slightly thicker pressings of Reynolds Wrap. Dickie had dents in his car, and he was furious with me for provoking this and demanded that I share in the cost of repairs. I felt terrible for the car and even more terrible that I had done something that stupid. I had made Big John scream at me. I don't remember what he said but his rage rang in my ears, as I awoke to a new and blazing sense of remorse: *Shit, I can never go back to Big John's again.*

Cavagnaro's Bar & Grill (closed)
107 Newton Lane
East Hampton, New York 11937
Bill Barich

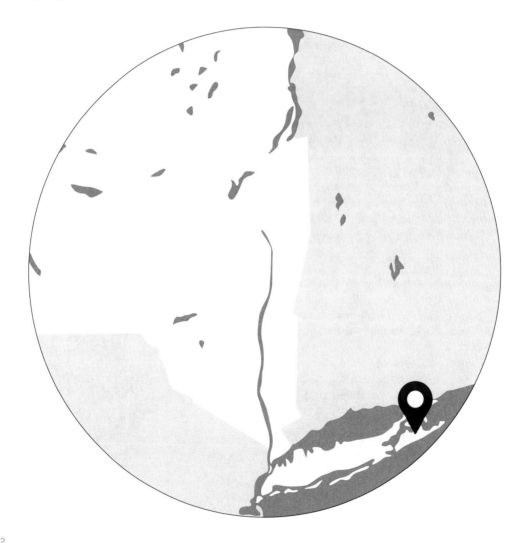

In the summer of 1980—the summer I adopted Cavagnaro's Bar & Grill as my local—I rented a house in the woods of East Hampton as a form of therapy. I hoped to recover the social skills I'd lost while writing my first book in near total isolation, in a dilapidated trailer in the northern California wine country, where my only regular visitor was a 75-year-old fishing buddy. Jack and I played cribbage for a nickel a point, and drank shots of Old Overholt with Brown Derby beer back. I don't recall either of us mentioning books or literature.

All that would change in East Hampton, I assumed. With so many authors around, I'd be able to catch up on the literary shoptalk I'd been missing. I imagined long, boozy evenings discussing the latest controversy in *The New York Review of Books* at the same taverns where James Jones and Truman Capote used to hold forth. I had just one contact in town, an old friend married to a columnist at *Time*, but she turned out to be very well-connected and invited me to a Saturday morning softball game for writers. Perfect, I thought. Exactly what I had in mind—a lazy summer devoted to idle pursuits.

A lot of writers showed up that Saturday, some quite famous. I realized with chagrin I'd never read any of their stuff. They produced thick nonfiction blockbusters and plot-driven novels destined for the big screen. Maybe the trick wasn't to live cheaply in a trailer and pray a publisher would like what you wrote. It might be better to come up with a marketable idea and sell it for a big advance before you'd put a single word on paper. Deals had probably been cut right there at second base. The scales were falling from my eyes.

The *Time* guy was the official scorekeeper and kept elaborate statistics. If you needed to know what Carl Bernstein batted last season, he could tell you. He rigged the game according to seniority. The writers who'd been around the longest—years in some cases—always got to play, but newcomers like me usually had to ride the pines even if they'd been (also like me) a high-school hotshot. Everyone took the softball seriously, too, and they didn't bother with drinks afterwards. Instead they behaved as they did in Manhattan and rushed off to their next engagement. Clearly, I'd been deluded about the literary shoptalk.

Even if nobody else craved a post-game beer, I did and stopped at Cavagnaro's on the outskirts of town. It occupied the ground floor of an ordinary three-story brick building. I'd driven past it several times, but I'd never noticed any activity and wondered if it was still in business. When I peeked inside, the answer appeared to be, "No." The place was empty except for a short, stocky man of 70 or so sitting at the far end of the bar reading *The Daily News*.

He did not glance up from the paper when I entered. Instead he buried his nose more deeply in it, determined to ignore me. This was Al Cavagnaro, who'd been on duty since 1951. His father had opened a restaurant and deli on the site in 1923. Al and his wife still lived in quarters behind the bar, and he cooked when he was in the mood to cook, which wasn't every day.

In spite of the chilly welcome, I climbed onto a stool. Cavagnaro's was a relic of the 1950s, a classic Italian joint with Sinatra on the box and red sauce in the kitchen. I tapped my fingers until Al finally rose from his seat with an audible groan and tossed a coaster in front of me. "What're you having?" he asked warily, then brought me the beer I ordered and returned to his paper. That was fine with me. I felt comfortable in the quiet room with its worn wood and vintage appointments. The bar offered a pleasant refuge from the glitzy nonsense of the Hamptons.

Al was a true Bonacker, I recognized—crusty, flinty, someone who didn't suffer fools gladly. The name derives from Accabonac Harbor, where the baymen and fishermen plied their trade. Most Bonackers regarded the summer people with dismay or worse, as I should've guessed from Al's cold shoulder, but I respected him for not caring if he made a buck off the tourists. "See you later," I called as I left. Al spoke not a word.

When I came back the next day, he was watering the shrubbery out front. "You want another beer?" he asked. I nodded. "OK, I'll open up," he muttered, handing me the keys to unlock the door. By such fits and starts, we lurched toward a conversation. After six visits, Al asked where I was from and, after my eighth, what I did for a living. He'd never had many writers as regulars, he told me, but the painters from Springs, like Jackson Pollock, used to drop in on occasion. "He'd pull up in his coupe with a babe on his arm"— not Lee Krasner, I gathered—"and hit the whiskey," Al confided.

Al didn't drink himself, but he had a terrible sweet tooth. He wasn't supposed to indulge it because the doctors had put him on a strict diet—they were treating him for bladder cancer—and his wife made sure he stuck to it. But he'd devised a strategy to get around her. Whenever she went out, he'd sneak into the deli next door for a pint of ice cream, then melt it in his microwave and slurp it down as fast as he could before she could catch him at it.

The bar was seldom crowded in the early evening. Most customers were Bonackers, guys off the boats or in from the potato fields still in their work clothes. They sold me freshly dug clams and taught me how to surfcast for bluefish. If they were hungry, Al might grill a burger for them, but he couldn't stand to cook all the time. He'd make lunch on Tuesday and be closed on Wednesday. I don't remember a menu. Once he boasted that he'd fixed prime rib, and I was sorry I hadn't ordered it when I saw the huge slab of juicy pink beef he served.

So Cavagnaro's became part of my summer routine. I'd write at home, then visit Al most days. If things had gone well at my desk, I'd celebrate with a bourbon or two, but more often I felt I deserved no better than a Beck's or a Heineken—microbrews and IPAs not yet on tap in that distant, deprived era. Sometimes I sat at a table to read a book, while at others I joined in the ongoing conversation about the farms and the sea. Four months flew by, and I got ready to move on to London at the end of September.

Al's face fell when I informed him. He looked genuinely wounded, and I was surprised. I'd never seen him show any emotion before.

He saw the makings of a Bonacker in me, apparently, and couldn't believe I'd decided to leave instead of settling down. It was as if I'd refused an O.B.E. or declined some other honor. He bought me drinks and insisted on feeding me a platter of homemade sausages, worried I'd risk starvation in faraway Europe.

"You're one of a kind," he said, patting me on the back. That was a high compliment to pay a summer person, and I was grateful for it. He wanted a photo of us together behind the bar, and enlisted a slightly tipsy customer to snap the picture. I still have it somewhere in storage. I'm holding up a glass of beer as though for a toast, and Al's smiling broadly. I sent him a postcard from London, and later heard he'd beat his cancer and lived on into his eighties—still a curmudgeon, no doubt, and much admired by all who knew him.

Weeds
1555 N Dayton Street
Chicago, Illinois 60642
Neal Pollack

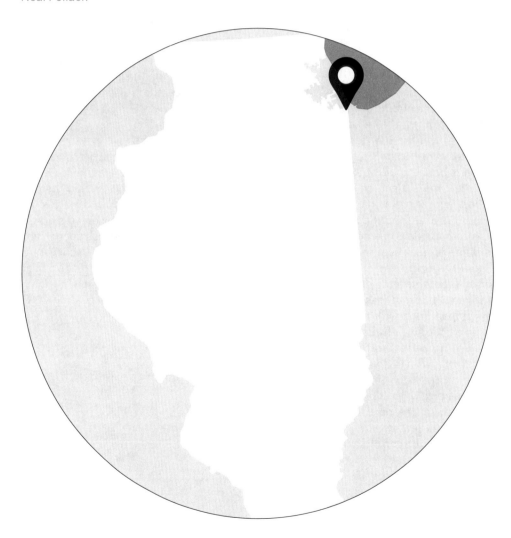

When I lived in Chicago twenty years ago, I hung out in a lot of bars. I did this because I was young, and that's what you do, and also because I'd grown up in Phoenix, a city that barely has neighborhoods, much less neighborhood bars. Dingy, massive, provincial Chicago, with its tavern on every corner, represented the opposite of my childhood. There were other reasons, too: I didn't own a car. The drinking night can really stretch on if you don't need to drive home. But more than anything, I hung out in a lot of bars because it was my job.

After I graduated from college in Chicago in 1992, I took a train trip around the U.S. for a couple of months, then I worked for a miserable season at a magazine in Indiana, and then I returned to Chicago. Within a few weeks, I'd scored a part-time gig as a stringer for a series of neighborhood newspapers, covering water board hearings and doing stories on eccentric neighborhood characters. The latter was my specialty. A crusty old copy editor told me, "You can put together a pretty good feature story, but you have a hell of a long way to go before you're a real reporter."

I didn't want to be a real reporter, not in the way she meant. So I pushed my chips toward local color, choosing piano lounges and urban weirdoes over zoning issues. By early 1994, that decision scored me a job at the *Chicago Reader,* the massive doorstop free weekly that defined mainstream "alternative" Chicago culture at the time. It had a big liberal heart and a massive editorial well. There was ample room for 2,000 words, twice a month, of bar talk.

I hung out in Polish bars and black bars and Mexican bars, gay bars and the straightest of straight sports bars. Each one told a story, or hundreds of stories, and I wrote them down for the newspaper. Most nights I'd be sitting on some barstool listening to people. Sometimes I felt like the Angel of Death as I covered one dying bar after another, watching the North Side slowly making the transition toward a more sophisticated drinking culture, where the booze and beer tasted better but the conversations were much less interesting.

Occasionally, I'd happen into a bar that was worth writing about more than once. An old Pole named Joe Danno operated a still in the back room of his joint on Cicero, which he called Bucket O'Suds. His liquors were vile concoctions, viscous hell-syrups that were hardly worth the wait, but the place had a spirit that kept it alive from the end of Prohibition to the grunge era. I spent a memorable night licking Lucifer Elixir off a placemat with infamous rock groupie and penis-mold artist Cynthia Plaster Caster, and was also there the night Joe closed the doors and shuffled off to Vegas, where he soon passed away, sad and sober.

But when it came to weird liquor-slinging establishments, Weeds topped them all.

The bar was presided over by a gruff, horny mid-forties pinko named Sergio Mayora, who, in the bar's glory days, would blow into Weeds around 9 o'clock, his dark hair in a ponytail. He always wore OshKosh overalls, a white T-shirt, and dark sunglasses. In his prime, he looked like he could lift a horse.

Weeds was dark and smoky. There was an elk's head on the wall that had a plastic skeleton dangling from its antlers whether it was Halloween or not. A burning stick of incense protruded from the eye of a mannequin head. Christmas lights hung everywhere. It was a carnival of unironic bohemian kitsch. There were also high-heeled shoes and dozens of brassieres hanging from the ceiling. Sergio liked it when women showed him their tits.

Sometimes he asked, sometimes the women volunteered. Sergio had a way of making the girls go wild; he was charming and shameless. In 1994, he installed a painted plaster bust of himself holding a bottle of tequila and giving a thumbs-up.

Weeds had been owned by the Mayora family since the late '50s, but they used to call it the 1555 Club until Sergio took it over in 1979. It had catered to factory workers, "back when there were factories in the area," he once told me for one of several articles I wrote about the bar. "My father, me, my uncles and aunts, we all worked here." The place was also a restaurant, but Sergio stopped serving food in the '80s, when the refrigerator broke. "I took it as an omen," he said.

His father and mother both came to Chicago from Mexico, and Sergio grew up in various neighborhoods on the West Side. Sergio was the artist in the family—a sculptor, part-time lounge singer, and poet. He decided to make Weeds a permanent home for his many friends. The bar hosted a cavalcade of painters, freaks, cholos, rockers, and assorted bohemians from across the city. The MC5's old manager, John Sinclair, hung around, making trouble. Thursdays were for jazz, and there were often theme nights. Birth Control Night was always a popular promotion, and no one got in the door on Halloween unless they were in drag. If nothing special was going on, Sergio and his buddies would sit on the stoop outside and loudly pass around a bottle of tequila.

In 1986, disc jockey, rock critic, and former White Panther Party "propaganda minister" Bob "Righteous" Rudnick approached Sergio about staging "literary bouts." The idea was based on the competitive readings started by local poets Al Simmons and Terry Jacobus around 1980; these poetry "fights" would eventually abandon the boxing metaphor in favor of wrestling, becoming more commonly known as "slams," a term believed to have been first coined by another Chicago poet, Marc Smith, around the same time.

Sergio said his family "was not at all interested in poetry. They wouldn't know how to spell it. If anyone else had come in, I don't know how I would have reacted. I was still a little rough around the edges, but I could tell Rudnick was for real. He was a great guy, man, and I said do it."

Weeds attracted poets who belonged nowhere else, including Joffre Lamar Stewart, who was 70 years old when I met him in 1994, and is still, incredibly, reading at open mikes in Chicago, as he's been doing since the '50s. He was immortalized in Allen Ginsberg's "Howl," and carries the poem around just to show disbelievers. Ginsberg wrote of Stewart having "big pacifist eyes sexy in their dark skin passing out incomprehensible leaflets." In 1993, Stewart was thrown out of a Barnes & Noble in Evanston because they thought he was homeless. He was trying to attend a poetry reading in the bookstore, but instead wound up getting arrested and spent eleven days in jail. Afterward he would not show up in court and told a reporter, "Not believing in courts, I do not try appearing in them." Stewart's poems were distinctly terrible and very anti-Semitic, and people at Weeds frequently booed him, but he was always welcome.

At some point in every Weeds poetry night, Sergio would read. He'd written two poems in his life, he told the crowd, and he always performed them in the same order. One was called "The Hole." It went:

We see outta holes.
We smell outta holes.
We eat,
We talk,
We hear,
We breathe,
We sweat outta holes.
We all piss outta holes.
And we all shit outta holes.
When we were born, we all came out of a hole.

And when we die, they put us all in a hole.
Life is one big hole.
It's a can of worms any way you open it up,
So you might as well dive right in and enjoy
your whole life.

I left Chicago in 2000, but I never forgot those
soaring words.

Sergio remained at Weeds for another decade,
by which point his nephew John Martinez was

puppets representing Tim Geithner and Larry
Summers. That old radical spirit lives on.

One of the last times I saw Sergio was in 1998,
when a bunch of friends had a party for him
at Pop's On Chicago, a spacious and then-
ungentrified tavern just west of Damen. As a
friend of his said to me, "People are saying, 'Is
this a benefit for Sergio? Is he dying?' No! Why
do you have to wait until someone's dying or
dead to have a party for him?"

A BURNING STICK OF INCENSE PROTRUDED FROM THE EYE OF A MANNEQUIN HEAD. CHRISTMAS LIGHTS HUNG EVERYWHERE. IT WAS A CARNIVAL OF UNIRONIC BOHEMIAN KITSCH.

running the bar. But the neighborhood got too
gentrified, the bar too yuppified, for Sergio's
taste. When they took down the bras from the
ceiling, it was time for him to leave.

He's still kicking around Chicago. There's
YouTube footage of him playing the guitar and
singing songs at the great Old Town Ale House,
one of his favorite non-Weeds joints, from 2011,
and, more bizarrely, a video of him playing the
guitar and singing about the financial crisis to

It was a fun time, though it started to wane
around midnight. Sergio and the Weeds crew
couldn't party like they used to. I mostly hung
back and watched. Before Sergio left, he was
asked to step outside for a brief video interview
by a guy who was taping the event for public-
access cable.

"Sergio," the guy said, "you just heard some
words talked about you. I've interviewed a
bunch of people who think you're a real nice

guy. Whaddya got to say to them?"

"They don't know no better," said Sergio.

"Except for my aunt and my sister. Everybody else is lying."

The cameraman looked nervous, and Sergio laughed sadistically.

"I'm very happy to be here," he said. "I hope I'm here a little longer. I feel like it's just a change of address. I'm either going up there . . ."

He pointed up.

"Or down there . . ."

He pointed down.

"But I think I'm going down there. Actually, I'm going to heaven. I'm going to Mayberry. Yeah, Mayberry's heaven to me. When I used to watch TV I thought, that's what heaven is like. Except there weren't enough fucking Mexicans there. I mean, we're all getting there soon anyway. I'll set it up for you guys. That way it'll be a lot easier for the rest of you dumb fucks."

Shots
1256 Weathervane Lane
Akron, Ohio 44313
Sean Manning

It was the summer before our senior year of college, the last summer that we would spend in Akron before getting real jobs and moving to other cities. We knew the significance. We didn't talk about it, but our understanding was evident in how much we saw each other. Unlike summers past, nobody ever made excuses. It didn't matter how early you had to be up the next morning for your internship in Cleveland, or how much homework you had to do for your MCAT prep course, or if your brother was in town visiting from Chicago for just that night, or, in my case, how exhausted and demoralized you were after a long day working a shitty shoe store job: you hung out. We hung out practically every night that summer. And we always hung out at Shots.

It sure as hell wasn't because of the bar itself. For starters, it smelled like shit. Actual human feces. It was located in the Cuyahoga Valley section of Akron, a mile down the road from the city's sewage treatment plant. Every night that god-awful smell would come wafting over. There was an outdoor area with tables and chairs but the stench was so bad you couldn't sit out there. Not even the doormen would stand outside.

The doormen were real dicks—ten times more power hungry than your typical bouncer. They'd sit their fat asses on a stool just inside the door and only let one person inside at a time. Then they'd take a good minute studying your ID, holding it up to your face. It took longer to get into Shots than to get past the most stringent airport security checkpoint. I'm positive those sadistic bastards did it intentionally, so that the rest of the people wanting to come in had to wait outside and suffer the smell of the poop plant.

Shots was divided in half, each with its own bar and vibe. In back was the nightclub half. It had fluorescent spotlights and a tiny dance floor that could fit six people at most. It didn't need to be any bigger. Nobody ever used it. There was never any dance music. The only albums that played on the jukebox that summer were Kid Rock's *Devil Without a Cause* and Creed's *Human Clay*. In front, by the entrance, was the sports bar half. There was a pool table and air hockey and three or four TVs always tuned to ESPN. This was no different than any other bar in Akron, but that didn't make it any better.

Really, Shots was a terrible bar. We only started going there because of the owner, Terry Deane.

He was friends with a couple of my buddies' parents. He'd just opened the place and he needed the business. But as it turned out, Terry was the reason we kept coming back.

Terry also owned the old Highland Theater. The theater had opened in 1938. It was run-down when Terry took it over. Few of the light bulbs worked on the original marquee and the seats were the same as when my parents went there as kids. Supposedly Terry put $250,000 of his own money toward renovations. This included turning the concession stand into a bar and, behind it, installing a huge, white neon sign that read "China White Lounge." He hoped to turn the bar into a hip, young hangout. He started screening art house and indie films. I saw *Mulholland Drive* there. But it never caught on, and eventually Terry sold the Highland, focusing all his attention on Shots.

The rumor was that Terry had made his money from being some hot shit Hollywood producer back in the '70s as well as managing some big-time rock stars. I never bought it. Who in their right mind would want to live in boring Akron with its sub-zero winters after hobnobbing with the rich and famous in sunny California? Then again, he definitely looked the part of a 1970s film producer or rock-and-roll manager. He had a full head of white hair and bushy eyebrows, and he always wore a button down shirt with three or four buttons open to show off his chest hair. He looked exactly like the actor Albert Finney. He constantly had a drink in his hand. His face was always flushed and there was always an excitable, mischievous gleam in his eyes, as if at any moment he might jump into his car and set off on some wild adventure. His car was a black Corvette. The bartenders called it the Terrymobile.

The bartenders were our age, and pretty— brunettes mostly, one or two blondes. One was pregnant, and smoked, which made us all very uncomfortable. Terry made the girls dress in all black. Tube tops weren't mandatory, but that's all I remember them wearing. A lot of people thought Terry was a dirty old man. Even I said so on occasion. I don't remember why. I don't have any specific examples. More likely, I was—we all were—a little threatened by Terry. We may have been in our twenties, but we were far from adults. We were still very insecure. Terry wasn't. He was comfortable with himself. He didn't give a fuck what anyone thought of him. We were jealous.

Terry usually sat by the entrance, on his own stool near the bouncer. Anytime anyone came in he'd shake their hand and say, "Terry Deane. How the hell are ya?" I heard that at least fifty times that summer. We went to Shots four or five nights a week. We'd stay until close at 2 a.m. then drive downtown, twenty minutes away, for Rally's Big Buford burgers. We rotated designated drivers. We always had one, ever since a friend was killed in a crash a couple years before.

When we first started going to Shots, it was empty. Aside from Terry's convivial presence, that's the main reason we kept going back. Shots felt like our own private clubhouse. We didn't have to wait to get served or deal with any wasted asshole meatheads trying to pick a fight, as was usually the case with the three or

He'd walk over and put a hand on our shoulders and say something nice about us to the girls or something witty in a way that acknowledged we were different from the rest of the crowd—we were a part of the fabric of the place. The girls would totally go for it. We'd go out to our cars and fool around, holding our breath as we ran hand-in-hand across the parking lot.

But of course Terry himself was the reason Shots became the place to be. Like most of northeastern Ohio, Akron is politically liberal. It's

NATURALLY ONE OF THE MOST ICONIC FIGURES OF MY ADOLESCENCE WOULD COME WALKING INTO SHOTS. IT WAS THAT MAGICAL OF A PLACE.

four other bars in the Valley. It made up for the smell and the doormen and the Kid Rock and the thoughts of smoking-related birth defects and the neon-colored shots the girls passed around in test tubes, which were fucking disgusting. We still did them. But they were fucking disgusting.

As the summer went on, the bar got more and more popular. We liked to take credit for it—and often did when trying to impress girls. "When we started coming here, there was nobody," we'd tell them. Terry would always do his part to help.

had the same Democratic mayor for more than twenty-five years and Summit County is always colored blue in presidential electoral maps. Otherwise, though, the city is very conservative. There's little tolerance for eccentricity or panache. Yes, Devo is from Akron. So is Chrissie Hynde. Jim Jarmusch hails from neighboring Cuyahoga Falls. They all moved away. An art-house theater showing David Lynch films can't make it. There are few genuine characters. Terry was one. It was impossible to resist his bravado and charm. He infused the bar with an aura I can't rightly explain. He just had it, whatever *it* is. I mean, I only exchanged a few sentences with the guy, ever, and here, nearly fifteen years later, he left a big enough impression that I'm writing an essay about him. He's still that fresh in my mind.

Shots became such a hotspot that one night the actor who played Principal Belding on the TV show *Saved by the Bell* showed up. He was in town as one of the annual Soap Box Derby's celebrity guests. (Suffice it to say, the Derby was in steep decline since its 1940s and '50s heyday, when Jimmy Stewart and Dinah Shore were regular attendees.) Like most kids my age, I'd been obsessed with *Saved by the Bell* growing up. Had you told me one day I'd be standing in the very same room as Belding, I would've freaked out. Most of the bar was—throwing their arms around him, buying him drinks, posing for photos with their disposable cameras. But to me it was no big deal. Naturally one of the most iconic figures of my adolescence would come walking into Shots. It was that magical of a place.

Inevitably, the bar became way too crowded and overrun by the meatheads. Some nights it was so packed we wouldn't even see Terry. This made it a little easier to leave Shots behind and head back to college—but only a little.

Shots would never be as popular as it was that summer. Soon, the Double Olive became the new hot bar, then The Nuthouse, then The Dorm, then The Double Olive again. Those first couple holidays, we'd stop in at Shots to pay our respects to Terry. He was still planted on his stool, still his usual gladhanding, gregarious self. But the place was so empty there was no longer any bouncer. It was really depressing. We'd have one quick drink then leave. Shots stayed open another two or three years, then Terry sold it.

It wasn't until after he died that I heard about his new bar. One of my buddies whose parents were friends with him told me. Around 2008, Terry decided he wanted to open a new place: an Irish pub. So he jumped on a plane and flew to Ireland and did some research. When he came back, he bought an old, barn-sized restaurant-bar just down the road from Shots, closer to the poop plant. He renovated the entire place—put in a new bar and floor and tables, all in the same beautiful, honey-colored wood. The old restaurant-bar was dark and cave-like. Terry's place glowed like a damn leprechaun's pot. He even changed the tile on the roof to look more authentically Irish. He called it Terry Deane's Irish Pub.

Or that's what he was going to call it. He was diagnosed with cancer and died two months later, before the bar could open. Somebody else bought it. It's still in business and does well.

It was only in reading Terry's obituary that I discovered the rumors about his past had been true.

> Terence F. Deane, 68, of London, England, left town early August 12, 2009. Terry immigrated to America from England in his teens when he found out he couldn't be King. After a tour of duty in the U.S. Air Force, Terry moved to Los Angeles and dove head first into show business, where he managed musicians and stars like The Mamas and the Papas, Louis Gossett, Rob Reiner, Tuesday Weld, and Albert Brooks. Terry also produced dozens of Hollywood movies, including *I Never Promised You a Rose Garden*, which was nominated for four Academy Awards. Terry married his wife, Julie, in 1976 and moved to Akron shortly thereafter, where he became Senior Vice-President of Mohawk Rubber and later opened and managed several local nightspots like The Highland Theater and Shots. . . . He enjoyed a good glass of wine and laughs with his friends, and his life had no shortage of either. . . . Terry died of the trendiest disease out right now—cancer—joining Farrah Fawcett, Paul Newman, and Sydney Pollack to name a few. Terry was diagnosed in early June and fought the disease with his trademark humor, wit, and easygoing attitude. Well, his humor and wit at least.

Humor and wit is right: Terry wrote the obituary himself.

Gabby O'Hara's
123 W 39th Street
New York, New York 10018
Andrew W.K.

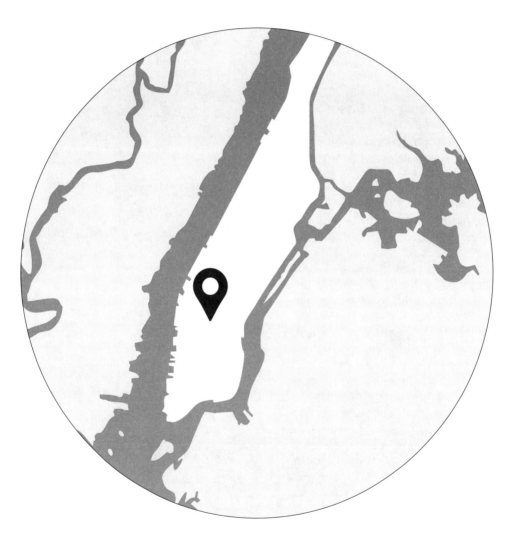

A lot of people don't like Midtown Manhattan bars—or Midtown Manhattan in general. For me, it has always been the best part of the city: the swirling whirlpool of personalities and pressures. The place where all sorts of people could be found crammed together—everyone from business workers to construction guys, from tourists to students, from crazy people to wealthy shoppers. It's why I wanted to live in New York City in the first place, and why I worked year after year to make my way closer and closer to Midtown. I don't like the area because it makes sense to me. I like it because it doesn't make *any* sense to anyone. It makes me feel out of place in the best way. Other parts of the city have lots of people who remind me of myself: similar interests, similar social circles, similar styles and backgrounds. That's too easy and too comfortable. Give me Midtown, with all its off-kilter, commerce-driven chaos. There's no way of knowing who is from where, what they're doing here, or where they're going next.

One of my favorite things about Midtown is Gabby O'Hara's Irish pub. I've probably gone to Gabby's more than any other bar in the world. Actually, I've probably gone there more than any other *place* in the world, other than

my own house—well, that might be a slight exaggeration, but only slight.

I never really had a favorite bar before Gabby's. I'd usually order drinks at restaurants or at venues when I was seeing a show or performing my own. Or I'd just go to a liquor store and buy a bottle of something. Why spend $25 on two drinks in an establishment when you get an entire bottle for the same price? But after randomly walking into Gabby's for the first time in 2009, I realized exactly why people do go to bars, and why some of those bars become their favorite places to go, period.

A friend of mine had suggested we meet at Gabby's for lunch. It was a spot he had been to many times, and even though I lived in the neighborhood, it had never really occurred to me to go inside. It's next to a big chain hotel and the exterior is attached to an office building, so I didn't really notice what it was offering. When I walked in, I was shocked by how well-finished and complete the pub looked and felt. It seemed like it could've been there for thirty years, despite being much newer. That feeling of familiarity and worn-in style didn't come from artificially-aged patina or efforts to appear old; it came from the employees, and how perfectly they inhabited the space—as though they, and the bar, had always been there.

Now, for me, what makes a good bar has little to do with the price of the drinks, the selection of drinks available, the clientele, or even the decor and atmosphere; it has everything to do with *the bartenders*—it all comes down to who's serving the drinks.

Don't get me wrong: Gabby's has an excellent selection of just about every sort of beer, wine, and liquor you could want, as well as really, really great dinner and lunch food. (I've eaten full meals there plenty of times, including Thanksgiving dinner.) The place is very cozy and comfortable, with a beautiful dark wood bar, plenty of seats and tables, and warm lighting. But it's the people who work there that truly make it remarkable. I'll even say that the service at Gabby's is amongst the best service I've experienced anywhere, whether it be at a bar, a restaurant, or just dealing with service from people in general. And the high-quality service isn't just for the regulars. I've seen plenty of first-time visitors treated with the same perfect blend of attention and low-key respect that I've enjoyed over many years of patronage. In fact, I've learned how to be a better person by watching how the bartenders at Gabby's approach their craft and treat their customers. At some point in day-to-day life, everyone ends up serving someone else, and when it's done with the kind of care that Gabby's puts into it, the very idea of service is elevated to an angelic realm. In other words, it's *humanity at its best*, and it makes me happy just thinking about the place.

Gabby's is a true Irish pub, meaning it's owned and operated by people from Ireland. I think everyone working there, except some of the cooks, was born in Ireland. Out of respect for the other excellent pubs I've visited in Manhattan, I've noticed that the bartenders at genuine Irish pubs have a similar level of focus and excellence. This seems to be a tradition and part of the appeal of the Irish pub specifically. Because of this, whenever I'm in another town and am looking for a drink, I would always choose a proper Irish pub over any other breed of drinking establishment.

I've found Gabby's to be the best Irish pub in New York City—at least for me and what I'm after. It seems to be the place I'm meant to be, and that's a special and rare thing to find in a city. There may be sexier bars, or older bars, or cheaper bars, or fancier bars, but I have NEVER been to a bar with better bartenders than Gabby's, anywhere in the world, and that's what matters most to me.

The bar service revolves around a core group of five main bartenders. There are also lovely cocktail waitresses, but I've only really ordered at the bar, so the fellows tending to it are the folks I'm most familiar with.

Martin usually works the early shifts when they open for lunch around 11 a.m. I think he's the oldest one and has a very soothing, fatherly quality—but in a completely non-judgmental and warm way. Plus, he has a wonderfully heavy pour. I've seen him come in to Gabby's on his nights off to show the place to friends and family. He's even bought me drinks on those occasions, and made me feel like a member of his extended troop.

Desmond is closer to my age, and anytime I've brought a lady into Gabby's, they've always developed a crush on him. He's someone I would trust to do the right thing in just about any situation, and I've seen him handle plenty of ordeals in the bar with a level grace that far exceeds his years.

Andy was the mystery and the toughest nut to crack for a long while—he's the most serious of all the fellows. Earning his respect took a bit more time, but it meant all that much more when we finally hit it off. We share the same name, so that helped. He has the least tolerance for foolishness and that's part of his charm and

adds a sense of balance and integrity to the overall texture of Gabby's. He loves to talk about his kids and family, but always with a focused and stern delivery. He is the fastest moving and most determined bartender of the bunch and is quick to send food back to the kitchen if he doesn't think it looks right, even before serving it to a customer.

Aiden is the youngest Gabby's bartender, I think. He's often the one closing up at 4 a.m., but will take his time to make sure all is well, even if it means he's leaving at 6 a.m. or later. I've never met a nicer guy. Sometimes in the early morning, when I got up to catch a taxi to the airport, I would see Aiden walking home, having finished a shift at 8 a.m.

Then there's the owner, Tom, who may be about Martin's age, or older. Despite being hardcore Irish, he lives and breathes American country music, and I've learned a great deal about classic and modern country by listening to his jukebox selections. When Tom starts singing along to "Seminole Wind," you get the sense that he's living the true American dream—doing what he was born to do and being where he was meant to be.

These gentlemen have made my partying dreams come true time and time again. I've gotten so spoiled by their excellence that almost every other bar falls short by comparison. What makes them so great is their absolute focus, not only on the bar, but on the customers, too, and always with good cheer and a calm attitude—they never sacrifice the quality of their character for the quality of their service—a nearly impossible balance to maintain. I've never seen anyone wait for service, or have to fight for a bartender's attention, even on a crowded weekend night. I've never seen a bartender the bartender smirking and commenting, "Must be a bad day, huh?" I actually wasn't having a bad day at all. I was having a *great* day. So I quickly left that bar and found another with a better bartender. You will never hear unnecessary comments made about customers' drinking styles at Gabby's. They've perfected that rare and subtle blend of warmth and distance, work and fun, energy and relaxation.

AT SOME POINT IN DAY-TO-DAY LIFE, EVERYONE ENDS UP SERVING SOMEONE ELSE, AND WHEN IT'S DONE WITH THE KIND OF CARE THAT GABBY'S PUTS INTO IT, THE VERY IDEA OF SERVICE IS ELEVATED TO AN ANGELIC REALM.

at Gabby's try to avoid serving someone or disappear and leave the bar unattended. Even when a customer has gotten out of line, they've handled it as smoothly and as professionally as they would handle a bottle of rare whiskey. It really is a sight to behold.

I've gone into other bars in the city and asked the bartender a simple question like, "What's the highest proof bourbon you have?" only to find Gabby's isn't the realm of "mixologists" making drinks that take ten minutes to prepare and muddle (although they certainly possess the skills to do so). Instead, Gabby's is a place where you'll be served quickly and without any nonsense or chatter. Unlike other bars, I've never had a bartender at Gabby's give me a weird look when asked for a certain kind of drink or spirit, or try to make small talk, thinking it will guarantee them a better tip. At other places, the bartenders tried to strike up unnecessary and awkward conversations about my order, or my clothes, or my personal life. For me, less is more when it comes to bartending. At Gabby's, they only talk if you want to talk, and it won't be forced or overly aggressive, but charming, witty, and quick—so the focus can remain on the bar itself. They remember every regular's name and immediately understand what sort of demeanor each regular customer prefers. Some folks love to talk sports. Others don't want to talk at all and just prefer to listen.

I've enjoyed plenty of laughter-filled nights with friends at Gabby's, jamming out to perfect selections on the jukebox. I've enjoyed nights alone where I watched sports on TV and people perform karaoke with live bongos and tambourine. I've taken friends there from out of town who were treated like old regulars and even let behind the bar to prepare their own drinks (and serve other customers). But some of my best times were simply walking in when the place was almost empty, and just sitting quietly by myself, enjoying being there instead of somewhere else.

God Bless Gabby's. God Bless New York City. And God Bless This Book. PARTY HARD FOREVER.

Eddie's Club (closed)
428 N Higgins Avenue
Missoula, Montana 59802
Kevin Canty

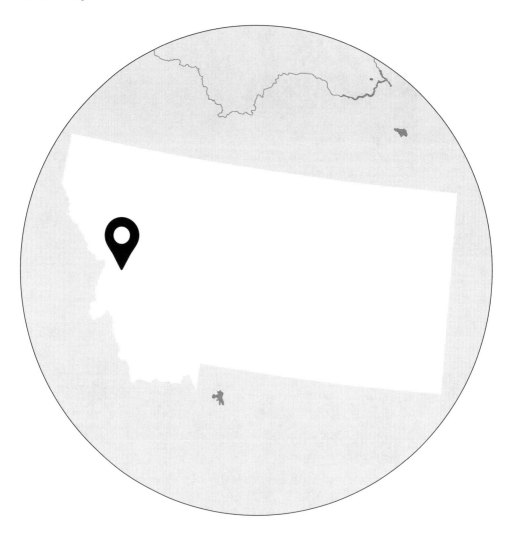

I came to Montana in the fall of 1972, nineteen years old, on a train called the North Coast Hiawatha. I dismounted in Missoula at the handsome old Northern Pacific station at the northern end of Higgins Avenue, the main street of town, and made my way to the Palace Hotel, where I rented a clean but threadbare room for $1.75 a night, bathroom down the hall. I then went in search of a bar.

I ended up in a place called Eddie's Club, for reasons I don't remember. Maybe it was as simple as thinking I wasn't going to get beat up. I was from the East Coast and I had a ponytail and I didn't know what the etiquette was in Montana bars, but this looked like a pretty free-and-easy spot. There were people who looked like college professors, people who looked like railroad bums, native Americans, cowboys, road workers, and even a few longhairs. It was not a crowd I had seen before and it amazed me with its variety.

A glass of beer was ten cents and a schooner was a quarter. The well drinks were tiny but cheap. All around the walls of the bar were handsome black and white portraits of men's faces, not pretty faces but lined and worn and well-used. This was confusing, more so when I recognized one of the faces from the wall drinking at one of the tables. This didn't seem at first glance to be the kind of place that would be decorated in original art: a long, dim room with a wooden floor and a battered backbar and a scattering of mismatched tables and a jukebox. In my imagination, it was playing "Kaw-Liga" by Hank Williams at the moment. It may very well have been.

The bartender was a tall, pale, balding man with the face of a 45-year-old baby. Was his name George? He was really very tall. Once, a couple of years later, I saw a drunk, angry, short woman take a metal folding chair by the legs and try to beat him with it. George just stood there with his arms folded across his chest while she hit him and hit him until she eventually spent herself. Then he threw her out.

I liked it here. I had quit high school a couple of years before and gotten a job as a construction laborer and had come to enjoy the after-work ritual of the bar, not every night but more nights than I should have. I recognized some percentage of the Eddie's Club clientele by their dirty jeans and hard hands. But even the ones who would turn out to be artists and musicians and even college professors were dressed like working men and women. The only ones wearing sport coats were the real down-on-their-luck types who wore whatever they could glean from St. Vincent DePaul.

The place was cheap enough, and close enough to the railroad tracks, that anybody could drink there.

I had been in and out of Montana for much of my life. My mother was from Billings. I had an uncle in Great Falls. I had come once with my grandmother Gertrude when I was eight or ten and gone a hundred miles an hour between Great Falls and Glacier Park, a number that impressed the crap out of me. But I didn't know Montana as an adult. Montana was different then, more different than it is now. There was no sales tax and no speed limit, no cable TV and no McDonald's. Missoula was not a cow town but a timber town—the minor-league ball team was for a time known as the Timberjacks—with seven operating mills in the valley, plus a number of teepee burners. Most of the locals heated with wood, too, so on a winter day when the inversion kicked in, the air was gray and toxic and smelled like a wet paper bag. It was a long, cold winter. That year, the high for the month of December was one degree Fahrenheit, and it only got up to one degree on one day.

Even if you loved it, I learned, there were moments in February and March when California or Arizona seemed like the only viable options. The people who stayed did so because they had jobs here or family here or both. It was a day's drive to the nearest major-league baseball game or art museum or French restaurant, and that day could stretch

infinitely if the passes (two major passes and a minor one between here and Seattle) were snowed under.

So people left: rich people, ambitious people. The riches of the mines of Butte paid for the building of San Francisco and the Corcoran Museum of Art in Washington, D.C. The tourists who loved it so in August were usually long-gone after a winter or two. The "Rocky Mountain High" that John Denver sang of was about a thousand miles south of us.

The ones who stayed were mostly working in the mills and the mines and the woods and the railroads. The smelter in Black Eagle was still going, as were the aluminum plant in Columbia Falls and the mines in Butte and the airbase in Great Falls. The Northern Pacific Railway and the Milwaukee Road still ran the width of the state, both of them, and the forests were checkerboarded with clearcuts. The people who got rich off these endeavors lived somewhere else. What you were left with was a big working class that shaded into a smaller middle class at one end, and genteel self-reliant poverty at the other. There were no rich neighborhoods but there weren't any really poor ones, either, unless you counted the trailer parks. And there was no particular shame in living in a trailer, either.

All this is just a long way of explaining what made Eddie's feel both common as dirt and also unlike anyplace else in the world. On the one hand, it was pretty basic: it was cheap, it was clean enough, you didn't have to dress up or dress down to go there. It wasn't really a wino bar, most of the time, but there wasn't anything fancy about it. On the other hand, that guy behind the bar might be Lee Nye, the photographer who took the beautiful portraits of drinkers and hoboes that lined the wall. He taught photography at the University and took portraits of the better-off, too. A few years later, I was leafing through a bookshelf and pulled down a first edition of *Love and Death in the American Novel* and there on the back jacket was a picture of the author, Leslie Fiedler, taken by Lee Nye in his unmistakable style.

That guy on the next barstool might be James Crumley, a Texas transplant and genius mystery writer. He liked the place so much that he renamed it Mahoney's and featured it in his first detective novel, even giving his hero an entirely imaginary secret office behind the bar. That guy selling prints off the pool table might be Jay Rummel, folk singer, ceramicist, and visual artist; the longhair cueing up another song might be a poet, or a philosophy professor, or a tree planter, or a bum. Richard Hugo, the poet, preferred to do his drinking elsewhere—he stayed at Harold's Club in Milltown, which was exactly as fancy as you'd expect a place named Milltown to be—but his students were at Eddie's.

I never really belonged there. I was a youth, a college student, and I was from Out of State.

Worse than that, I was from Back East. But the beauty of the place was that you didn't need to belong there. They took all comers. This was the same principle that had let me enroll at the University with a GED from Washington, D.C. Basically, I was tall enough to push my money over the counter.

It wasn't the only game in town, either: Missoula was a town of bars, one for every mood. If you wanted to dance there was the Flamingo Lounge at the Park Hotel, or the Cabin in East Missoula. The Stockman's and the Turf were good for Western flavor and the Flame was perfect for dangerous assignations, a long dim room that was mainly lit by a thirty-foot fish tank above the bar, through which an eel moved in sinister curves. There was Connies, the Silver Dollar, the Top Hat and the I Don't Know Tavern. You could walk from one end of the downtown to the other, from the railroad to the river, by going out the back door of one bar, across the alley, and into the back door of the next.

Eddie's was a certain mood: unpredictable, adventurous. It felt slightly dangerous though I don't think it actually was. You would end up in a conversation that you hadn't thought about before, about the Kennedy assassination or the impossibility of time travel. Or you could end up cornered by the world's drunkest bore, telling a story they really wanted to tell that was a little shorter than the Britannica but not much. Old tattoos and lined faces and stories to tell. If a girl wanted to go to Eddie's that meant something, especially if she also owned a fringed leather jacket. (The 1970s, remember?) Eddie's was where we hatched the plot to spring my friend's brother out of the state mental hospital in Warm Springs. It wasn't much of a plot—we drove to Warm Springs, my friend's brother jumped out a window, then we drove home—but it worked.

in and played the same song twelve times in a row, a country song from the viewpoint of a semi called "Hello, I'm a Truck."

So that's what I remember of the Nixon resignation: "Hello, I'm a Truck."

After a few years of this I moved on, stayed out west, came back to visit my sister a few times. The old parts of Missoula always seemed the same to me, but one time I came to town

THE TOURISTS WHO LOVED IT SO IN AUGUST WERE USUALLY LONG-GONE AFTER A WINTER OR TWO. THE "ROCKY MOUNTAIN HIGH" THAT JOHN DENVER SANG OF WAS ABOUT A THOUSAND MILES SOUTH OF US.

Eddie's was where I watched Nixon resign, too. My friend Brad and I had just come back from a week-long backpacking trip across the northern tier of Glacier Park, starving for ice cream, salad, cold beer, and news. We stumbled into the bar just as Nixon was starting his speech. The bartender had set up a little black and white TV on the back bar—normally there was no television in the place—and as Nixon started to warm to his task, a drunk from the very loud table of drunks behind us wobbled over to the jukebox and put a dollar

and Eddie's was gone. I couldn't seem to get an answer for why. By the time I got back here a decade later, to take a job teaching writing at the University, there was a new bar in the same place, called Charlie B's. It was not exactly Eddie's but they did have the pictures on the walls and the cheap drinks and the democratic spirit and a few of the regulars from the old place. At Eddie's, they used to put a gold star on the portraits of the ones who died. At Charlie's there got to be so many gold stars that it got depressing, and now you get one if you're still alive.

James Crumley used to drink in Charlie B's, too, at least in the afternoons, when it was most like the old place. At night the youth would take over and the music would be blasting and Crumley would move across the street to the Depot, a more sedate place, where a plaque now stands to commemorate his passing, right next to his familiar barstool.

These days Montana's more like everywhere else, of course, just like everywhere else is. We have a French bakery and four independent breweries and coffee shops everywhere. You can get fresh fish and instant news. We even have a few Internet entrepreneurs. The tattoos are back, of course, but they're the nice new fresh kind, not the woke-up-in-Sitka-with-a-hangover-and-a-tattoo kind. But sometimes, if you're in the mood for afternoon drinking—a beautiful Saturday in the summertime when the rest of the world is hiking or working or out on the rivers, or better still a winter Tuesday with a blizzard blasting outside—you can wander in to what used to be Eddie's Club and settle on a torn barstool and get a shot and a back at three in the afternoon and start a conversation with whoever's on the next barstool and smell the smoke of decades past and you can fool yourself into thinking that you really are someplace.

THE
MUSIC

THE LIGHT MUSIC OF WHISKY FALLING
INTO GLASSES MADE AN AGREEABLE
INTERLUDE.

—JAMES JOYCE,
DUBLINERS

Bradley's (closed)
70 University Place
New York, New York 10003
Written by David Hajdu; Art by John Carey

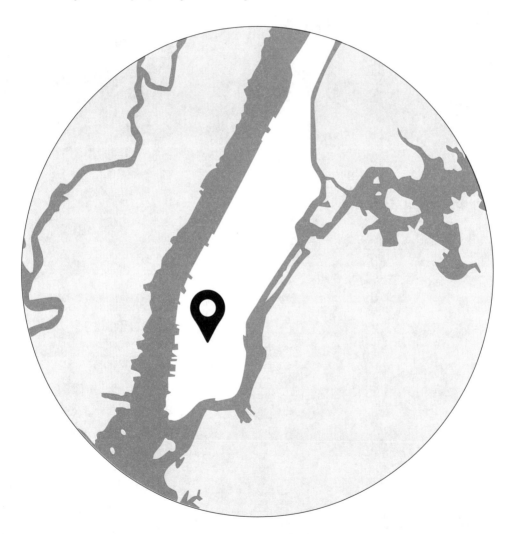

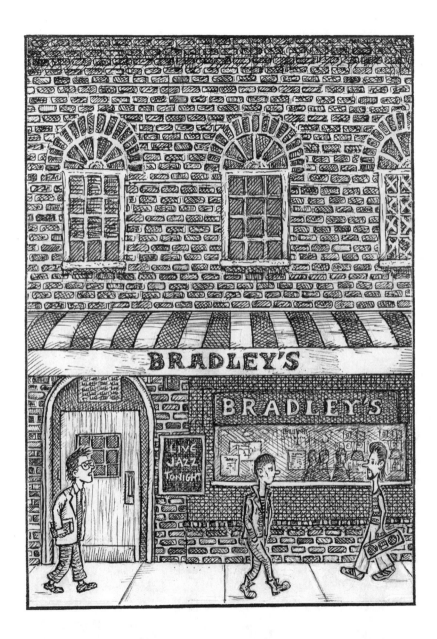

I GREW UP IN BARS. THERE WERE A THOUSAND OF THEM IN THE SWEATY LITTLE MILL TOWN IN NEW JERSEY WHERE I WAS RAISED, AND MY FATHER LIKED THEM ALL. HE WOULD PICK ME UP FROM SCHOOL AND TAKE ME ALONG WITH HIM ON HIS ROUNDS TO GUY'S AND SHORTY'S AND STEVE'S. I'D PLOP A BOOK ON THE BAR. HE'D GIVE ME A QUARTER TO PLAY THE JUKE BOX. I HAD A PRIVILEGED CHILDHOOD.

WHEN I WAS IN COLLEGE, AT NYU, I DID MY COURSE READING WHERE I WAS MOST COMFORTABLE, IN THE BARS IN GREENWICH VILLAGE. ONE NIGHT I HAPPENED UPON A SPOT A FEW BLOCKS NORTH OF SCHOOL, ON UNIVERSITY PLACE BETWEEN 10TH AND 11TH STREETS: BRADLEY'S. I COULD HEAR THE SOUND OF JAZZ SEEPING OUT FROM INSIDE.

I LOOKED THROUGH THE BIG PLATE-GLASS WINDOW IN THE FRONT, AND I SAW A BAR FULL OF PEOPLE NOT TALKING TO EACH OTHER. MEN AND WOMEN WERE SITTING TOGETHER WITH THEIR HEADS BOWED. ONE GUY WAS READING. THIS WAS A BAR FOR ME.

THE BRADLEY OF BRADLEY'S WAS BRADLEY CUNNINGHAM. HE WAS A LOOMING, BROAD-SHOULDERED GUY WITH HOLLYWOOD STUDIO-ERA LEADING-MAN LOOKS AND A WAY WITH PEOPLE. I EVENTUALLY LEARNED THAT HE HAD BEEN A MARINE IN THE PACIFIC THEATER DURING WORLD WAR II, AND HIS ASSIGNMENT HAD BEEN TO INTERROGATE JAPANESE PRISONERS OF WAR. HE WAS SAID TO HAVE WRANGLED VALUABLE MILITARY SECRETS OUT OF HIGH-LEVEL CAPTIVES. AFTER THE WAR, HE CAPITALIZED ON HIS SKILL AT GETTING PEOPLE TO OPEN UP, AND BECAME A SUCCESSFUL BARTENDER IN NEW YORK. HE WORKED FOR A WHILE AT CHUMLEY'S, A FORMER SPEAKEASY IN THE WEST VILLAGE, AND THEN RAN THE 55 BAR ON SHERIDAN SQUARE. WHEN HE TOOK OVER THE 55 BAR, HE REMOVED THE TV AND PUT IN A JUKEBOX. WHEN HE OPENED BRADLEY'S, HE REMOVED THE JUKEBOX AND BROUGHT IN A PIANO.

BRADLEY LIKED BEBOP, ALCOHOL, AND CIGARETTES, AND HE COULD PLAY CHORD PIANO IN A STYLE THAT WAS IMPRESSIVE IN SHORT DURATION. HIS CLUB PROVIDED JAZZ AND COCKTAILS IN AN ATMOSPHERE OF UNDERSTATED ARTINESS AND FRIENDLY SERIOUSNESS. BRADLEY'S AS A CLUB SEEMED LIKE A REFLECTION OF BRADLEY AS A MAN, AND BRADLEY CAME ACROSS AS A CERTAIN KIND OF MAN BECAUSE OF THE CLUB HE RAN. I LIKED THE PLACE IN PART BECAUSE I WANTED TO BE A PERSON LIKE BRADLEY. I KEPT COMING BACK, AND THE GUY AT THE DOOR -- LARRY WAS HIS NAME -- STOPPED ASKING ME FOR THE COVER CHARGE.

READY FOR ANOTHER SCOTCH?

SURE, THANKS!

BRADLEY'S WAS A BAR THAT HAD PIANO MUSIC, BUT IT WASN'T A PIANO BAR IN THE USUAL SENSE. THE PIANISTS DIDN'T TAKE REQUESTS, AND THE CUSTOMERS DIDN'T SING ALONG. THE JAZZ THAT I HEARD AS I SIPPED MY COCKTAILS WAS NOT BACKGROUND MUSIC OR COCKTAIL JAZZ. IT WAS SERIOUS BUT UNPRETENTIOUS, SUBTLE BUT VIRTUOSIC. THE VILLAGE VANGUARD, WHERE SONNY ROLLINS PLAYED, WAS THE JAZZ CLUB FOR HORN PLAYING. SWEET BASIL, WHERE GIL EVANS PERFORMED, WAS THE SPOT FOR LARGE-ENSEMBLE MUSIC. BRADLEY'S WAS THE PLACE FOR PIANO JAZZ.

BRADLEY HIRED ONLY FIRST-TIER PLAYERS -- HANK JONES, TOMMY FLANAGAN, JIMMY ROWLES, KENNY BARRON, CEDAR WALTON -- AND THE MUSICAL STANDARDS AT BRADLEY'S WERE SUCH THAT BEING HIRED AT THE CLUB ESTABLISHED SOMEONE AS A FIRST-TIER PIANIST. BRADLEY'S _WAS_ THE TIER. I REMEMBER SEEING FRED HERSCH PLAY AT BRADLEY'S WHEN HE WAS ONLY IN HIS TWENTIES, HALF THE AGE OF MOST OF THE PIANISTS WHO USUALLY PLAYED THERE, AND I KNEW HE WAS GREAT IN PART BECAUSE HIS PRESENCE AT THE PIANO AT BRADLEY'S TOLD ME SO.

ONE NIGHT IN THE EARLY 1980S, THE FRENCH PIANIST MICHEL PETRUCCIANI CAME INTO THE CLUB TO PLAY. PETRUCCIANI, WHO SUFFERED FROM OSTEOGENESIS IMPERFECTA, THE "GLASS BONES DISEASE," HAD A PERSONALITY TOO BIG AND STRONG FOR BRADLEY'S TO CONTAIN.

BILLY STRAYHORN, THE JAZZ COMPOSER AND ARRANGER LONG ASSOCIATED WITH DUKE ELLINGTON, WAS HELD IN SPECIAL ESTEEM AT BRADLEY'S. STRAYHORN'S MUSIC WAS SMART, LYRICAL, AND HARMONICALLY RICH, BEAUTIFULLY SUITED TO THE INTIMACY OF BRADLEY'S. IT WAS AT BRADLEY'S THAT I FIRST HEARD SOME OF STRAYHORN'S MASTERPIECES, SUCH AS "THE STAR-CROSSED LOVERS" AND "SOMETHING TO LIVE FOR," PLAYED BY TOMMY FLANAGAN AND JIMMY ROWLES. THE MUSICIANS AT BRADLEY'S WERE TALKING ABOUT STRAYHORN BEFORE I KNEW MUCH ABOUT HIM.

JIMMY ROWLES
RECORDED "JIMMY ROWLES PLAYS
DUKE ELLINGTON AND BILLY STRAYHORN."

CEDAR WALTON
RECORDED "LUSH LIFE: THE CEDAR WALTON
TRIO PLAYS THE MUSIC OF BILLY STRAYHORN."

TOMMY FLANAGAN
RECORDED "THE TOKYO RECITAL," WITH NINE
PIECES BY STRAYHORN, TWO BY ELLINGTON.

JOHN HICKS
RECORDED "SOMETHING TO LIVE FOR:
"A BILLY STRAYHORN SONGBOOK."

FRED HERSCH
RECORDED "PASSION FLOWER: FRED HERSCH
PLAYS THE MUSIC OF BILLY STRAYHORN."

BILLY STRAYHORN

IN THE MID-1980'S, I DECIDED TO WRITE A BOOK ABOUT BILLY STRAYHORN. TO INTERVIEW MUSICIANS ABOUT STRAYHORN, I NEVER HAD TO MAKE APPOINTMENTS. I JUST WENT TO BRADLEY'S, AND THERE THEY WERE. JOHN HICKS WOULD BE AT THE BAR, LISTENING TO TOMMY FLANAGAN. JOANNE BRACKEEN WOULD BE THERE, LISTENING TO JOHN HICKS. JUNIOR MANCE WOULD BE LISTENING TO KENNY BARRON.

LATE ONE NIGHT, TOMMY FLANAGAN BROUGHT ME OVER TO THE PIANO AND SAT ME DOWN ON THE BENCH. HE TOLD ME THAT BILLY STRAYHORN HAD ONCE TAUGHT HIM HOW TO PLAY HIS INTRICATE SIGNATURE PIECE, "LUSH LIFE," WITH FOUR FINGERS. FLANAGAN INSTRUCTED ME TO HOLD OUT MY THUMB AND FOREFINGER IN EACH HAND, IN A "U" FORMATION. HE STOOD BEHIND ME, LAY HIS ARMS OVER MINE, AND GRIPPED MY WRISTS WITH HIS HANDS. AS TOMMY FLANAGAN MOVED MY HANDS AROUND THE KEYBOARD, I PLAYED "LUSH LIFE," IN A MANNER.

HAVING PLAYED "LUSH LIFE" AT THE PIANO AT BRADLEY'S, I FELT, FOR A TIME, EVEN MORE FULL OF MYSELF THAN I USUALLY WAS.

I KNEW THAT A LOT OF COCAINE WAS BEING SNORTED IN THE BACKROOM AT BRADLEY'S DURING THE '80'S. THEN AGAIN, A LOT OF COCAINE WAS BEING SNORTED EVERYWHERE IN NEW YORK DURING THE '80'S. NEW YORK HAD BECOME A GIANT BACKROOM FULL OF COKE. AFTER ALL THE TIME I HAD SPENT IN BRADLEY'S, I FELT SLIGHTED BY NOT BEING INVITED TO SNORT UP WITH THE COOL CROWD.

IN 1988, BRADLEY CUNNINGHAM DIED OF LUNG CANCER, AT AGE 63, AND HIS WIFE WENDY, A FORMER WAITRESS AT THE CLUB, TOOK OVER THE MANAGEMENT. SHE DIDN'T CHANGE A THING, AND THE OLD REGULARS STARTED TALKING ABOUT HOW THE CLUB WAS NOT THE SAME ANYMORE. I STARTED TO PANIC THAT THE CLUB WOULD CLOSE. I HAD COME TO CARE A LOT MORE ABOUT BRADLEY'S THAN I CARED ABOUT BRADLEY. I HAD NEVER GOTTEN TO KNOW HIM WELL, AND I DIDN'T END UP VERY MUCH LIKE HIM, APART FROM MY WEAKNESSES FOR JAZZ AND SCOTCH AND CIGARETTES.

WENDY KEPT THE CLUB GOING FOR EIGHT MORE YEARS -- LONGER THAN MOST PEOPLE AT THE BAR SAID THEY EXPECTED. IN THE SPRING OF 1996, JIMMY ROWLES DIED. THAT SUMMER, MY BIOGRAPHY OF BILLY STRAYHORN WAS PUBLISHED, AND TOMMY FLANAGAN PLAYED "LUSH LIFE" AT THE BOOK PARTY, WITH ALL TEN OF HIS FINGERS. THAT FALL, BRADLEY'S FOLDED. JUST A FEW WEEKS LATER, NEW OWNERS REOPENED THE SPACE. THEY REMOVED THE PIANO AND PUT IN A TV.

The Uptown Bar (closed)
3018 Hennepin Avenue
Minneapolis, Minnesota 55408
Craig Finn

I like Apple products. I own a MacBook, an iPad, an iPod, and an iPhone. However, there is a particular Apple Store that makes me sneer when I walk by. It is located at 3018 Hennepin Avenue in the Uptown area of Minneapolis. It is a predictably sleek Apple Store. It has smart displays of their newest products. I'm sure the service is very good. But it occupies the space that, for many years, was The Uptown Bar. I know the Apple Store didn't push them out exactly, but they represent something that did, and I need someone to blame.

There are many bars I love. In Manhattan, I love HiFi. In Brooklyn, I love the Pencil Factory and Lake Street. In London, I love Quinn's. In Leeds, I love Mojo. I love First Avenue in Minneapolis like a brother, but in my mind that's a club more than it is a bar. In modern day Minneapolis I love the Triple Rock and Grumpy's. But in my lifetime, and in my memories, my all-time favorite bar was The Uptown Bar.

As a kid we used to go to the Uptown area just for something to do. I lived in a nearby suburb and it took about fifteen minutes to get there by car. Once parked we would walk around, check out the preening punks in front of McDonald's,

poke through records in various stores, or watch street musicians. Sooner or later we'd cross over Lake on Hennepin and slow our walk to look in the darkened front windows of the Uptown. It was beery and mysterious to us, all smoke and neon. There was a stage on the far wall and sometimes a band might be setting up.

The Uptown was a bar and thus it was always 21 and over to get in. This was massively frustrating to me because I loved music. The Uptown had music seven nights a week. First Avenue, the legendary club downtown, had a lot of shows that I couldn't get into due to age, but they did have some all-ages shows. The Uptown was completely off-limits, so it seemed extra interesting to me. Also, I had read articles in *City Pages*, Minneapolis's free alternative weekly, mentioning that members of the Replacements and Soul Asylum drank there. It sounded to me like it was a clubhouse for Minneapolis rock royalty.

I had a rock gig flyer collection that covered the walls of my bedroom. Many of the advertised shows had taken place at the Uptown, but I was unable to get past the doorman. Each week I would look at the Uptown's show calendar in *City Pages*. The shows would taunt me: local favorites like Arcwelder and Babes in Toyland played there but also hip touring bands like Nirvana and The Flaming Lips. Minneapolis at the time had a thriving music scene but it was all a little older than me and a bit out of reach. I was pretty sure I was really missing out on all the amazing stuff that happened at the Uptown.

Finally I realized that the place was not just a bar but a restaurant. To feel a little closer to the action a friend and I met there for breakfast one day. It was not the same as rocking out to a flannel shirt with a Grain Belt in your hand, but it was something. We could get inside and feel some part of the scene.

The restaurant was slammed. Breakfast was popular at the Uptown. The food was pretty good and the portions were huge. HUGE. The hash browns on my plate were roughly the size of a football. It was especially good if you were just going to eat one meal that day, which was likely for many patrons. The crowd was mixed: some older folks, but mostly hungover artist and rock-and-roll types. There were no children there. Most people were washing their food down with Bloody Marys, which the bar boasted were the best in Minneapolis. The Bloody Marys came in a souvenir pint glass that said Uptown Bar. While we were too young to be served alcoholic beverages, we did negotiate two of those pint glasses from the waitress.

From our booth I took stock. There was a front room with a rectangular bar and some TVs. Elevated booths lined one side. Beer signs hung on the walls. In the other room were more booths and tables. There were even tables on the stage, and the waitresses walked up and down the stage steps to serve food to the diners seated there.

So now I had entered the building at least. It didn't quite feel like I had really "done" the Uptown given the absence of rock and roll and booze, but it was a start.

•

In 1989, I left Minneapolis to go to school in Boston. My sophomore year, I got a pretty terrible fake ID but it worked at a bunch of places in Boston. When I went back to Minneapolis that summer it worked even better. But I was scared of using it at music venues, as I had heard their doormen were tougher on fake IDs. Eventually, I worked up the balls to try my luck at the Uptown. I went alone. I walked up to the bouncer and handed him my ID. He looked like he didn't really buy it, but after a few seconds he handed it back and motioned me inside. I was in. Free to drink, free to rock, free to mingle with the rock-and-roll people that were suddenly within reach.

I walked to the bar and got a pint of Leinenkugel's. It was the cheapest draft, and the first of very many pints of Leinenkugel's that I would drink over the years at the Uptown. I walked around the place, expecting at any moment that the bouncer would change his mind and come kick me out. A band played. It was a historically uneventful group but at the time it sounded fantastic. I had another beer and then called it a night. I was driving, and I didn't want to ruin a good thing.

I went back a few times that summer, always alone. While I had gained access, I didn't really have a lot of people to talk to. Still, I was able to grasp what was special about the Uptown: it was not a rock club so much as a neighborhood bar for people who loved rock-and-roll. There was a cast of regulars that you'd see each time you went. Guys in dirty suits, spiky hair, weird framed glasses. It wasn't unusual to see Bob Stinson or Dave Pirner saddled up to the bar. There were also a lot of older regulars, people who liked the food or drinks or conversation. It was conveniently located for a lot of people. It was a meeting place, somewhere you could stop in and see if anyone was there you knew. You didn't have to make plans to meet at the Uptown, you just went. That said, I just went and didn't know anyone, so would mainly just quietly nurse my drink in the corner.

It struck me that summer that one thing that made the Uptown especially unique was good live music, but no cover, at least on weeknights. On weekends you might pay $3 or $5 to get in to see one of the bigger local headliners like Cows or Run Westy Run, but mostly there was no cover charge. Bands were paid off the bar receipts rather than a cover, so there was very little risk as a music lover. You could just pop in, grab a beer and poke your head in the other room to see if the band was to your liking. If not, you could spend the evening drinking in the room with the bar, where it was quiet enough to have a conversation. This no cover situation at the Uptown was a huge reason the music scene flourished in Minneapolis in the '80s and '90s. It was a great bar to hang out at, and as a bonus you might catch a cool band you'd never heard of before.

•

The following summer I came back to Minneapolis with an even better fake ID. It was an actual Minnesota driver's license passed down by a friend's older brother. He was old enough to drink but not too much older than me. The photo looked a lot like me, and I even had his college ID as backup. The guy was named John Miller, and I practiced answering to that. I went to the Uptown a ton that summer, at least four times a week. The doorman started saying "Hey, John" when he'd see me, and I stopped having to show ID at all. I was interning at a local record label and made a bunch of cool new friends. Most of them lived walking distance from the Uptown, and we met there after work. I even got friendly with a few bartenders. I felt a part of it.

I saw Pavement play at the Uptown that summer, along with a hundred other great bands. Leinenkugel's were $1.90 a pint, and a few more quarters made a tip. It was glorious.

At the end of the summer came my 21st birthday. My parents took me and three friends to dinner at a downtown steakhouse and then we went over to the Uptown for drinks. I didn't even have a beer at dinner because I wanted my first legal drink to be at the Uptown.

When I got to the door, the doorman said, "Hey, John."

I paused and took out my now legal actual ID, saying, "Actually, it's Craig."

He smiled, figuring out the joke.

"Hey, Craig," he said and handed it back to me.

I was in and it was legal.

My friends and I drank a bunch of beers and a few people, including the drummer of Soul Asylum,

bought me shots. I was to head back to college the next day and I didn't want to go. My summer had ended at the Uptown in a perfect way.

•

After graduation I left Boston and returned to Minneapolis. I got an apartment in the Uptown area and went about my goal of finding a job and starting a band. I did both but also found time to hit the Uptown four nights a week. Sometimes I would get a bit tipsy and get up the courage to go introduce myself to someone cool from a band or label. I found that if you complimented them furiously, they usually were pretty willing to talk to you for a while. My band Lifter Puller got a demo tape together and we played our first show at the Uptown. It went fantastic and we were asked to play again. It was easy to get people to come check it out with no cover charge.

A few months later I walked into the Uptown hoping to catch a band from Seattle called Steel Wool. When I walked into the bar I noticed a big crowd around the TV in the front room, but no one in the band room. I expected to find a down-to-the-wire NBA playoff game, but instead saw a white Ford Bronco cruising down a Los Angeles highway. That is one of my most memorable evenings at the Uptown, all of us watching that strange American history unfold while sipping at our Leinenkugel's.

Another memorable evening was seeing Guided by Voices there when they played Minneapolis for the first time. It was predictably great. I saw a lot of other great bands and some mediocre ones too. I went to some birthday parties there. I went to some going away parties there. I slid into the vinyl booths and my shoes stuck to the floor. On big snowfalls we would bundle up and make our way to the Uptown, trudging through huge snowdrifts. When we got there it would be steamy and loud and welcoming. Those snowy trips to the Uptown were some of the best nights of each year. The bar brought me great joy as well as some crushing hangovers. A few hours later I chased many of those hangovers away with hash browns and Bloody Marys in the same place.

•

In 1996, the Uptown stopped doing music, or at least music in the way we knew it—forgoing rock-and-roll for more upscale local blues and jazz combos. The bar stayed open but without the rock-and-roll traffic I didn't go too much. In 2000, I moved to NYC and I'm pretty sure I only visited the Uptown once after that. But it wasn't just the bar that changed—I changed too. When I went home I wasn't looking for a scene much anymore. Instead, I was trying to stay inside, recuperate from touring, and see the family and friends that I had grown up with, unbothered.

The Uptown neighborhood was getting nice and then nicer still. Rents went up and big brand stores became tenants. There used to be a head shop next door to the Uptown. That is now an Urban Outfitters. That is all fine and normal.

When The Uptown Bar finally closed for good in 2009, much was said in eulogy. In the *Minneapolis Star Tribune,* someone commented that the Uptown was like a rock-and-roll Cheers: somewhere you could go where everyone knew your name. That sounded about right to me. While certainly everyone didn't know my name there, some people did, and I was at the age when that mattered the most to me.

Fireside Bowl
2648 W Fullerton Avenue
Chicago, Illinois 60647
Joe Meno

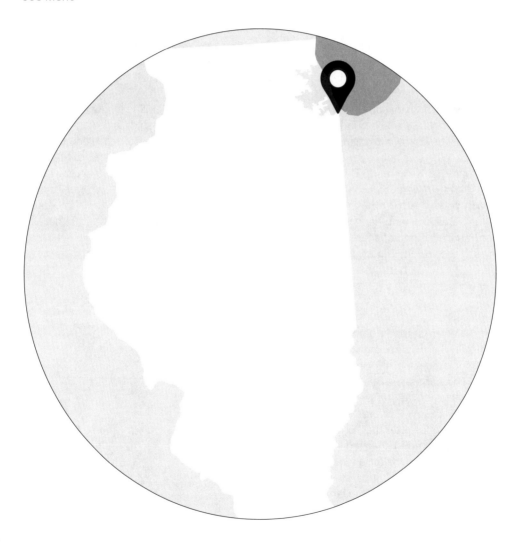

1.

It was the end of the century. Everything we had ever known or had been told to believe was coming to a close. The way light worked somehow seemed different. Everything was fluorescent. Buildings, monuments, and institutions once been thought to be permanent were no longer permanent. The Cold War was over; no one needed to fear being suddenly irradiated. Al Gore invented the Internet and shared it with everybody. You could fall in love without ever seeing somebody's face. You could end a relationship with the assistance of a computer. Music was free. Albums you had spent years of your post-adolescent life trying to track down—haunting used record store bins, visiting garage sales, hitting swap meets—all of it was available somehow. No one thought to call it stealing. Girls who hadn't been pretty— bookstore clerks in turtleneck sweaters, twenty-year-old librarians in thick-framed glasses, art school students who wore too much black eye make-up and carried copies of Kant around— now seemed alluring.

2.

Everyone was in a band at the end of the century. People with absolutely no musical talent—your older sister, your parents, your bearded elementary school teacher—were all recording music. There were bands that only played one song, bands with no instruments, people in bands who bravely announced that they actually hated being in bands. It did not matter if these bands were good or not, only that they made flyers, booked gigs, printed T-shirts, made phone calls asking you to come see their shows.

3.

In 1997, I was living in Chicago. I was twenty-three years old and in a band. In Chicago, in 1997, if you were in your twenties and in a band, and your band wasn't famous, wasn't ever going to be famous, you had no choice but to play the Fireside Bowl.

4.

The Fireside Bowl sat quietly on the north side of West Fullerton, near Western Avenue, with a broken neon sign in the shape of a gigantic bowling pin, stoically offering BOWLING. Among the other crumbling storefronts and brown brick facades on the street—an abandoned-looking mechanic's shop, a kitchen-and-bath supply store—the Fireside was like the woman in Nelson Algren's poem: "Like loving a woman with a broken nose, you may well find lovelier lovelies, but never a lovely so real." Originally built as an ice factory, the Fireside was a long, rectangular, wooden structure, its exterior and interior painted a plaintive red and beige. In the 1940's the ice factory was converted to a bowling alley, following widespread national interest in the sport.

5.

For nearly fifty years, the Fireside Bowl existed solely as a bowling alley, until owner Rich Lapinski handed operations over to his son, Jim. In 1994, the Fireside Bowl began to host its first live music shows. By the late nineties, the Fireside had become the cornerstone of Chicago's explosive underground, punk, post-punk, indie-rock, and avant-rock scenes. It was one of the only local music venues that offered all-ages shows, which meant kids of any age—minor-age college kids, high-schoolers, even brave junior-high-schoolers—could come see the music being played. Instead of introducing an awkward division to the musical proceedings, the presence of the younger kids engendered a sort of older-sibling kindness. You could pretend to be the cool older brother or sister you always wished you had. If the shows got violent—and sometimes they did, with pits and aggressive dancing, not to mention the inter-politics of various Chicago skinhead groups—older kids in

their twenties would usually watch out for the younger ones. It sort of felt like summer camp, for kids who were too weird to go to the real thing.

6.

Once at the Fireside, I saw a boy who had to be eleven or twelve years old getting his head shaved into a Mohawk between bands. I thought about the hell the kid would catch when his mom or dad came to pick him up in their suburban minivan. Then I thought about the memory that kid would have—the incandescent feeling of a beautiful, pink-haired twenty-something girl leaning close, breathing against the back of his neck, as the clippers shaved away the rest of his bowl cut—to keep him company during his forthcoming puberty. I thought that, in the end, the kid had probably made the right choice.

Once the Fireside hosted a benefit for local college station WLUW. It was promoted as a slumber party and high school kids and twenty-somethings jumped around in their pajamas and nightgowns. Somebody brought pillows for a pillow fight. Dan the Fan—who danced relentlessly near the front of the stage at every show he attended—took out a switchblade and tore open all the pillows. By the end of the night, small white feathers had filled the air. There were at least a hundred kids dancing in what appeared to be snow.

Once I saw a band I had never heard of named PAL play a blistering set of George W. Bush-inspired screeds. It utterly reaffirmed my faith in live music, the idea that a band like that could even exist, could make music so riveting, though no one had ever heard of them.

Once, when I was 25, I thought I was dying. I had to get an endoscopy because a doctor thought I had the early symptoms of colon cancer. I didn't have health insurance and spent hours and hours at Cook County, the public hospital. My friend Jake picked me up after the procedure and immediately drove me to a show at the Fireside Bowl. Soon the music started and for the next few hours I did not need to contemplate my illness, my lack of resources, or the future.

7.

I don't know how many bands I saw at the Fireside over the years; hundreds I guess. I don't know how many shows I played there in various bands. Again, most of the bands I saw, and most of the bands I played in, were not that great. Which was sort of the point. The most important thing about the Fireside was its complete lack of pretense; it was hard to imagine the trappings of fame and fortune when you were playing in a bowling alley to a bunch of high school kids. There was no backstage. There was no door on the men's room. During the summer, condensation dripped from the ceiling. Chunks of drywall would sometimes rain down during a particularly loud set. If a band was awful, if it was your band and you bombed, it didn't really matter. There was always a good chance a worse band would play after you.

There were genuine underground artists like Tortoise, Sleater-Kinney, Mustard Plug, Less Than Jake, Shellac, Ted Leo, At the Drive-In, and hundreds of others that overcame the dive-bar scenery and created moments of true musical transcendence, distilling the hope and anxiety of the late-'90s with an incredible rawness and heartfelt immediacy. Their music was almost always loud, almost always familiar-sounding, because these were the kind of songs young people had been singing to themselves for years. Few people danced, but everybody, at least for a few minutes, listened. Just as there was the chance that the next band would be worse than the one currently onstage, there was also the feeling that at any moment the next band, the next song to be played could upend your thoughts about the possibilities of both art and music. By 1999, the Fireside was hosting eight shows a week and no one ever talked about bowling.

8.

Then there was the bar, amid the sweat and peeling paint, like a secret club within a secret club. I remember walking through the peeling wooden door on springs, past the scruffy-looking doorman checking IDs, feeling like I was going into one of the bars my dad used to frequent when I was growing up, those mysterious corner saloons, permeated with the silence of working-class men. The Fireside's bar had that same allure of adult mystery; comfortably small, with a few tables, a faintly-lit jukebox, an unassuming pool table, Budweiser bottles and half-sipped bourbons in square-shaped glasses lining the L-shaped bar. There were always two bartenders: an older woman who looked like she had been there since the Fireside first opened and some younger girl who looked like Wednesday Addams. Were there posters on the wall celebrating the city or maybe the recent Chicago Bulls dynasty? I seem to remember those, but I could be wrong.

Even more than the shows, the bar was the best part about the Fireside, and if you weren't old enough to go in, you might never have known. What made that small, dimly-lit wooden room so special were the young faces, the awkward voices—bright men and women not yet at their best, adventurers, weirdoes, slackers, freaks, druggies, burnouts, stoners, quasi-hippies, a few trust-fund kids. Tough-looking girls with dyed black hair breaking off at the roots from being colored so many times, S and M jewelry around their necks, facial piercings poking out of their lips. Androgynous, overweight

creatures with silver, faux-leather pants and glittery makeup handing out vegan pamphlets. Punk guys with face tattoos who looked like they had been squatting somewhere in the Pacific Northwest and had, for some reason, been forced to rejoin civilization. A post-teen science fair geek talking about his band that featured a theremin.

You could overhear conversations about what the greatest Misfits record was or who was screwing who or who was self-recording a new record or what art installation someone was putting on. Here was a zine your friend had just made. Here was a demo tape for a noise-core band someone was trying to start. I was twenty-four with an art degree, but I was delivering flowers for a living, with artistic ambitions I still did not fully understand, surrounded in that place by people with the same ambitions and the same total lack of understanding.

9.
Looking back now, the importance of the Fireside—the importance of that small bar and all those loud, awkward sounds—seemed to best represent the importance of being in your twenties, of having not quite figured yourself out, of being willing to fail at something, and then having to get up and try again. Which is what happened at the Fireside each and every night. People would gather in the bar and drink.

Bands would play. People would meet back in the bar and talk about what they had seen. Night after night. Make something. Talk about it. Make something again. Five years of those kinds of people, those kinds of conversations, never-before-played songs rattling around in the background. A rough draft; a Xerox; a demo-tape of adult life.

10.

By the start of the new millennium, the threat of worldwide terrorism had begun to appear, with attacks in Africa and the bombing of the USS Cole. The dot-com bubble had suddenly burst. The President got a bad blowjob and lied about it. Most of us had gotten bad blowjobs and had tried to lie about it, with ex-girlfriends or roommates or ex-girlfriends of roommates or girls who lived out on the street. Or girls we met at the Fireside bar. These girls always left weird make-up marks on the pillows when they slept over. Some of them had a hard time waking up, because it turned out they were on a lot of anti-depressants. All of them had surprising tattoos on the backs of their necks—an off-colored rainbow, a happy dolphin, an amiable Strawberry Shortcake—that belied just how inexperienced everyone was.

We watched the President and the impeach-ment trials, saw the Bush and Gore debates, the 2000 election, and felt guilty for some reason. An era of fear, confusion, adult apathy suddenly began.

People began to graduate college, get day jobs, fall in love, move away. Bands I was in played shows one week and never existed again. It seemed to be a lesson the new century was trying to teach us. Don't get too comfortable. Don't go on believing these things last forever. Everything is impermanent.

11.

In 2003, the Fireside stopped having shows. After years of the threat of eminent domain from the city of Chicago and complaints from neighbors, the owners decided to upgrade the bowling alley and stop hosting music altogether. Seven years went by. The Fireside Bowl started having shows again in 2010, about once a week, on off-nights, Tuesdays or Wednesdays, but by then the music scene had moved on to venues like The Empty Bottle, The Hideout, The Bottom Lounge, and Reggie's. Since then it's been co-opted, first by Myspace, then Facebook, then YouTube, and the idea of going to see a show with a band just learning to play their instruments seems less exciting than it should.

12.

I haven't been to the Fireside in ten years. I'm married now and I have two kids. But the real reason is I don't do anything just for fun. I drive by the red and beige Fireside facade and feel like wincing. It's like being confronted by an old photograph of yourself—one from the mid-'90s where you're dressed like Robert Smith. It's horrifying and pathetic but not for the obvious reasons. It's not that you look like an idiot; it's because you don't have the ability to try something and fail and then laugh at yourself anymore. More than the bar, more than the music, more than the sense of camaraderie, this is what I miss. I can still put on the old records, I can still wear the hand-printed T-shirts, now faded, but what is gone is the daring, the ignorance, the guts. Everything I do now happens at the same time, every day. I sync up our calendars and annotate our schedules. I get my cholesterol checked. I fall asleep at 10 p.m. Fourteen years into the new century and I miss being lost.

SOME MEN ARE LIKE MUSICAL GLASSES;
TO PRODUCE THEIR FINEST TONES YOU
MUST KEEP THEM WET.

—SAMUEL TAYLOR COLERIDGE

Club 7
HaMelacha Street 7
Tel Aviv, Israel
Shani Boianjiu

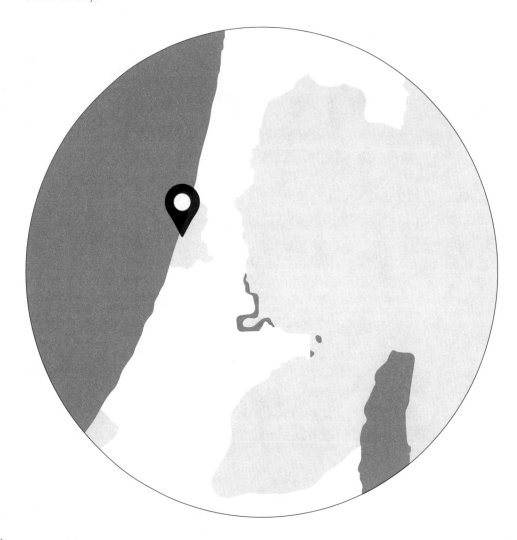

I have only been inside Club 7 once in my life, but whenever I am in Tel Aviv, which only happens if I have to go there for errands or work or to meet my only Tel Avivian friend A., I stand on line just to watch how I don't get let in.

There is so much joy inside you can feel it even as you get hit by people punching and begging the bouncers when they try to claw their way inside. This, as the Lana Del Rey song goes, is my "idea of fun."

It's called Club 7 because it is on HaMelacha Street 7, among the warehouses. The only description it gives of itself online is that "The number 7 circles the world of the Jew, 7 represents perfection, 7 is the number which rules our rhythm of life, and it influences whether we want to or not. Therefore dear friends we have established for you the Club 7 in Tel Aviv. One of the most beautiful places in Tel Aviv, a giant dance bar, several sitting areas, a giant dance floor, several spread out bars."

The truth is Club 7 is very small, compared to any bar I have been to outside of Israel or where I am from in the Galilee, where most bars are in the open air. It is survival of the fittest trying to get in, and I was not excited to hear my friend A. invited another girl, a Russian immigrant, so that now I had to make three people survive the line.

"You invited a little Katyusha?" I asked.

He insisted that I'd like her.

Katyusha is the pet name for the Russian-made missiles that have fallen and are continuing to fall on my village six miles from the Lebanese border. It used to be that my area was full of only Israeli Arab, Moroccan, Iraqi, Romanian, Lebanese, Syrian, and Iranian Jews, but when I was a child this all changed and we became fifty percent Russian. This caused tension. Explosive tension.

It was winter, but like me Katyusha came dressed in a very low cut top that revealed as much as possible. I appreciated this as we needed all the help we could get. She was tiny, and had the face that she admitted many times made people think she was 10. My friend A. knew her from the army, where they were combat medics. I was already done with my service. She escaped persecution for being a Jew in Russia, and came to Israel as a teen, all alone with no family; she stayed with a foster family in a poor peripheral town in northern Israel near my village, until it was time to join the army. All of this she was excited to tell me about, while touching and admiring my hair and body and asking me about my life and appreciating my courage and accomplishments and journey as a fellow Israeli and challenging my assumptions about the road that awaited me while constantly asking me to challenge hers as well, casually.

The line outside of Club 7 was getting dangerous. Groups were fighting among themselves because only some of them were being let in, people were either cursing or crying in front of the gatekeeper, a beautiful 18-year-old blond girl with a clipboard, who was surrounded by seven muscular bouncers.

I was worried about us. Katyusha was European-looking, but her Russian accent and mannerisms were working against her. I was Iraqi and Romanian and Galilean acting. A. was half American-Indian, half Polish, and gay, and not the good type of gay—he was not muscular and he was losing his hair. I told Katyusha not to speak, and A. to try not to look lame and remember he is rich and Tel Avivian. I hoped that the perfect Tel Avivian Hebrew I could use when I wanted to would save the day and that my face would not cause too much trouble.

When Katyusha arrived to Israel, she was told that it couldn't be proven that she is technically Jewish. Now she was using the army's free resources to officially convert in the proper way. A. claimed she was taking it all to the extremes, becoming very devout about following every single rule and regulation.

"What have you learned so far about Jewish rules?" I asked her.

She could tell that I was probably joking.

"Like, you don't steal. You don't lie. You don't covet. You don't . . ." She recited most of the Ten Commandments, out of order like that. Then she lowered her head like a child soldier and asked me how I thought she did.

"God. I think you have a lot more to learn if you want to become one of us, kiddo," I said and saluted, dismissing her.

I was joking but I was also displaying bad behavior that had nothing to do with Katyusha and more to do with all the Russian girls and missiles that have hurt me in the past, and all of this Katyusha also knew, miraculously, and it hurt her, because Katyusha was also smart and all-knowing, and that's why I actually loved her, not liked her. I have never been to a temple in Israel or celebrated the Sabbath.

It took us two hours to get into the club, after a lot of talking, moral-reasoning, threats, flirting, promises, tears, and begging on my part and Katyusha's part. It turns out one of the muscular protectors of the gatekeeper spoke Russian, so Katyusha could flirt with him in Russian so much so that even A. was let in, which at the beginning of the night seemed like an impossibility, because when the blond with the guest list saw him she just pointed and laughed, saying that A. had "made her night."

I would like to tell you that it was not all that great inside of the club, but the truth is there is nothing quite like being inside an Israeli club. Everyone loves and trusts each other and everyone is so endlessly happy. It might sound like I am bragging, but I think Katyusha and I were the best dancers there that night. As A. brought us drinks from time to time, we danced to every single song—a mixture of Jewish Arabic songs and classical Hebrew music and the current army radio hits and American songs and Euro songs and Russian songs. I think we were the best because the highest number of people surrounded us out of any girls or boys who were dancing there. I was counting. We complemented each other's dancing well. We were always in sync, and when we changed styles the other one understood where the first one was heading and went along with it, adding her own ideas. All the time we kept on shouting our life stories to each other over the music and asking each other questions about our ambitions and how we were going to accomplish them and questioning each other's future actions. We didn't stop dancing for anyone, and we let any person who wanted to join us dance with us and be as close as they wished to be. It was the best thing ever, like air, or love, or freedom, or music, or safety.

•

In order to get to the selection line in Club 7 I take taxis. Taxi drivers in Tel Aviv, like in most of the country, are usually Jews of Arab or North African or Persian or Post-Soviet decent or Israeli Arab or Ethiopian, and they are obsessed with this one specific question. Usually I get in the cab and then there is a news report that is related to this question, and then they start sharing with me their theory about it, right after they ask me questions about my background. This happens almost every time I take a taxi in Tel Aviv.

I first get asked where I am from, and then I say the Galilee. Because I say the Galilee, they ask what my "exodus is" to know if I am Muslim, Christian, Druze, or Jewish, because most people in the Galilee are not Jewish, and thus are slightly less fascinated by the question that bothers taxi drivers most in Tel Aviv, or at least that's what it seems like to me. I then say I am Iraqi, but also

Romanian. What happens then is that a relevant news segment comes on the radio.

A recent relevant news segment that came on said that the deputy CEO of one of the only three Israeli HMOs has been accused of sexual assault by dozens of his employees. It actually happened to be the HMO I have been getting healthcare from in the Galilee all of my life and where my mother worked as a medical secretary when I was a little girl.

The taxi driver, who informed me he was Jordanian Jewish, was enraged that news reporters, all of these Ashkenazi, meaning European and North American Jews, were giving this any coverage and behaving as if the fact this man had been caught means something: "People with power and money will always do these things and this is just the way of the world. This is just self-righteous hypocrisy." Then he went straight to analyzing the question that truly drives taxi drivers mad: What was former Israeli president Moshe Katsav's mistake?

Moshe Katsav was the president of Israel when I was a soldier. He is Persian, the first non-European president Israel has ever had. He was born Musa Qasab. He is now in jail for the rape and sexual assault and harassment of his female subordinates throughout his long political career as a local and national politician,

a scandal that blew up while he was president. He got seven years, which is a long time for such crimes by Israeli standards.

My Jordanian taxi driver thought that his mistake was a classical Persian mistake. He claimed that Persian men are seen as Mizrahi Jews, meaning Arab Jews, but really they are just like European Jews, meaning entitled. He wanted to rape all these married ladies, some of them even European, and then also not promote them or even fire them and not pay them enough, which was ultimately unkind, and even he, a man, thinks one has to respect women and a man, even a president, must pay for his mistakes. "The woman asked for 5,000 dollars, and the Persian would not pay because he was now the president and thought he was just like all the Ashkenazim, and this is the result."

When he dropped me off at Club 7, Rihanna's "Stay" was blasting from the inside, and I wished Katyusha was with me. By then Katyusha was married to a Palestinian Israeli man from East Jerusalem and wearing a full hijab. After the army, she failed her conversion test. She answered all of the hundreds of technical questions correctly, about rules and history and the Bible. But she got one question wrong. She was asked whether or not she would send her children to a religious school.

Her foster family was of the rare minority in Israel who were very observant, but even they did not send the children to a religious school because there wasn't one in their town. She wanted to be like them. She said no. She was wrong. She should have just said yes. She flunked the test, after four years or prepping for it and following all the regulations that she was asked to follow during the conversion process.

involved for years in an underage sex ring along with his father and managers. It has already been decided that Eyal Golan will not be indicted, and he has recently released a new song about the ordeal called "Praying," which is very beautiful and successful.

When the radio started talking about Eyal Golan and the Moroccan taxi driver started asking me about my background, I told him the Jordanian

WE DIDN'T STOP DANCING FOR ANYONE, AND WE LET ANY PERSON WHO WANTED TO JOIN US DANCE WITH US AND BE AS CLOSE AS THEY WISHED TO BE. IT WAS THE BEST THING EVER, LIKE AIR, OR LOVE, OR FREEDOM, OR MUSIC, OR SAFETY.

Anyways I did not get let into Club 7 because I was alone and wearing Galilean clothes.

The radio news story that prompted my Moroccan Tel Avivian taxi driver to tell me about his opinion regarding the Moshe Katsav question was Eyal Golan's case. Eyal Golan is Israel's most successful singer today. He is half Yemenite, half Moroccan. Two months ago it was revealed that he is suspected to have been

taxi driver's theory about Moshe Katsav's mistake before he could tell me his own theory. He strongly disagreed.

"She did not ask for 5,000 dollars, it was 15,000. He was not a greedy Persian, that is just a stereotype. Like, for example, I can see you are a beautiful young Iraqi girl. I want to ask for your number but you won't give it to me because I am a taxi driver. I can't do anything to you, because if I did and you come back with some boys or your dad, I can't pay because I am a Moroccan taxi driver. So the questions of his mistake, these are complicated issues, and there is never just one answer."

My friend A. doesn't like it that it makes me sad Katyusha is not a Jew. He thinks that makes me a racist. He is a hardcore leftist political activist. I don't mind it if people aren't Jewish. Most people aren't Jewish and that is fine by me. It is just that I think in the specific case of Katyusha, she is very Jewish and has always been Jewish. She really couldn't shut up about how her great grandfather was one of Russia's most brilliant rabbis. So, they should have let her pass the test, because she really wanted to. I think the test was flawed, that's all. I worry about her getting caught one day by her strict Muslim husband when she goes to visit a Druze Galilean friend or boyfriend or to dance or whatever. Because she is very extreme but also very free. She loves clubbing. So do I. A. says that's what Russian girls are like, but I think this is a racist thing to say. I think that's just what Katyusha and I are like. I think, like the Taylor Swift song says, that she belongs with me.

I wish I could go back in time to when I was standing with Katyusha in the line after she recited some of the Ten Commandments and

instead tell her: "You are the most Jewish there is. You know all the answers, Katyusha."

Like I bet if I asked her right now what she thinks former president Moshe Katsav's mistake was, she would come in like a wrecking ball and say: "Like, you don't steal. You don't lie. You don't covet. You don't . . ."

MUSIC IS THE WINE WHICH INSPIRES ONE
TO NEW GENERATIVE PROCESSES . . .

—BEETHOVEN

Slim's Last Chance Saloon
5606 First Avenue S
Seattle, Washington 98108
Duff McKagan

It's a bit funny for me to write about my favorite bar at this juncture in my life. As a professional rock-and-roll musician, I am certainly no stranger to watering holes—from the highbrow-Manhattan-$250-bottle-service-beautiful-people-scenester club to the very low-down Frolic Room II in Hollywood. But having filled my life's quota of these joints before the age of 30, I eventually tired of that old drama starring booze and a strong supporting cast of drugs. These days I'm not much of a drinker, and things I look for in a good bar have switched dramatically. At one time I'd judge a bar by its darkened spaces to debauch within. Now I judge a bar by its menu—staggering out only if I've sampled too much to eat. Yes, it's food and ambience I seek out these days.

Seattle is my favorite place on this planet. The different neighborhoods here each have their own distinct air about them. There is ultra-hipster Capitol Hill, super-blue-collar Georgetown and parts of Ballard and Fremont, cosmopolitan downtown Seattle, and the straight-up seediness of parts of First Avenue left over from the days when the city survived largely on boats, piers, fishermen, and sailors.

I also love Seattle for the food. Maybe it is because Seattle is a rather small big city, and you can't really serve shitty food here and get away with it for very long, but the choice of great places to eat out is an embarrassment of riches: The Wild Ginger, Il Fornio, The Palace Kitchen, Ivar's Salmon House—I could go on and on.

But there is one place that rises above the rest for me: Slim's Last Chance Saloon. Located on an otherwise empty stretch of First Avenue, one mile south of downtown Seattle, Slim's stands alone for its dedication to great fucking chili, a great booze and beer selection, free peanuts, plenty of motorcycle parking, and kick-ass rock-and-roll.

The ambience at Slim's is somewhere between gritty punk-rock tattoo parlor and a family get together. The staff are thoroughly tattooed and always friendly (often remembering the specific chili order from your last visit), the music through the stereo ranges from Cheap Trick through Zeke, and the walls are decorated in crusty old-school rock posters and sundry cheek whatnot.

On winter weekends at Slim's, live rockabilly and punk bands play inside. In the summer, a whole outdoor back-section opens up with a separate bar and a truck flatbed as a stage. Being outside in Seattle come summer is the ultimate place to be, and Slim's back-section is the ultimate place to be outside. I got to play a gig there with the Walking Papers a couple summers back. It was one of those perfect warm Seattle nights, when the sun doesn't set until 10 p.m. Seeing people teeter-totter from drink in the enduring evening sunlight reminded me just how north Seattle is. It's akin to the latitude of Northern Europe, and people in Seattle can—and will—drink with the best of those Norse descendants.

Back to that chili. The meat comes straight from the bar's next-door partner restaurant, Pig Iron BBQ. Top-notch beef, turkey, and pork go into four different chilis, and the thing to get for sure is your choice of chili over Jalapeno mac n' cheese, with a side of sweet potato fries. Ridiculous.

As I'm a history buff, I also love Slim's for the old-Seattle nostalgia it holds. Slim's and Pig Iron sit all by their lonesome on the furthest southern outreach of the Sodo district (short for "South of the Dome"). They say that back in the pre-Interstate 5 days, when this part of First Avenue South was still Highway 99, the Last Chance Saloon was literally that: a driver's final opportunity to get something to eat before a long drive. The fact that Slim's does sit way down there also enables those outdoor summer gigs to never be shut down because of noise complaints.

Owners Mike and Celeste Lucas have made a point that Slim's remains a sort of non-caste environ. From Hell's Angels to suits-and-ties, everyone is welcome and made to feel at home. It makes for interesting people-watching, if not some colorful and often intellectual conversation. (Seattle is the most literate city in America after all.) The "cool factor" is kept to the dullest of roars. You will be accepted. Your biker friend will be accepted, as will your accountant and your grandma. I have brought a cross-section of my huge family to Slim's as well as touring rock friends, and they all leave with the voiced intention of coming back as soon as possible.

I certainly feel accepted at Slim's. No big deal is made because of such-and-such band I may have played in. And at this point in my life—in my hometown, away from the fray of touring and all—being a "regular" is exactly what I crave. (Though still not as much as that chili.)

Slim's Last Chance Saloon: it isn't just my favorite bar—it's the *perfect* bar.

IT IS THE WINE THAT LEADS ME ON,
THE WILD WINE
THAT SETS THE WISEST MAN TO SING
AT THE TOP OF HIS LUNGS,
LAUGH LIKE A FOOL—IT DRIVES THE
MAN TO DANCING . . . IT EVEN
TEMPTS HIM TO BLURT OUT STORIES
BETTER NEVER TOLD.

—HOMER,
THE ODYSSEY

ROMANCE

DO NOT CEASE TO DRINK BEER, TO EAT,
TO INTOXICATE THYSELF, TO MAKE LOVE,
AND TO CELEBRATE THE GOOD DAYS.

—EGYPTIAN PROVERB

The Mint Bar
151 N Main Street
Sheridan, Wyoming 82801
Will Blythe

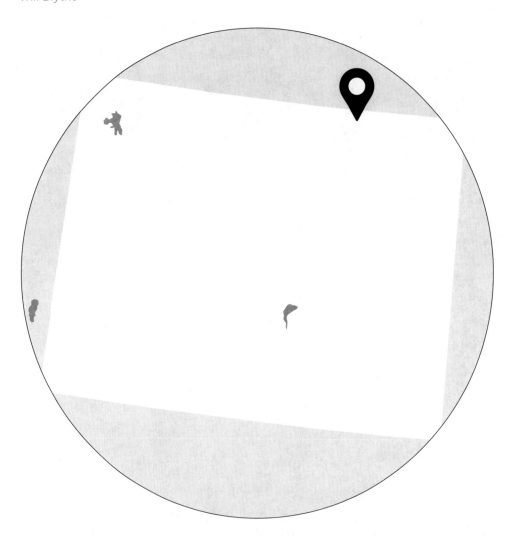

In my long and varied drinking life, which over the years has averaged out to moderate but steady though occasionally spectacular consumption, mostly of gin though I like bourbon too, I've discovered that there are two types of bars. There are the bars that due to location and style are like walking into your own kitchen—for me, the Subway Inn in New York, with its alluring neon sign and dinged-up tables and generous pours and anomalous location just across the street from the loading docks of Bloomingdale's on the Upper East Side, where employees in basic black gather under the awnings for a smoke, come heat wave or blizzard. In an age when the city's "mixologists" invent rococo cocktails the way teenage entrepreneurs create Internet companies, the bartenders at the Subway Inn slap down a shot and a beer in front of you with no visible sense of inferiority.

The second type of bar is to the kitchen what the soul is to the body, another realm altogether, a change of venue, a portal to a new existence as surely as a shaman's ayahuasca. You don't even need to drink in such a bar, though a few drinks will not compromise the vision quest in the least. That the second type of bar may represent the first type for a local simply reveals that, as usual, context is everything. These bars come to you as if in a dream.

And so it came to us.

•

We had been driving west for days, having started out of Minneapolis where we'd dropped off the kid at the airport so she could fly back east to see her dad. Time had stilled and the world had shrunk to the size of a motel bed. Not even the Great Plains seemed too great for us, the famously big sky a simple sheet of infinite blue mounted behind the stage of our romance. This is how it always begins, though it rarely ends that way.

Through the Red River Valley of Minnesota we went, across South Dakota, over the Missouri River and across nearly half of Wyoming, with its low hills and wind-whipped grasslands stretching to the horizon. We rolled down the car windows and allowed the sage-scented air to blow clean through us. An exorcism of a thousand miles. We each had difficult histories trailing us that we had vowed to reclaim the same way the local mining companies promised that the landscapes they had gouged beyond recognition would one day bloom again. The wind drowned out the radio, which was all right, though at times in all that open space, particularly toward dusk, we welcomed the sound of human voices other than our own, western voices doling out cattle and grain prices, even the rants of the politically impaired. Eventually we left the highway at Sheridan, Wyoming, on the northern edge of the state, just down the pike from where Custer met his last at Little Big Horn. We checked in to a motel, washed our faces, made ourselves presentable, and headed downtown. The streets were crowded with ranchers and cowboys, or maybe just people wearing cowboy hats—accountants and electricians and cell phone salesmen, those sorts of folks. Everyone says the Old West is gone forever. The hats, however, remain.

It turned out that we had arrived during "Rodeo Days," a weeklong celebration every summer. Even if the Old West was indeed gone, it didn't seem right that the cops in Sheridan had to wear shorts and ride bicycles when back in our hometown of New York City, there were fully dressed police officers mounted on imposing horses clattering down the avenues.

•

On Main Street a big dance was taking place. We started to join in but these Wyoming guys and gals were simply too good. It would have been like jumping up from the audience and crashing a Broadway chorus line. All of our dancing lives, we had gotten over by enthusiasm, by faking dance moves so intensely that they looked real, at least to us. And if our dancing didn't look real to others, at least the witnesses might appreciate our high spirits. Not in Sheridan.

The men wore iron-hard jeans, white shirts tucked in at the waist, billowing out as they dipped and swooped their partners. Their hats stayed on, no matter what they did. So did their boots.

"I've never seen white people dance like this," I said. I meant: so well. Or so whitely. In this little pocket of the universe on the northern border of Wyoming, it was as if hip-hop had never been invented. In fact, it was as if black people had never been invented.

The dancers commanded the street. Old men and women, former dancers perhaps, now unable to bend from the waist, looked on with beaming admiration. There was a family of dancing brothers who outdid all the other men in gallant movement. The women who were their partners couldn't help but smile at their good fortune. The men tried to look as if they did these moves as naturally as the wind blew.

Up here on the High Plains, our aesthetics were changing. I tucked in my shirt. And my gal bought a pair of cowboy boots right there on Main Street.

Outclassed as dancers, we followed the crowd to ranker forms of entertainment, at which we felt very much at home. We hauled ourselves up into bleachers set up in the middle of Main Street and watched young women (and the occasional drunk dude) stick a quarter between their legs and attempt to hold it there while circumnavigating a tricky obstacle course that included a series of little jumps—all of this without the quarter tinkling dishearteningly to earth. The event was timed, the competition intense. At the end of the course, as the final test, the contestant had to stand astride a plastic cup and drop the quarter into it. No use of hands was permitted. It was inspiring how talented some contestants were at this.

The competition came to a rousing end when the judges were unable to find the quarter between the legs of one woman who appeared to have completed the course successfully. They asked her to jump up and down a few times and even respectfully checked out the situation while surrounding her for privacy's sake but they simply couldn't find the coin.

"This has never happened before," a smiling judge announced to a wildly cheering crowd.

"That's my girl!" a man in the bleachers stood up and announced, either in fact or hope.

"If I'd had another rum and Coke, I would have done it," my girl said. She was the wildest shy girl I had ever met. Or the shyest wild girl. Whichever way that works.

Back at the motel, she did indeed try this and I am pleased to report that she plunked that quarter into her cup on the very first try.

·

The next morning found us in sore need of early refreshment. And there on Main Street showing us the way was an extravagant neon cowboy gripping the reins of a bucking bronco and practically tipping backward into the street. We passed under the sign, the beckoning glow of which we had spotted the previous night, into the bedlam of The Mint Bar at eleven in the morning on the day of the WYO rodeo. The place was dense with drinkers. Above the bar stretched a rattlesnake skin taken from some mythical giant that once crawled the local earth.

We undertook the considerable pleasure of drinking in the daylight hours, which gives the day an expansive feel, voluptuous with pleasure and possibility, right up until it's time for a nap. Already there were a couple of cowboys snoozing in the back of The Mint Bar, oblivious to the choruses of "Sweet Caroline" being raised to the rafters by fellow inebriants in Western wear.

"You were amazing with that quarter," I said.

"Wasn't I?" she said.

"Next time you're going to show the public what you can do."

"Oh dear," she said. "I don't know about that." The shy Wisconsin girl was back. But it was only morning.

During Prohibition, the owners of The Mint Bar had rigged a dress shop for the ladies in the front and served bootleg liquor in the back. When Prohibition ended, the dresses disappeared but not the drinkers. This being the West, those drinkers may have included horses. We studied a photograph of a horse in the bar, barely noticeable for all the patrons. Some kind soul is holding out a bucket for the animal. Maybe it's water, maybe it's booze, maybe the horse felt it had earned a stiff drink after a hard day on the ranch—who knows what elixir lurked in that bucket?

There is a long history of this kind of thing, I know from experience. Frat boys back in my hometown of Chapel Hill, North Carolina, used to smoke weed with our dog, blowing the fumes into his damp nostrils. They also let him lap up bowls of beer. Then they'd call our house and say, "Do you have a dog named Freckles? He's been partying pretty hard." Freckles would be duly retrieved, sleep off his binge for the next few days, and then escape back to campus at the first opportunity to hang out with his boys.

According to local historians, The Mint Bar once had its own dog to entertain the drinkers, though by all accounts, Rounder, the owner's faithful companion, was a teetotaler. The *Sheridan Post* of 1911 states that he was known as "the brightest, keenest, wittiest, and altogether the most remarkable dog in Sheridan—perhaps in all the state of Wyoming." Say what you will about Rounder, it is clear that for all of his intellectual attainments, much admired in the greater Sheridan metropolitan area, he was not nearly as convivial as my family's dog.

•

Easterners can't help but measure the West by its closeness to the movies they've watched about the West, by its nearness to legend. Even now, with the lowest number of cattle being raised in America since 1952 and ranches on the decline, the West is still a credible version of its celluloid self. Trout still swim in the streams, mountains still rise in the distance, men and women still ride horses—and then dismount and enter their pickups and SUVs in the gingerly fashion of people with joints aching from years of backbreaking work. Or maybe they're just getting old.

"You're too young to be walking like that," a geezer in an army jacket told me back at Wounded Knee. He was a Vietnam vet who unfolded himself from a sports car with the aid of a cane. But I felt like one of the gang every time I extricated myself from a midsize SUV. Limping around as if I had just dismounted made me feel like a true Westerner.

So did drinking. At The Mint Bar, a former owner and diligent artist of the close-at-hand had burned different cattle brands into hundreds of cedar shingles that comprised the walls of the joint. Taken together, they looked like the untranslatable hieroglyphics of an alien civilization that had beamed down without notice on the Great Plains.

The alcohol spoke our language, however. We understood it. It was communicating directly with our synapses, bypassing our language centers. And it felt good to be drinking a "ditch" (whiskey and water) before noon in a bar where they were already singing. To feel a buzz rising before the sun had hit its peak in the big sky.

"I could live here," I said.

"So could I," she said. "But what about the kid?"
"If she came out here she could learn to ride and shoot and lasso. She could be in 4-H. She could raise prize-winning cows. She could marry a strapping cowboy and come into town with her brood of children and get a big table at the Rib and Chop House."

"The thing is, she really loves dance."

Back in the Bronx, the kid danced as part of a competitive dance team. She was especially great at hip-hop.

"They surely have hip-hop out here," I said. "Somewhere. Or else we could start it. It could be our mission to bring hip-hop to the Bighorns. We could go down in history for that."

"We could," she said. "We really could."

"You're humoring me."

"Not entirely," she said. "I could see us living here. And I've got the boots for the job."

She kicked them together under the bar in a charming display of footwork.

That's the sort of optimism a joint like The Mint Bar can inspire. With no expectations beyond a drink and a bar stool, we had stumbled upon a power spot, admittedly not a ring of rocks on a high ridge that a Crow warrior might have sought, but a visionary place for us, no matter what happened in the years to come, no matter even if the pulp of the memory we were making

good," she said. "But I don't do it anymore. It's for the young gals."

She liked it in Sheridan just fine. "This place is all right," she said. She didn't live in town anymore. Maybe she never had. But for her, The Mint Bar was still a known commodity, maybe in the way of dull and dutiful husbands, reliable if not exactly exciting. Of course there is something to be said for those who stick around. Her ex had been in the rodeo. She didn't appear to like him

WE STUDIED A PHOTOGRAPH OF A HORSE IN THE BAR, BARELY NOTICEABLE FOR ALL THE PATRONS. SOME KIND SOUL IS HOLDING OUT A BUCKET FOR THE ANIMAL. MAYBE IT'S WATER, MAYBE IT'S BOOZE . . .

was one day extracted and all that remained was the husk.

That's what we were feeling when a blonde of a certain age took a stool beside us. Ridden hard and put up wet, that's what they say. She ordered a Pabst Blue Ribbon and a shot of whiskey.

"I used to be a barrel racer," she told us. Rodeo confessions seemed apt this day. "I was pretty

so much anymore. Or else she liked him and he didn't like her. "He was a good rodeo rider," she said. Maybe she told us his name, though we wouldn't have known it.

The story was coming out in fragments, if story it was. She talked to us as if we already knew everyone she was talking about. In a way, we did. We had to lean in to hear her, what with the Neil Diamond Revue in the back. Her wrists were dainty, her skin brown. She was no stranger to the sun.

There was a lull in the music and she told us once again: "I was a barrel racer."

•

Several drinks past noon, we settled up.

"Are you hungry?" my gal asked. "Let's go to the Rib and Chop House and eat ribs before the rodeo." We said good-bye to our barrel-racing friend who smiled toward the bar and kept drinking.

We ate ribs and pork chops and wedges of iceberg lettuce with blue cheese among long tables filled with three generations dining together and then we went to the rodeo at the fairgrounds, having bought the last available seats. The barrel racers were lovely and strong. The bulls threw nearly every rider within a couple of seconds. And a Crow Indian competing in the pony race spoke favorably of the Great Father, General Custer.

"Did he just say that?" I asked. We knew the Crow hated the Sioux and had served in the U.S. Army as scouts and fighters but it was impressive how ancient loyalties still lingered even at a pony race on a summer evening in the twenty-first century.

The next morning at the hotel, the desk clerk, an enterprising young fellow who seemed determined to rise in life, said to me, "I see you've been living it up."

"What gives it away?" I said.

"Your hair," he said, pointing at his own, which in contrast to mine was as neat as a Mormon's.

My gal laughed. "It always looks like that," she said.

We left Sheridan and The Mint Bar behind that day without looking back. The West was still westward and we had a long ways to go. With luck, we still do.

Downtown Beirut (closed)
158 First Avenue
New York, New York 10009
Elissa Schappell

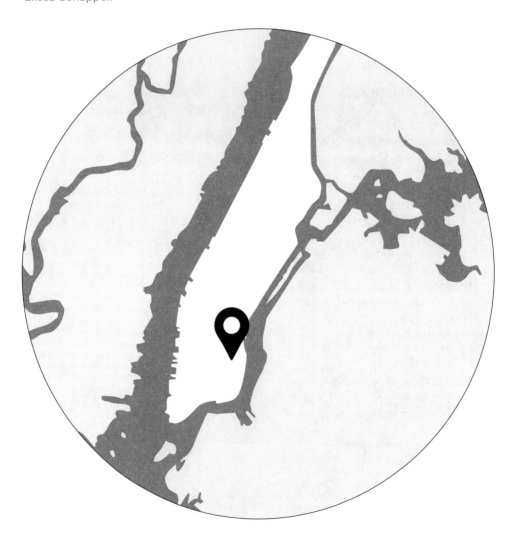

My future husband might have suggested we meet at another bar. There were lots of other places downtown that were, well, a lot more *welcoming*. At the Blue & Gold, the Polish bartender who could pass for Pope John Paul II's disgraced brother greeted you with a wave of his grimy bar rag. At King Tut's Wah Wah Hut, a tattooed art student with a yellow beehive and tangerine lipstick shook her hips to the B-52s and every third drink was on the house. The Holiday had red leather banquettes, Sinatra and the Smiths on the jukebox, and a pool table. Instead, he picked Downtown Beirut for our first date.

It was a Monday night. I'd met him the previous Friday, on the Amtrak to D.C. He was going to a party in Baltimore. I was going to visit my college roommate and hook up with an ex. But the train broke down, and by the time I arrived in D.C., six hours later, I was so smitten I canceled my booty call.

At the time I was living on the Upper East Side with two other girls in an illegal sublet where we couldn't even get mail. Before that I'd lived in Hoboken. So most of my experience with New York bars was in places like Maxwell's, the Surf Club, and Pedro's. I'd gone downtown to Danceteria and Area but Downtown Beirut—located on First Avenue between 10th and 11th streets—wasn't even on my radar.

He'd said to meet him there at 7:00, so I showed up at 7:15—only he wasn't there. I ordered a beer and began to wait, getting increasingly anxious and pissed off. *Nobody puts baby in a corner!* Finally it dawned on me that I was in the wrong bar. I wasn't in Downtown Beirut but—*quel* irony—next door at the The Village Idiot.

It was an understandable mistake: Aptly named, Downtown Beirut looked as though it might have sustained a mortar blast and brazenly risen from the ashes. "Beirut" appeared in big white block letters, "Downtown" seemingly added later, in a box set at a jaunty angle. On the black awning, the name appeared once again, the lettering cockeyed and off-kilter, as if the bar had been buried in rubble and some thoughtful soul had scrawled the name on it so the faithful could find it. In the front window a ragged string of Christmas lights burned like the embers of Candy Land.

Inside, it took a moment for my eyes to adjust to the darkness. Finally I spotted him by the jukebox, blasting the Beastie Boys. He was wearing a Flipper T-shirt, black pants, and looked like he cut his own hair. And he'd brought a friend.

I could blame it on the beer I'd just chugged or nerves, but I believe it was more a sense of freedom and lawlessness that the bar sparked in me: so that when he introduced me to his friend, I kissed him—the friend, not my future husband.

He showed no outward reaction. Neither of them did. Downtown Beirut was the kind of bar where you kiss your future husband's friend on the mouth, and nobody raises an eyebrow. It was no mistake that a sign behind the bar announced: *Good Girls Go to Heaven, Bad Girls Go Everywhere.*

•

How can I romanticize a bar with the aura of a war zone, a place psychically wrapped in barbed wire?

In the '80s I felt that every block on the Lower East Side had the potential to change my life. After all, there was Allen Ginsberg heading home to East 12th Street with a bag of groceries; Joey and Marky Ramone, in black leather jackets, striding down St. Mark's Place like kings; Thurston Moore and Kim Gordon flipping

through art magazines at Gem Spa. Every day new art galleries were literally bursting out of holes in the wall. Keith Haring was alive, Jeff Koons was revving up his shell game, and Julian Schnabel was smashing plates. The streets were alive with the sound of punk and hip-hop, every wall tagged in graffiti, the sidewalks glittering with crack vials. Tompkins Square Park had become the squalid Tent City and the scene of a riot. Half the tenement buildings on the Lower East Side looked burned out, and seemingly held together only by the CBGB Sunday matinee posters plastered to the bricks.

Downtown Beirut flaunted a similarly appealing squalidness. The bar always felt sticky; with what, it was hard to tell, as it was perpetually dark—in the daytime, defiantly so. The bathroom was plastered in band stickers, the walls magic-markered with proclamations of love and hate, philosophical rantings and explicit hieroglyphics depicting human genitalia. Unlike the bathrooms at CBGB, this one-seater was a poor altar for debauchery . . . but it would do.

Happy Hour was from 10 a.m. to 10 p.m. They never carded and no drink was over $5. There were dollar drafts for the day drinkers, and three-buck Rolling Rocks and PBRs at night. I can't remember ever seeing Downtown Beirut empty; at all times of the day, under the persistent heavy cloud cover of cigarette smoke, there was someone lodged at the bar either drinking or passed out.

It was a diverse crowd of regulars. There was the gray-bearded, pot-bellied biker who kept his motorcycle helmet on at the bar, and the two women who might have been secretaries who stared as though sightless into the crowd, their pupils so dilated their eyes appeared full of ink. Near the back were the girl and the guy both with hair the color and texture of straw who could've been brother and sister and who by night's end would either be licking each other's faces or screaming obscenities in the street. There were of course the punks: the girls in cat's eye glasses and black band T-shirts, their hair dyed or fried black, white, or bright blue; the guys with matching piercings in their ears and lips and eyebrows, decked out in studded leather jackets, their shredded T-shirts and jeans suggesting that they'd been mauled by tigers on the PATH train.

Then there were the girls and guys like myself who hadn't grown up in New York City, but after only a few months called it home. Guys in Buddy Holly glasses. Girls in black tights and minis, who did their eyes like Sophia Loren and their mouths in MAC Russian Red and carried copies of *I-d* in their bags.

I stepped out of my life when I entered Downtown Beirut. There was a kind of anonymity that came when I slipped into the low light and smoke, my voice distorted by the pounding jukebox. I wasn't the girl from a small town in Delaware, who was working as the junior books editor at a woman's magazine, whose first job in the city was selling diamond earrings at Tiffany's. I was a writer. I was the girl with the white buzz cut, in a black leather jacket and Doc Martens I'd bought from Jimmy at Trash and Vaudeville, with the last of my paycheck. I was in love with a boy I'd met on a train, a boy who'd moved to NYC with a suitcase full of books and $150 in the pocket of his Harris Tweed coat (all the money he had in the world). A boy whose favorite bar was Downtown Beirut.

Eventually we were going there two or three nights a week. Even so it took a while for us to be acknowledged as regulars. No one at Downtown Beirut was going to throw open their arms and welcome you in. Certainly not the bartenders, and not just because no one was getting rich off tips for dirt cheap beer and $5 shots of Jack. The female bartender with a green bob who played in a hardcore band took particularly perverse delight in waiting on as few customers as possible; waiting until they were clawing their way over the bar to reach the taps before she deigned to serve them. She had a taste for torturing the newbies in particular, those suspected of slumming. It was a point of pride when after months and months she finally served us without making us wait.

The jukebox could be just as intimidating, like a fearsome mythological beast hunkered down, blasting punk and hardcore: Throbbing Gristle, Dead Kennedys, the Misfits. Fortunately this was the music I loved, and Downtown Beirut was the only place outside of the shitty apartment my future husband was sharing with three other people on Staten Island that I heard it.

·

After a few years, ironically after we moved into a place on 8th Street between B and C, the bar's exoticism faded. We went out less and less. The crowd, like the neighborhood itself, began to change. Our friend Eddie was beaten up by a fucked-up frat boy—an act more unsettling for all of us than the night a drunken ex-Marine, lamenting the death of his girlfriend from an overdose, stabbed a bowie knife into the bar where we were sitting.

The evil forces of gentrification had begun closing in. We couldn't feel all that aggrieved. After all, we had been a part of that early invasion, fallen prey to a bait and switch on the starving artists drawn to the art and music

scene on the Lower East Side and cheap rents, which a few years later would be jacked up so high no one, save for the bankers and trust-fund babies, could afford to live there.

But for a time I had my place, a place where I felt myself being transformed, bounced around and elbowed at the bar while Glenn Danzig screamed in the background, arguing about whether Bret Easton Ellis was a genius or just a brilliant bullshit artist, holding hands with my boy, feeling alive and a part of something exciting and slightly dangerous, feeling that anything could happen and everything was about to happen. That *I* was about to happen.

Today, there's a back- and foot-rub parlor on that spot. And I've become one of my least favorite kinds of people: that superior bitch who, hearing some younger person going on about how *cool* the Lower East Side is, feels compelled to shit on their experience. *You have no idea, fetus. Have you ever even heard of a bar called Downtown Beirut?*

WINE COMES IN AT THE MOUTH
AND LOVE COMES IN AT THE EYE;
THAT'S ALL WE SHALL KNOW FOR TRUTH
BEFORE WE GROW OLD AND DIE.
I LIFT THE GLASS TO MY MOUTH,
I LOOK AT YOU, AND I SIGH.

—WILLIAM BUTLER YEATS

Pueblito Mexicano (closed)
Avenida Abraham Lincoln
Ciudad Juárez, Mexico
Karen Olsson

A flushed Japanese man held a microphone with both hands, giggling convulsively. There were tears in his eyes, on his cheeks, and while he was trying to sing, his laughing and crying made it all but impossible. He had been drinking at a table with some other guys, likely all managers from the local manufacturing plants, when he was summoned by the Mexican emcee to come forward into the middle of the busy restaurant. I wasn't sure why he had been asked to sing. He wobbled back to his buddies, and then came the next part of the strange variety show: a sanitized cockfight, in which handlers clutching live roosters approached each other, letting the birds bristle and hiss, before backing away. This was repeated a few more times, then the roosters were removed. At some point, mariachis played, but this was more than sixteen years ago, and I don't recall whether they played during the show or beforehand.

The restaurant was part of Pueblito Mexicano, a failing indoor mini-mall that, come evening, became a bustling nightlife spot on Avenida Abraham Lincoln in Ciudad Juárez. The large space had been modeled after a colonial Mexican town: colorful facades, a white church, and a municipal building surrounded a square with a gazebo. In addition to the restaurant, there were two small open-air cantinas and a bigger, enclosed bar with a polo theme. Otherwise, most of the storefronts were empty. It had the feel of a passenger terminal in a remote airport.

A colleague and I had gone there on assignment for a national magazine that has since folded, having persuaded a editor in Washington, D.C. to let us write about the improbable existence of a polo-playing scene in Juárez and El Paso. I considered the gig a great stroke of luck, less a job than a junket, a free trip with L., who'd become a friend and also the object of my furtive affections. At that time he was my boss at another, smaller magazine, in Austin, and we'd reported and written a couple of stories together, which had taught me what little I knew about reporting. I've since met other women who, in their first jobs, were infatuated with both the work and with an older man in the office who taught them the work, the two enchantments all tangled up in one another. That is to say, now I can recognize the outlines of a common-enough story, but at the time it was all my own, a romance that would reach an apex of sorts that night.

Earlier, we'd gone to watch a casual polo match played on a field east of El Paso, in New Mexico. It had been a perfect late-spring afternoon, and the field was so pretty—a lush, irrigated section of green surrounded by orchards and purplish mountains, a world away from the parched chaos of Juárez. I'd never watched polo before and had been taken with the game's beauty, the horses thundering back and forth, the mallets swinging and meeting the ball with a satisfying *thwack*. The season was just starting, and the polo club's owner, an overweight dentist with a clinic in Juárez and a home outside El Paso, brimmed with happiness. "It just keeps getting better and better and better," he told us, "all summer long."

The same could not be said for Ciudad Juárez in 1997. The city, in the words of a Juárez newspaper editor who met us for breakfast a day or two later, was bursting at the seams. Dust clouds rose from its unpaved streets, sewage flowed in open ditches, and the population just kept on growing—said to be one million or maybe two million, nobody knew, since more people were arriving every day from other parts of Mexico. Many of them came to work in the *maquiladoras*, foreign-owned assembly plants. The pay was so low that they typically lived in neighborhoods with the look of refugee camps, the houses fashioned from warehouse pallets or sheets of opaque plastic. Many were young,

single women, and by 1997 the murders of some of those women had drawn international attention.

If the population boom and the poverty and even the murders all had links to the factories, naturally so did the wealth there—or at least such wealth as wasn't tied up in the illegal drug trade—and by extension, so did polo. A man named Antonio J. Bermúdez had helped design the *maquiladora* system in the '60s, and he and his brother Jaime built a big industrial park (at the time, the world's largest) for the plants. The Bermúdez family also promoted polo in the city and established a polo grounds, and it was the family's Grupo Bermúdez that had created Pueblito Mexicano in the early '90s. It had been built with the family's signature ambition, but American shoppers had not come as readily as corporations to the industrial park: the mall was a flop.

The restaurant and bars seemed to be doing fine, though. One of the proprietors, a gracious man who'd played in the afternoon's polo match, had offered to take us there, and we'd followed his big white Chrysler across two borders, from New Mexico into Texas and then into Mexico. He was still dressed in his polo uniform—red jersey, white breeches, riding boots—and still smoking the cigar he'd lit after the game as he led us into the polo-themed bar, where he showed off polo trophies and framed photographs of Juárez polo players, including a picture of himself on a field in India, a turbaned groom by his side. Then he urged us to have a meal and take in the show, before he departed for his office, located behind the façade of the false town's municipal building, where the mayor's office would be in a real town.

Maybe we took advantage of his hospitality. Although we'd told the polo players that we planned to write about Juárez, no doubt they anticipated a more flattering article than we had in mind. The fat dentist had copies of *Town & Country* in his office and must have imagined something along those lines. But we wanted to write about their polo game in its desolate context, about a city where the inequalities of the global economy, the third-world suffering that enables our first-world consuming, were all right there, jammed together, the workers' shacks pressed up against the American border. This wasn't directly the polo players' fault, no more than it was the fault of those of us who bought the products of RCA and Toshiba and Ford and GE and all the other companies operating along the border. But because of the starkness of the contrast between their privilege and the surrounding destitution, they weren't going to look that great in the article.

Okay, we did take advantage. After dinner our host returned, sat us down at one of the cantinas, and started pouring tequila, exemplary tequila, a liquid the likes of which we'd never tasted before and which I will not even try to describe. He poured and he talked, though I lost track of what he was saying. Techno music blared from a nearby speaker, and I was sitting farther away from him than L. was, and my Spanish was only so-so to begin with, while L. was fluent. Soon enough I was drunk. They talked, and I wondered what he and his polo buddies thought of me, of us, what these Mexican men were assuming was the relationship between the man who asked most of the questions and his much younger companion. In fact, the two of us had undertaken the story together because I was the one with the connection to the magazine, which I'd written for before, and while L. was the better reporter I was the more fluid writer. But I doubt that's what the men were thinking. It wasn't even what I was thinking after a few drinks.

Not that it mattered any longer, for I'd arrived in an absurdist paradise, thanks to the Japanese non-singer, the non-cockfight, and the fake town whose pseudo-mayor was treating us to very fine liquor. The entire kitschy complex was suffused with nostalgia for the sort of towns that Mexico's economy could no longer support, the towns that young people were fleeing in order to go to Juárez or to the U.S. And this man who droned on in words I couldn't understand, he was being very generous, and all the while my heart was aflutter for reasons of its own, so that while the setting was one thing—entirely false— the delight was another, inflated by alcohol but entirely genuine.

Nearly two decades later, that Ciudad Juárez presents itself to memory wrapped in its own haze of nostalgia. In spite of the ongoing murders of women, it was a time of relative

of Chihuahua had agreed to buy the building and convert it into government offices. The restaurant, bar, and one of the cantinas had still been operating, and one of the owners, the same man who'd plied us with tequila, announced that the bar would close for good, while the restaurant and cantina would move to other locations in the city.

I also searched for the dentist's name, wondering whether anything had come to light that

NOT THAT IT MATTERED ANY LONGER, FOR I'D ARRIVED IN AN ABSURDIST PARADISE, THANKS TO THE JAPANESE NON-SINGER, THE NON-COCKFIGHT, AND THE FAKE TOWN WHOSE PSEUDO-MAYOR WAS TREATING US TO VERY FINE LIQUOR.

calm compared to what the city experienced a decade later, when the drug cartels went to war and thousands of people died. Until very recently, the era when two Americans might drive across the border to go to a bar seemed to have ended—though by 2013, the mayhem had subsided, the cartels apparently having come to an agreement of sorts.

That truce came too late for Pueblito Mexicano. I learned via the Internet that in 2012, the state

would explain how the owner of a modest dental clinic in Juárez could afford to own twenty-eight polo horses. Sure enough, he'd been arrested and charged with insurance fraud and money laundering a few years back, and had pled guilty to the fraud. I also wondered whether that editor we'd had breakfast with had survived, given that so many journalists along the border had since been threatened or killed by agents of the drug cartels. I came across his name in a newspaper columnist's list of fallen colleagues, though he'd died of lung cancer, not assassination. When we'd spoken all those years back, he'd poked fun at Pueblito Mexicano's failing mall. "Not the work of any marketing genius," he'd said, treating it as a silly vanity project by a family that had enriched itself through government concessions.

It was indeed a ridiculous business, an elephantine tourist trap, and I loved it there. The culmination of the night, the trip, the crush on my boss: after parting ways with our host, the two of us linked arms and took a drunken stroll around the empty plaza, as couples do in the towns that had inspired this replica. We walked past the empty storefronts, arm in arm, and I couldn't have been happier. Then we returned to the parking lot and our rental car, drove back up Avenida Abraham Lincoln and across the bridge to our own country, to our separate motel rooms in El Paso. Before we parted, he tenderly gave me two Tylenol.

It now seems to me that the best romances of my early twenties were the unconsummated ones, the flirtations that never would've panned out in the real world but bloomed for a night in some alternate universe. A month or so later I left Texas to go to graduate school. The day I said goodbye to L., I told him, *We'll always have Juárez*, which was a joke. But I still meant it.

The Bar (closed)
68 Second Avenue
New York, New York 10003
Mike Albo

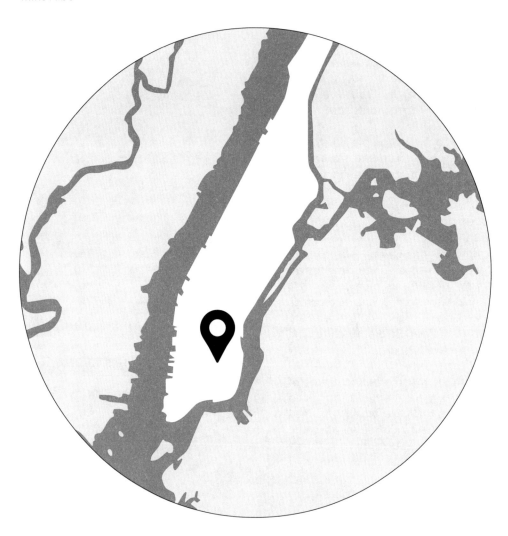

Sundays was Sugarbabies, Mondays was Crowbar, Tuesdays was Tunnel Bar. On Wednesdays we went to Flamingo East, which drew a snotty fashion crowd, and we paraded around like flamingos. Thursdays was Foxy at The Cock and Fridays was Squeezebox. But at the core of the '90s gay East Village scene was The Bar: a basic, nondescript watering hole on the corner of 4th Street and Second Avenue. It was unsung. It was underwhelming. It was just there. And we all passed through it like an airport customs gate, on our way to sex or love or what we thought may be both those things.

The Bar was bare bones, with seating around the wall and a pool table and a jukebox that played Nirvana and Hole and Elastica and anything else that we thought separated us from the past. Drag queens lip-synched to Jefferson Airplane or Kate Bush rather than Judy Garland or Madonna. We stood there drinking Rolling Rock or vodka, wanting each other, while the neighborhood coke dealers—a surprisingly young gay boy in his twenties and his female friend—wandered through. This was not only a gay bar. This was a gay dive—or was trying to be one. It was tough—or felt tough. That was what we gay guys were trying to portray: I can take care of myself. I will still be sexual even though death surrounds me. I don't give a fuck what you think.

You have to understand: when I started going out, in the late '80s and early '90s, there was an emptiness everywhere, a feeling like every gay area had been evacuated. I remember when I first got to New York I would walk down Christopher Street—arguably the birthplace of modern gay liberation—and feel like I was walking through a graveyard, surrounded by ghosts. I had missed all the fun and now everyone was dead. That was the fate of my generation of Gen X gay guys: too young to have experienced the so-called golden age of gay life, and also too young to have seen all my friends die of AIDS, but also too old to just listen to Britney Spears and ignore it all. We came of age when kissing was risky. But desire is stronger than fear, and we kissed anyway. We needed a place that wanted to be basic again, where we gay guys could reinvent ourselves. The Bar was a corrective. It was stripped of all style or pretense. It was a wooden box with bourbon.

•

I was 19 when I first went to The Bar. It was spring 1990, my junior year of college, and I was on a two-week "externship" (I still have no idea what an externship is) and staying with my ex-boyfriend, who was sharing an apartment with a straight couple on 16th Street and Fifth Avenue. They were both waiter/actors. The city was pulling itself out of bankruptcy, or gentrification was just beginning, or both, and working actors could still afford apartments on 16th and Fifth. The couple were in their forties, around my age now. They both seemed so cool, but also so tired. Every night

how I spent most of my bar visits in 1990—alone, with one beer, watching people like I had activated some kind of invisible button. Sometimes I wonder if the gay scene then was as funereal as I recall it to be, but I remember countless nights at so many bars where I sat by myself back then, waiting for something to happen. Maybe I was the ghost.

That night, a gorgeous man walked in. He had green eyes and mounds of hair, and an angular

BARS ARE THE LITTLE KNOTS IN THE ROUTINE OF OUR LIVES—WHERE SEX AND DEATH AND LOVE AND LONELINESS ALL SNAG. WE STAND AROUND IN THEM, HOLDING OUR DRINKS, AND WAIT FOR LOVE AND LONELINESS, SEX AND DEATH, TO GO HOME WITH US.

they would come home from their waitering jobs and watch TV and never go out and it seemed so sacrilegious to me. My ex-boyfriend had a full-time job and he didn't go out either. But it was my first time in New York, and I was bursting. Somehow I heard about The Bar. I had a vague idea of how to get to it and I walked there by myself.

That first night I visited, I sat there with a beer in the corner and a few people filed in and out. This is

face like a character in E.M. Forster's *Maurice*. He was in a tiny slashed-up shirt and was also haughty and busy, like a Forster character. He was carrying roller skates and told me he was about to head to the Roxy for ironic roller disco night. He seemed steeped in a social scene that I longed for. He asked me about myself and I told him I was visiting and I must have also conveyed to him in my posture and wanting, ready face that I was prepared to fall in love with anyone who approached me (which is how I was in gay bars until the age of 30).

He laughed, judgmentally. "You are young," he said. "You'll move here, get a boyfriend, have fun." Then he left.

•

He was both right and wrong. I moved to New York in 1993 soon after graduation, but my romantic life wasn't that simple. By then, something had lifted in the mood of the city. I joined a throng of men in their twenties surging into the East Village. We wore cut off T-shirts and gas station attendant pants and chains dribbling off our wallets and went to The Bar at least twice a week. Like so many corner bars, The Bar became a kind of social vortex. This was before cell phones, so you would meet there first before heading out somewhere else—there or The Boiler Room next door, where for hours on end we roamed around and around the central pool table, looking at each other.

I remember meeting Jeff at The Bar, leaning on the jukebox, his blond hair backlit into a corolla of light around his head. I fell in love with him but he loved someone else. This was what it was like for me back then: I was too busy loving someone to pay attention to who loved me. I suppose I kept circling and circling the pool table. But then Jeff and I became friends, along with Chris and Vince and Roger and Pete and everyone else.

More and more guys came to The Bar. CK One released an ad campaign with "real" guys, half of whom were there the night before. Then, years passed in seconds. Chris became a crystal addict, Vince moved to Berlin, Roger became a CEO, and Pete disappeared. Jeff, right after 9/11, was beaten up by some kids outside his apartment in the Lower East Side. They were taking their fear and anger out on him and broke almost every bone in his face, and he spent months having it reconstructed.

I never see Jeff, but then suddenly I did, in Brooklyn, just last year, walking a three-legged dog. He was still gorgeous to me.

The gay scene moved to Williamsburg. Then that ended. The gay scene moved to Hell's Kitchen. Then that ended. The gay scene has now moved to Bushwick (and, of course, the Internet). Somewhere, right now, there is a young gay guy in a trendy bar, there in Bushwick, thinking that his scene has never happened before. And there is a younger gay kid in the corner of the bar with a cheap beer, thinking that he doesn't belong.

Recently, my friend David, who is older than I, told me about his heyday of bar-going in the '70s at the Boots & Saddle in the West Village.

He described it in the same sepia-toned, rough-edged hue that I remember The Bar. Rough, basic, sexy.

We remember our bars like no other, but all saloons share the same soul. They are the little knots in the routine of our lives—where sex and death and love and loneliness all snag. We stand around in them, holding our drinks, and wait for love and loneliness, sex and death, to go home with us.

Recently I was writing a story about the latest cool club entrepreneur and his new night at The Cock, down on Second Avenue, because I guess the perpetual wheel of trendy hotspots has turned back to the East Village again.

That night didn't start until 1 a.m., so I had time to kill. I walked north a couple blocks and stepped into the Queen Vic, which used to be The Bar. There were two or three guys my age on stools. They were all staring at their phones. A Dionne Warwick song was playing. A young male couple was snuggling on a couch. Back in the '90s, The Bar never, ever had couches. It also never had a giant touch-screen jukebox, but there was one here, turning all our faces blue with its light.

I spotted a tiny rainbow flag in the corner.

"Is this a gay bar again?" I asked the bartender. He had a graying beard like my own. "This was the first gay bar I ever went to in NYC."

"It was everyone's first bar," the bartender said. Some years back, he explained, the owners changed it to a straight beer-and-sports establishment called 2x4. Then around 2003, timed with the excessive aughts, it became a place called Evolution with expensive bottle service. Now the owners, said the bartender, are slowly letting it return to being gay.

"The whole staff is gay, at least," he said.

I looked through the same windows, out to the intersection.

"They never should have fucking changed it," the bartender said, and gave me a bitter IPA.

IT PROVOKES THE DESIRE, BUT IT TAKES
AWAY THE PERFORMANCE.

—WILLIAM SHAKESPEARE,
MACBETH

The Pillars (closed)
113 Marble Road
Guilford, New York 13780
Darin Strauss

I'm the wrong person to write this essay—to be in this book, at all.

You'll see.

One teenaged night, having illegally drunk crap beer with my best friends whom I almost never saw, I leaned over—this was out under a bug-circled sodium lamp—I leaned over to kiss a girl, and thus made it a pretty good distance toward fulfilling my ambitions for the evening. *This is it*, I thought. *This-is-it*. I was a virgin. Or sort of a virgin. (You'll see.) The girl kissed me and I was happy.

Is it the stupidity of youth that lobs the ball of life so advantageously into your court?

That night it was, I'm pretty sure; it *was* the stupidity of youth. To any 40-year-old, the stuff of adolescence may seem jackassy. Though what happens to us when we're dumb and innocent is no less real than what happens to us when we're old and smart—if we ever really do get smart. Sometimes a 40-year-old's precious world-weariness is actually just plain weariness.

Enough dicking around; tell the story.

The Pillars, the bar in question, stood battered in a battered upstate New York town. The beer was bad. I don't remember the décor, or the jukebox. They didn't serve wine or food. And the clientele (I thought) was unsophisticated and anti-Semitic and disliked my friends and me.

And yet.

For two months in the summer of 1988 I went there six nights a week. Despite myself, I look back at those times rather Bryan Adamsically as the best days of my life. My friends and I were working at Oxford-Guilford, an unofficially Jewish summer camp five hours north of NYC, in the green heart of Chenango County. I'd been going to OG for nine summers in a row—from the time I was ten—and I'd been hearing about The Pillars for almost that long. It's weird to think that there can be an innocent debauchery. But that's what there was, or at least that's how it seems twenty-five years later: the camp's owner provided a van, every night, to safeguard its underage counselors as they went out and drank illegally.

I loved my camp friends more than my home friends, though I only got to see them during the summers. There was D., a handsome wise-ass whose casual malice was, for his close friends, shot through with a huge and intensely sentimental kindness; M., a handsome and dumbly sweet kid so enthusiastic you wanted to offer him a dog treat; S., a frankly effete, overweight, Duckie-from-*Pretty in Pink* kind of guy who would, in two months, use the reboot-possibilities of college to overhaul himself into a handsome, outdoor sports type. Handsome, handsome, handsome.

was drinking that night, the first night of that summer. And I was kissing a girl.

I mentioned I was a virgin. That's not quite true.

About a year earlier I'd been on a high-school ski trip to Quebec. I picked up a girl I thought was Canadian (turned out she was from Jericho, two Long Island towns over from where I grew up). My jealous friend E. refused to give me a condom as I left the lodge on my way back to the

WHAT WAS IT THAT WAS SO MAGICAL TO ME? CHEAP ALCOHOL, A FREE RIDE EVERY NIGHT, FRIENDLY COMPANIONSHIP FROM PEOPLE I'D GROW APART FROM?

And who was I?

I was the shy kid who had not long before been in a terrible accident (it wasn't my fault, I was—and evidently still am—quick to say), an accident wherein someone died. I've written about that disaster in my book *Half a Life* and don't want to go into it here. I'm not up for that; it's still too emotionally strenuous. But suffice it to say I was in need of friends, and fun, and I

girl's hotel; in bed, once we'd started, I'd decided unprotected sex was too dangerous; I'd made it about halfway through a single, bare-skinned and inexpert thrust, before I'd stopped. And here I was, a year later, with little in the way of sack savoir-faire.

I didn't really know the girl I was now kissing; she was a counselor, too, but new to OG.

She and I continued our little smoochiad back in the van returning to camp. *I hope my friends can see me*, I thought. *I must look really freaking cool to them right now.*

I heard D.—my sometimes cruel buddy—laughing in the seat directly behind mine. "What's Darin doing?" he said, though he knew. I pulled back from the girl. This was familiar to me, the nervous flight from what I wanted, the all-purpose social doubt.

My friends thought the girl was ugly, or later they said they did. I hadn't agreed, but pretended I did. Anyway, I sensed their feelings, and thus had quit kissing the girl as soon as I'd heard the laughter.

"What were you thinking?" said D. later, back at our bunk, where we were supposed to be in charge of kids.

"I was so drunk," I said. Though I really hadn't been.

"She's gross," said J., a female friend who that summer had a crush on D. and would eventually marry him.

Here's where I should tell you that I realized what was morally right; that I told my friends the girl wasn't gross; that I at least talked to her again.

That didn't happen. Fine. I should at the very least write that, despite my dickish conduct that evening, when I look back now the summer is tainted for me—that my assholery taught me something.

But that's not true, either.

Those days *were* happy for me, and I can't look back on them as anything but golden. Though I was guilt-ridden about the high-school catastrophe I'd been a part of before that summer; though that first night I'd been cowardly toward the girl I kissed and then cravenly ignored; though I was probably negligent in my duties as a guardian of children; though the people who were my best friends that summer I would eventually outgrow—would see them as stunted, or immoral, or just dull—I find myself, when I think of that time, almost choked by a throat-clotting nostalgia.

People are complicated.

When I realized all this just now, I went to my computer and typed, at speed, the stuff you've been reading. I don't want to allow any of the usual filters, writerly carefulness or human shame, to trip me up, to keep me from telling the truth.

What was great that summer, what I really look back on fondly, was my time at the bar. The Pillars: that rat hole with the shitty beer and dirty looks and the van home. (The reason it was six nights a week and not seven was that one night a week, I was "on duty," watching the kids, and thus not totally an irresponsible a-hole.)

I mentioned before that I thought the Pillars regulars were anti-Semitic. There had been allegations that, in the late-70s, a Klan meeting had occurred across the OG lake, that some of the locals had said: "We don't want your Jew camp here." I don't know. What I know is true is that, in 1988, I interpreted the black looks my friends and I got as residual Jew hatred. What it probably was, instead? Understandable working-class annoyance at these underage, upper middle-class New Yorkers (though that was a category that didn't include me, as my dad was in the process of losing our house to the bank), drunk kids who plagued their favorite local bar every summer. Fair point.

What was it that was so magical to me? Cheap alcohol, a free ride every night, friendly companionship from people I'd grow apart from?

I started this essay by telling you I was the wrong guy for this book about bars. That's true,

you'll probably agree by now. The more I think about the subject, the more I think bars are sad places—even the nicest bars—and that the mythologizing of drinking is a bit pathetic. Sure, you might say, *your* favorite bar experience was balanced on creaky pillars—false friendship, hair-trigger cruelty, misreads. You might tell me, *That's you.*

But isn't that true of most bar relationships, bar memories, pleasures and sorrows, most bar days and bar nights?

SEX AND A COCKTAIL: THEY BOTH LASTED
ABOUT AS LONG, HAD THE SAME EFFECT,
AND AMOUNTED TO ABOUT THE SAME THING.

—D.H. LAWRENCE,
LADY CHATTERLEY'S LOVER

FRIENDS

IN SOUTHWERK AT THE TABARD AS I LAY
REDY TO WENDEN ON MY PILGRIMAGE
TO CAUNTERBURY WITH FUL DEVOUT CORAGE,
AT NIGHT WAS COME IN-TO THAT HOSTELRYE
WEL NYNE AND TWENTY IN A COMPANYE,
OF SONDRY FOLK, BY AVENTURE Y-FALLE
IN FELAWSHIPE, AND PILGRIMS WERE THEY ALLE,
THAT TOWARD CAUNTERBURY WOLDEN RYDE;
THE CHAMBRES AND THE STABLES WEREN WYDE,
AND WEL WE WEREN ESED ATTE BESTE.
AND SHORTLY, WHAN THE SONNE WAS TO RESTE,
SO HADDE I SPOKEN WITH HEM EVERICHON,
THAT I WAS OF HIR FELAWSHIPE ANON

—GEOFFREY CHAUCER,
THE CANTERBURY TALES

City Grocery
152 Courthouse Square
Oxford, Mississippi 38655
Tom Franklin

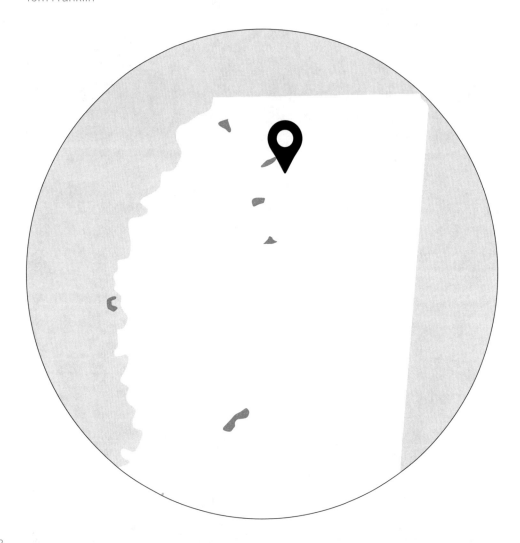

Oxford, Mississippi, where I live, is a famously literary town, shaded by the long, deep shadow William Faulkner cast, and home to many other writers including, at some time or other, Willie Morris, Barry Hannah, Richard Ford, Donna Tartt, Chris Offutt, Darcy Steinke, Mark Richard, Megan Abbott. The list goes on and on. Faulkner's house, Rowan Oak, is a museum now and part of the University of Mississippi. Oxford is also home to Square Books, recently called the best bookstore in America by *Publishers Weekly*. For eight years, until his second term ended, the bookstore owner was the mayor. Famous writers come through all the time, to read from their new books or simply to visit the town which, apart from its literary scene, has nationally recognized restaurants and amazing live music. It also has, to my great joy, one of the most literary bars in the country.

A couple doors down from Square Books, you go up a set of stairs. As you ascend you see, through windows to your right, the City Grocery Restaurant, for which the bar has its name— lively, sparkling with champagne glasses and silverware, loud even through the glass (beyond which you can see a shelf of books by local writers). You go on up and rise past the black floorboards and the bouncer on his stool reading *Lonesome Dove* into a long room centered by a brass bar behind which the bartender, Chip, is already there with your drink of choice.

For me, City Grocery will forever be tangled with one of my literary heroes. On Thanksgiving eve of 1994, I and two graduate school pals were en route from the University of Arkansas in Fayetteville, Arkansas, to Mobile, Alabama, where my family lived. My two friends were Irish and I wanted to show them a good ole down home Thanksgiving. On the way, one of them suggested we stop in Oxford, to see Larry Brown, who this friend had met at a writing conference a few years earlier. Brown had been a fireman in Oxford for twenty-one years before quitting to write full time, and still lived in Tula, not far from Oxford. I'd been a fan of his for years, had read every word I could find, and so I was thrilled at the chance to meet him.

We had trouble locating him because my friend had forgotten to bring his number, but a stop at the local fire station yielded results. Brown's old captain called him at home and told him about us, then hung up and turned back to us. "He says he'll meet y'all at City Grocery in half an hour."

My first time up those steps. The place was empty. It was the night before Thanksgiving, after all. We grabbed some beers and sat waiting at the bar, with its long brass counter. On it I noticed metal plates bearing engraved names. I began to read them, walking along the bar, delighted to find Larry Brown's name etched there along with his drink, Wild Turkey rocks.

Not long after that, up the steps came Larry himself, a skinny guy in a leather jacket and cowboy boots. He shook all our hands and ordered a Coke—he wasn't drinking these days, he told us—and we sat and talked for a couple of hours as my buddies and I drank several Bud Lights apiece. At some point I asked how you got your name on the bar. He grinned.

"You just spend a lot of time in here," he said.

We told more stories and eventually the evening ended and we walked outside into the cold and said our good-byes.

But I never forgot the town. Nearly ten years later, when I was offered the John and Renée Grisham Writer-in-Residence at Ole Miss, I took it immediately. My wife and I moved from Illinois to Oxford with our three-month-old daughter and fell in love with Oxford and never left. We were fortunate to both find jobs here at the university, a rare thing among academics.

A year after our move, when my wife got pregnant with our son Thomas, she found herself exhausted by 8:30 every night. Because I'm a night owl, she'd send me on my bicycle to City Grocery. I suppose I spent a lot of time there, befriending the bartenders, tipping far too much, and, finally, getting my name stamped on the brass bar. It happened to me, I'm here to report, faster than anyone else in the history of the place.

Tom Franklin, it says, in metal. *Bud Light*.

I'm proud of many things in my life: my kids, my marriage, my job, writing and publishing books, but perhaps I'm most proud of getting my name there.

During much of my childhood, my father practiced as a lay minister when he wasn't fixing cars in his auto repair shop. He always said a church was not its building but the people who congregated there. I feel the same way about City Grocery and the line of regulars that includes construction workers, chemists, doctors, professors and, yes, writers.

All writers stop by City Grocery when they're in town. One night David Simon visited. A bunch of us regulars had watched and loved *The Wire*. We'd been telling another regular, Syd, about it. Syd is curmudgeonly in a good way, a tequila-swilling blade of a man you could (in those days) find there every night.

When I introduced him to David, Syd said, "Buy you a tequila." Not a question.

"No thanks," David said. "I'll take a Jameson's, though."

Syd looked insulted. "Tequila," he growled.

David shook his head, no thanks. "Jameson's."

"Look, motherfucker," Syd said, gesturing around him, at the whole place, "these assholes have been bragging on how fucking good your show is."

I was a little uncomfortable by this point. "It's okay, Syd," I said.

"No," he said, locking twinkling eyes with David. "You're in here, you'll drink fucking tequila."

David drank it.

Later, as we were headed home, David said, "You know who I liked best in that bar?"

"Who?" I asked.

"That guy Syd."

I don't see Syd much these days. He's moved out west. But when I do, it's always tequila. I've learned not to argue.

The last time I saw Larry Brown was in City Grocery. The bookstore owner's mother had died. We all knew and loved her. I came up the steps after the wake and there was Larry, sitting at a table, the only time I'd ever seen him in a tie. We shook hands and chatted a moment. Not long after that, Larry had a heart attack and died. He was 53.

He's still in the City Grocery, though, and not just as a name on the bar. His picture hangs above the bar, too, and I don't go in the place without looking at it for a long moment. In the men's room the graffiti is well written. People write poetry there. There's an RIP line, too, including Larry Brown and Willie Morris and Barry Hannah and Dean Faulkner Wells and others.

One day (one distant day) I hope my name will be added. I'll have been hanging out in the bar, in my late nineties, and will be headed out, home, me and my walking cane. I'll start down those steps and perhaps my heart will give up the ghost after the second step or the third, and by the time I land at the bottom, I'll be gone.

But I'll live on. There I'll be, my name scrawled on the list in the men's room, my name stamped on the bar. The regulars that remember me will raise their glasses and from above I'll raise mine back, and then I'll go find Larry and Barry and Willie and all the others and we'll shut down heaven.

Shay's Pub & Wine Bar
58 JFK Street
Cambridge, Massachusetts 02138
Edith Zimmerman

This girl walks into a bar, in Harvard Square. She's there to meet her friends, because it's where they always go to meet up when they're all at home, usually for the holidays. It's a low-key bar, sort of on the outskirts of the square. She sits down at one of the tables and waits for the waitress to come over. She is the only customer at the bar. It is maybe 1:30 or so, and she thinks to herself that it's too early to be in a bar. But it's the day before Christmas, so whatever. But not whatever. When another customer lingers on the patio area out front—it looks like she's tying up a dog, although the dog is out of eyeshot and it's taking a weirdly long time—the girl thinks, *Lady, please come inside and be a customer at this bar so I feel less disgusting even though technically I don't care.*

The girl orders a glass of pinot grigio while she waits for her friends, who are slightly late. She sort of stares out at the middle distance, also at the Christmas tree that they have outside on the patio, trying to look comfortable and normal, like it would not even occur to her that it is weird to be drinking alone at 1:30 in the afternoon. Except that she *is* preoccupied with the amount of time she spends in bars, and she knows it should be reduced, or, more accurately, that she

definitely needs to drink less. It is a problem that she needs to solve, and it's no longer something that she can pretend isn't a problem, except she still doesn't know when she's going to deal with it or how it's going to happen, because as soon as she starts thinking of the things she has to do—*anything* she has to do—they seem impossible and she knows she can't or won't yet do them. It's terrifying and humiliating and sad and alienating and she doesn't know what the fuck is wrong with her. Her pinot grigio comes. *Yaaay*. Pinot grigio is amazing, especially in the afternoon.

Yes, it's "vacation." But this girl also doesn't have a job. She had one but then she left it, and although it was probably the "right" decision—not that there are technically right or wrong decisions, really, because there is only the decision that gets made, and it's the only one that ever could happen, meaning the other decision fundamentally doesn't exist—she has no job and she recently had to pay so much money in taxes that she is now broke and has to get a job again, which is probably a good thing, because her life feels kind of miserable and meaningless without a job, or a boyfriend, or whatever it is. She's also probably depressed.

Which is sort of a frustrating word. Because if there were no such word as "depressed," she'd probably be like, *Okay, I am not feeling so great because of some choices I made; time to make some other choices and try to turn this thing around.* But instead the word "depressed" does exist and it's all, "I'm depressed. She's depressed. We're depressed." And it's just like, *Can't people just be sad?*

Anyway, L. is the first of her friends to show up. They hug, and L. orders tea, and by the time it comes, the girl is done with her first pinot grigio, which is also when their friend A. shows up. They all also hug, and then A. orders a hot toddy, which is made with warm port, because the bar only serves beer and wine. It's sort of a joke-order because it is a strange drink, but A. orders it all the time there, when they meet up, so maybe it's not a joke anymore. Maybe it never was a joke. It's also really tasty.

One time when the girl was there about six years earlier, Ben Affleck walked in. He was radiant but low-key, basically perfect. He was with a guy who the girl chose to believe was his friend from high school, just like how she meets up there with her friends from high school. Just a bunch of regular old Cambridge people. Except the girl couldn't stop staring at him or focusing on anything other than the fact that Ben Affleck was there, right there, *right over there*, and

eventually she and her friend—who was also kind of stunned silent in his "presence"—left because they couldn't keep their conversation up, or have a conversation that wasn't about Ben Affleck.

There was also the time she was there alone, reading a book because she thought she didn't want to talk to anyone, but then this guy kept asking questions about the book and about her life, so she told him she was only in town because her dad was dying, which was true, but then he told her his own father had died a couple months earlier, and they ended up talking for a long time.

The girl orders a second pinot grigio. When it's time for a third, she's like *ahhhhhhh* (inwardly). Because although she wants one, and although she just wants to drizzle her head into the ground and make the day swish away—she doesn't want to think; she doesn't want to be trapped with herself; she doesn't want to have to be herself around other people; she doesn't want to be around other people; she has no idea; she feels like one of these is the answer, the thing that's true, although she really has no idea—she also doesn't want to get too drunk in front of her friends because she wants to seem more together than she is, and she gets too drunk in front of her friends too much. So she doesn't order one.

Then things kind of wrap up and they all part ways for the day. The girl is tempted to go to the liquor store to buy a bottle of vodka to keep in her bureau in her childhood home (beside the other empty bottles of vodka), because drinking all day sort of takes the corners off being home, or whatever it is that she tells herself. But she tells herself that she can handle not having vodka in the drawer for ONE day. Plus there's plenty of wine at home.

Weeks later, she has an epiphany about her weaknesses and shames and secrets, and she makes some hard choices and sticks with them, and at one point when she's on the other side of all this shit, she thinks to herself that she's really glad she did it all because life's even better than she could have imagined, and she's proud and relieved that she wasn't as weak as she'd been afraid she was, that she isn't so lonely anymore, that she's finally really connecting with people. No, actually she still has no idea. But maybe she will someday.

8-Ball Saloon
208 S 1st Street
Ann Arbor, Michigan 48104
Davy Rothbart

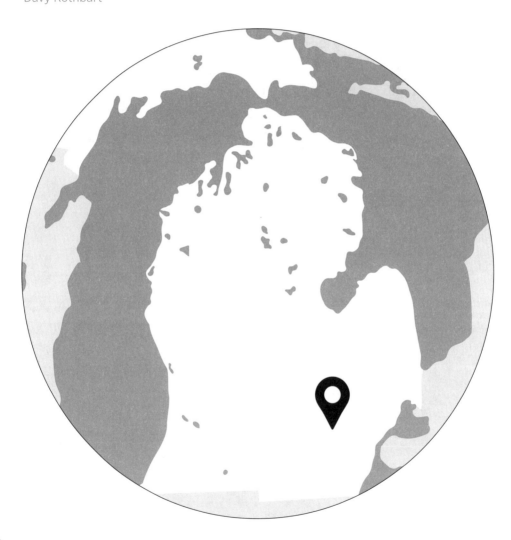

One particularly dead Sunday night, nursing my fourth PBR on a stool at the 8-Ball, I caught sight of my old friend Sam, who I'd been close with in high school but hadn't seen in years. We hugged and slammed down a couple of whiskey shots. Then he looked at me somberly and said, "Today was my grandfather's funeral."

I remembered getting to know the guy when Sam and I were in high school. His name was Max—a cheery, talkative old-timer who always got after me for wearing a baseball cap indoors. "Better show off your hair while you still got it," he'd say with a smile. His story, as I'd heard from Sam, was that he'd been a barber in a small town in Poland, and during the war had been shipped to Treblinka, his young wife to another camp. He'd survived only because the Nazi soldiers needed someone to cut their hair, and he was apparently damn good at it. His wife, meanwhile, had perished. Later, after the war, he lived in Denmark for a couple of years, and then tracked down a distant cousin who'd found his way to Detroit and followed him there, marrying again, eventually, and raising a family. For decades, he'd helped his cousin manage a small appliance store, and had cut hair for family members and friends from synagogue on a barber's chair he kept in his garage. In high school, I'd had my hair cut by him twice myself.

I bought Sam another shot, and he wound from one story about his grandfather to another. Sam had gotten to know the guy pretty well the summer between tenth and eleventh grade, when he'd spent three months working at the appliance store and living with his grandparents in Royal Oak. One night, Sam said, after he'd been there for a month, he'd bounded into his grandfather's bedroom to ask him a question, and came upon an eerie, astonishing sight—his grandfather was half-naked in the middle of the room, dressed in only a woman's antique slip and high-heeled shoes, struggling to pull a skinny, frayed dress over his head. "I turned and bolted right outta there," Sam explained. "I was pretty sure he had no idea what I'd seen, which made things less awkward, I guess, while still being somewhat awkward. I mean, it was like I'd caught him in the dressing room at some crappy women's clothing store at the mall. But I never told anyone what I saw." Sam paused. "Although, for most of that summer, I used to refer to my grandfather as 'T.J. Max.' You remember that?"

I shook my head. This all felt like a pretty weird story to relate to someone the night of your grandfather's funeral. On the other hand, we'd both been drinking heavily, and Sam seemed relieved to have run into someone to share stories of Max with, especially since I'd actually known him.

"Well, whatever," he said, "I didn't use that nickname long." At the end of the summer, Sam went on, his grandfather had called him some kind of unknowable heartbreak or dark twist that I was afraid to hear about.

"Yeah, we fucked each other's brains out!" Sam cried, his face gone mad. Then his smile skedaddled and his eyes drooped. "No," he said. "My grandfather just told me he wanted to explain something to me. He knew I'd seen him in women's underwear and wanted to explain who these clothes belonged to." Sam looked me in the eye. "Well, you can guess.

THIS WAS MY LAME PLOY TO INJECT LEVITY INTO A STORY THAT SEEMED, TO ME, LIKE IT WAS CREEPING TOWARD SOME KIND OF UNKNOWABLE HEARTBREAK OR DARK TWIST THAT I WAS AFRAID TO HEAR ABOUT.

into his room, saying he wanted to talk to him, that he had something to show him. Laid out on the bed, Sam said, were the same old-school women's underwear, ornate high-heeled shoes, and drab but pretty dress that he'd seen his grandfather wriggling into a couple of months before.

I stopped him. "Wait, did you guys *bone?*" This was my lame ploy to inject levity into a story that seemed, to me, like it was creeping toward

They belonged to his first wife. The one who died. The one who was killed. It was her favorite dress, he said. Her favorite pair of shoes. Years and years after she died, I guess, some relative of hers tracked down Max and gave him the clothes, and a couple of other trinkets of hers. 'I love your grandmother more than anything,' he told me that day, 'but it doesn't mean I don't miss Hedda sometimes. When I'm missing her, I put on her clothes. Maybe it's just my imagination, but when I'm in her clothes, I feel her close to me, like I can still smell her, can still feel her touch.'"

"Holy shit. What did you say?" I asked.

"What could I say? I just said, 'Okay, Pops.' He never mentioned it again. I never brought it up either. But then, we were going through his stuff yesterday, me and my mom. I was helping her clean out his house, sort through all his stuff, empty out the closets. And I saw the dress. I'm sure it was the dress."

At this point, I realized that Wolfie, the bartender, and a few other guys close by who Sam and I half-knew had been pulled into the story. "So, what'd you do with it?" Wolfie asked.

"What do you think? I tried that fucker on!" Sam roared. "When my mom was out of the room!" He laughed too hard, then seized up. "Well, it didn't fit me. I don't know, man. Shit. We just donated it to Goodwill, with all the rest."

Wolfie poured one last round of shots and passed them silently around. "These are on me," he said.

Sam held up his glass, whiskey spilling over the edge, down his fingers, dripping to the floor. "To T.J. Max," he said quietly.

"Cheers," we said. "To Max." And we all drank.

The American Colony Hotel Bar
1 Louis Vincent Street
Jerusalem
Janine di Giovanni

A long, long time ago—around the time of the first Palestinian intifada, or uprising.

I was due to meet Richard Beeston and his wife, Natasha, at the bar of the American Colony Hotel in East Jerusalem on a Thursday night in May. They were living at the Colony, in a room overlooking the lemon-scented courtyard, until they found a proper apartment. They were very young, but very worldly and very glamorous. So was the American Colony, a former Pasha's palace that was the headquarters for all the Middle East press corps—the ones in the know.

Rick was a real journalist—the bureau chief of *The Times* of London. I was a freelancer with no expense account. I was writing my first book, and I had a contract in my pocket to do it, but I felt— quite rightly—like a fraud. I was one year out of graduate school, and I knew quite enough about *Anna Karenina* and *Crime and Punishment*. But a book about Israel? The thought of what lay ahead of me—reporting, research, and writing— kept me awake at night with horrid anxiety.

Even a nasty Italian journalist—a woman who hated other women—had said to me in front of a crowd of older reporters, "And YOU. Yes, YOU. What do YOU know about the Middle East? Why are YOU writing a book?"

Not much, I had to admit. I knew very little. But I was about to find out. Baptism by fire? More like baptism by gunfire.

Outside, the first intifada was raging, and I had never covered a war before. Palestinian kids were throwing rocks through the windows of journalists' cars. In a quiet room, the American Colony manager had installed a wire machine for reporters to read about where the conflict was moving in between cocktails. I did not even know how to send a Telex.

More importantly, I didn't even know what one wore to a war zone. That chic and wonderful writer Martha Gellhorn had insisted on handmade Belgian shoes during the Spanish Civil War, when she fell in love with Hemingway. But I could not afford kidskin slippers, even if I knew where to buy them. No, I decided, on the plane—a one-way ticket to Jerusalem—I was going to have to rely on my guile, my wits, and my guardian angel.

Like the Beestons, I was also staying at the American Colony. But mine was a cut-rate, cheapo room—$40 a night—found for me by the sympathetic blue-eyed Palestinian Christian manager named Hani. It was right underneath the muezzin, which woke me at 4 a.m. with the call to prayer. The whining, tinny voice would rouse me from sleep. I would put in earplugs, cover my head with a pillow, and fall back into my single bed wondering what the hell I was doing in this godforsaken place.

I had no friends and I felt utterly self-conscious, utterly alone. Then I found the American Colony Bar, and Ibrahim the barman, and suddenly I had a million friends.

I arrived early for that first Beestons dinner in my best baggy white linen shirt and a pair of beige silk Nicole Fahri trousers. How do I remember that particular outfit? I remember because it was my Year of Living Dangerously outfit. I had worn the exact same thing my first night of my very first story, in Nicaragua, again a place where I did not know what the hell I was doing. It made me feel slightly more secure.

I was so young that I remember being embarrassed about my age, my inexperience, and my lack of knowledge of everything, from sex to Middle East politics. I had married very young, and had lived a fairly sheltered life. I was so naïve I did not even realize how incredibly potent and seductive that combination might

have been. If I'd known how to use it, which I did not. Anyway, I was happily married, to a wonderful man, and I was going to become an academic, finish my Ph.D., write this book, then go on to have babies, and teach at a university. I was certainly not cut out to be a foreign correspondent.

At the bar, I began to feel racy. I ordered a glass of mineral water with lemon (in those days, I did not yet drink) and picked at the peanuts in a silver dish. The barman, a Palestinian with a moustache in his early thirties, dark and rather chic—Ibrahim, I would later learn—watched me with an amused air. Eventually, he began to talk to me, deciding, I guess, that I was worth it. He flirted as he mixed drinks and poured expensive whiskey.

Several older men sat at the bar near me and watched me silently, like I was fresh flesh. One was called Mr. Tim by the rest of the guys at the bar. He got up at one point, leaving his whiskey, and danced alone, boogying down to some soul music while Ibrahim looked on approvingly.

A blonde woman who worked for *The Independent*—the new, cool newspaper—came rushing in. A woman who wore a red T-shirt emblazoned with TIME MAGAZINE on the front went rushing out, with cameras around her neck. Everyone looked like they had a purpose, a place to go, and knew what they were doing.

Everyone except me.

Eventually the Beestons turned up and we got horribly drunk on bad overpriced red wine. Natasha was a diplomat's daughter and looked it: all long and lean in tight, faded Levi's and a man's white shirt, like Lauren Bacall. She had olive skin and green eyes and shiny hair. She was fresh out of Cambridge and very clever. She knew about the Middle East, as did Rick, who had started covering the first Lebanese war straight out of high school. They talked about Sykes-Picot and Gertrude Bell. They had just recently married, and held hands.

Rick was blond and easygoing and already, at 25, a Fleet Street legend. After our boozy dinner, he paid the bill. "These guys don't deserve me," he joked, meaning the bean counters at the *Times*. "I cost them so little."

We became great friends, friends for decades, friends in Jerusalem, London, Moscow, Bosnia, Chechnya, Iraq, and Afghanistan.

But how could we know, in light of that early, youthful drunken dinner, how life would turn out? How could we know that twenty-five years later, Rick would die of an agonizing cancer leaving behind his beloved wife and two children? How could we know that I would pixie-spin through my life reporting war after war, writing five more books, never going back to academia, and burning out my youthful marriage (and a second one, too), trying to put out a fever that would start those very weeks in Jerusalem?

"There you were, bright-eyed and utterly beautiful," Natasha would later write to me, of that first meeting.

We all were, in those lost Fitzgerald-like years. Bright-eyed. Utterly. Beautiful.

·

Five years later—around the time of the Oslo Peace Accords.

JC, who looked like Che Guevera, sat perched at the bar, a foggy glass of something toxic in front of him.

"Come here sweetheart," he crooned. He was sitting with a leering, handsome blond man named Julian and another man, a funny Egyptian named Yusuf.

"Don't you dare go over there," hissed my mate, P., a famous foreign correspondent, and a Catholic like me, drawing on his Silk Cut. He was teasing. "Those are BAD men."

"Bad men," I said dreamily. "Just my kind of guys."

Of course I went to their table, and of course I stayed up all night partying with them. They were hilariously funny, they drank Johnnie Walker Red, and they were all the cleverest of the clever of the Middle East correspondents. I felt good just being in the same room with them.

As we moved from story to story, major Middle East event to more Middle East events, we always met at the American Colony. By now I had a real job at Beeston's paper, the *Times*, and a fat expense account. Now I had the Pasha's room at the Colony.

JC called the bar at the American Colony the "Chamber of Horrors." It was our office: underground, dark and smoky, a place of deep regrets. JC was best friends with Ibrahim, and said that Ibrahim knew where all the bodies were buried. Boy, did he.

Ibrahim saw everything. He never drank, so he recorded it all in his enormous memory. The rest of us get drunk and embarrassing. But it's okay—we're foreign correspondents. We cover war and see horror. It's expected that we drink and drink and behave badly. It's in our DNA. We transport the party all over the world, wherever we go to report: after the sun goes down, after

we file, after we count the bodies, we gather to party. Bosnia, Somalia, Rwanda, Sierra Leone, Iraq, etc., etc.

Later, JC goes to rehab. JC gets married. JC gets separated. JC goes back to rehab. One night, JC and I are partying all night in my flat in London, and at 5 a.m., he gets up to go, weary and shuffling in his heavy body.

At the staircase, he turns to blow me a kiss.

"Goodnight, kiddo." Despite the fact that I was growing up, the older male correspondents still called me "kiddo." "I won't be seeing you for a long time," he added gloomily. "Not for a long, long time."

"But I'll see you next week," I said, surprised, "at Melissa's party." Then I understood what he meant.

"Oh God, NO. You don't mean that. Please don't do that. It's much worse down there."

He put his hand on my arm. He smiled woozily.

"No, you don't understand. It's time. It's just time."

A few months later, JC was dead by his own hand, in his native Bolivia, a gunshot to the head.

I was in Somalia when I found out, by satellite phone. Julian had phoned me and tried to shoo away my tears from a million miles away.

His third or fourth wife, I forget which number, Marie, who would also die too soon—of a rocket shell in Homs, Syria, in 2012—would say, "JC saw too much."

•

Around the time of the assassination of Rabin.

P. and I have been drinking for hours at the American Colony bar. My father has just died and I am grieving. Now I know how to drink. I spent the day at the Church of the Sepulcher, saying prayers for my beloved father, then I met P. for sundowners.

We pick at food and continue our boozing. At one point, I have a brilliant idea.

"Let's go for a swim," I say, slurring, no doubt. With the nonchalance of practiced drunks, we take off our clothes and skinny dip in the pool in front of some ultra-conservative Palestinians, who are horrified by the naked flesh.

"Stop staring," I shout at them, as P. dives sloppily into the pool and crashes his head on the bottom. I have to dive down, holding my breath, to fish him out, naked. I think he's dead but eventually he opens his eyes.

"Christ," he says woozily.

"What are you, voyeurs?" I shout as I rise to the surface. I get out of the pool starkers and walk slowly to get a towel, giving them a full view.

Laughing hysterically, thinking we are the funniest people on earth, P. and I stumble back to our rooms, stopping off for a nightcap. Or three.

The next morning, we are both hung over and full of remorse, popping Nurofen and sipping lemon water.

"God, how embarrassing!"

For years after, Ibrahim will say to me, with a sly wink: "Hey Janine, want to go for a swim?"

•

A few years later—the second intifada.

S., a close male friend and a great reporter, is urging me to have a baby. He has two and is ecstatic about being a dad.

"You don't want a kid because you think you aren't going to be sexy anymore, right?" he says, laughing.

"Go to hell," I say.

"You'll still be sexy."

"Go to hell," I say.

Little do I know, but I am three months pregnant. I am engaged to a French journalist I met in Sarajevo. I am very much in love.

But he is in Africa, and S. and I are reporting the carnage at the Jenin massacre. I live on the road, in hotel rooms, reporting story after story, war after war, and I am so out of touch with myself that I don't know I am pregnant.

In Jenin, we run through olive groves past Israeli tanks, to get into the leveled Jenin camp. "Holy shit," S. says when we get inside. "Look at what the fuck they did in here."

We go back to the bar and drink and drink and drink away all the bad stuff. After a while, all the bad memories melt into one. The next week, I find out that I am pregnant. I lose the baby.

•

Some years later—post 9/11, post-Afghanistan, post-Iraq. Everyone has forgotten Palestine.

I'm five months pregnant, with a huge belly. My great friends Judah and Alex, both photographers, take photos of me waddling through refugee camps, breathing laboriously. Alex photographs my belly in Ramallah. I am in love. I am married (again) and wear a ring proudly. When I go into camps to interview women, the Palestinian mothers make me lay down and they rub my belly.

Something is wrong, they say, frowning.

We are going down to Gaza when I feel like my water is breaking. But wait! I'm only five months pregnant. This can't be happening!

My friends rush me to the emergency room. The doctor says, "Do you want this baby? Tell the truth. Because you are not acting very responsibly. GAZA?"

I'm kept in the hospital overnight. They decide to ship me home to England. After the hospital releases me, Alex and Judah and I go back to my room in the Annex section of the American Colony—now I am on big expenses—and they watch as I pack to go home.

In the bar, Ibrahim makes me a tea. The boys drink Coke.

"You'll be okay," Alex says.

"This is what my life is going to look like," I say. "You are looking at responsibility."

Alex looks amused.

"Responsibility? What the hell is that?"

•

Sometime around the Arab Spring.

At last, I have a baby, a son. He is my redemption. He is my angel. I have a reason to live. I have a reason to stay alive, not to die of depression like JC or die from a rocket like Marie. Or get shot in the head by some unknown rebel soldiers like Kurt Shork, the Reuters war correspondent and my friend from Bosnia, who is murdered in Sierra Leone while we are on assignment in 2000.

P., too, is a father.

S.'s daughter is a model.

Alex has two children, with two different women, and is the President of Magnum Photos—not yet 40 and full of responsibility.

After Rick's death, Natasha became a mega-agent in London.

Julian became a successful businessman in Africa and fell out of a helicopter and was injured but survived.

Yusuf left journalism.

I ask about Mr. Tim—who I'd never forget boogying by himself my first night at the American Colony bar. No one seems to know.
But Ibrahim is still there, behind the bar. I order a mineral water with lemon. I can't hold my alcohol the way I used to—I get furious hangovers. Half-heartedly, Ibrahim jokes about taking a dip in the pool.

"I am respectable now—a mother," I sputter. "I don't skinny dip."

I like being respectable. Going to bed early. Getting up to do the school run. War zones done in a careful fashion. Being called a doyenne instead of "kiddo."

But sometimes, once in a while, I miss it. Being back in the day. Especially when I see new reporters coming into the bar. Bright-eyed. Utterly. Beautiful.

Manuel's Tavern
602 N Highland Avenue NE
Atlanta, Georgia 30307
Jack Pendarvis

I lived across the street from Manuel's Tavern for fourteen years. I went in—let's be conservative—at least three times a week. Not until my very last *days* in Atlanta did the bartender perk up when he saw me and call me by name. It took me about a decade and a half to become a regular. That's what I call a bar with integrity.

There are bars I truly love in Oxford, Mississippi, where I live now, and in them I have "drink drinks." Chip upstairs at City Grocery makes a gimlet the way I like it. See Brian at Snackbar for a perfect Manhattan. But I can't remember drinking anything but beer at Manuel's. God, it was a great place to drink beer. I just wanted to eat hamburgers and drink beer under a murky portrait of President Kennedy while everybody blew cigarette smoke in my face. And my wish was granted.

Manuel's is as big as a barn, though the areas within it where a person could smoke got smaller and smaller during the years I spent in the neighborhood. I'm no huge fan of smoking. It has killed a lot of nice people I used to know. But smoking is better than change. Even when I stopped in alone at an odd hour of the afternoon,

when the only other visible customer was an old man providing supplemental narration for the *M*A*S*H* reruns playing above the bar, there were smoky ghosts in the air. Manuel's smelled like my departed grandfather's moustache. Manuel's is where I often watched my Muslim mother-in-law take a deep, luxurious drag while semi-conscientiously removing the forbidden specks of pork from some sausage gravy she had ordered on the side. So I was upset about the incremental smoking ban. And I was outraged when they started cutting the J.J. Special into two pieces instead of the eternal four.

The J.J. Special was a cheeseburger with onions on toasted wheat bread, and it came with fries *and* onion rings. In its most perfect and holy original incarnation, it was divided into four beautiful little quarters, a toothpick proud in each one—those special toothpicks with fluttering cellophane in fireworks colors.

When they brought me a J.J. Special cut in half, I freaked out. I actually complained to the kitchen. It was okay, because I knew the woman in charge back there. She was a former co-worker of my wife, Theresa, and had been at our wedding. She had been hired to shake things up. I think she added sweet potato fries to the menu. Okay, whatever. I remember what Clint Eastwood said about movie scripts, that you don't want to "kill them with improvement." But she was patient. I liked her a lot. She showed me step by step the ergonomic benefits of this blasphemous distortion of my J.J. Special.

I got used to it. I guess. It took a while. You know, maybe I didn't get used to it. Manuel's is not where you go for something new and different. I remember eating with my friend Caroline at a French place on Cheshire Bridge in Atlanta: duck à l'orange and cherries jubilee while a woman with her long, straight hair shimmering in the candlelight strummed her guitar and warbled Jacques Brel. What's the opposite of irony? It was that. We felt like Burt Reynolds and Catherine Deneuve in their prime. This was the twenty-first century. There were these weird, eternal pockets all over the city, and Manuel's was one.

Manuel's is heaven, and you want it to be like heaven in that Talking Heads song, "a place where nothing ever happens." I swear that when they first added the "smoke-free room" you could literally sit in there and be ignored forever if you had enough patience. It seemed like a just punishment, or one of the early stages of grief, or maybe a transdimensional barrier no one could cross.

Manuel's abhors a barrier. Look, I kind of hate to see little kids where I'm trying to drink. I keep thinking they're going to fall down some stairs and there might be a scene. Yet at Manuel's I was always like, "Aw, look, cool, some little kids." It was a real family place. Everything was fine there. Everybody was welcome. I remember a kid who lined up all his action figures according to height on a table and said, "I'm looking at all my friends."

That was Ward's kid. Ward and I worked at TBS, making promos and junk, and we'd stop by after work and get sloshed trying to think of all the art we were going to make instead. We'd write down stuff on a napkin that later nobody could read.

Once Ward went to the bathroom and came back and said in a sincere voice, "I've got an idea for a TV show." Dramatic pause. "Urine AI." Two more beers, please.

After that I worked for a sister company, TNT, making a kids' show with my friend Barry. We had these marionettes and a live goat that hosted cartoons. Somehow, the president of the network managed not to see it for two years. Then one day he called us into a conference room and asked to see a sample of what we had been doing, so we showed him and he chortled and beamed with delight and then he fired us. We drove to Manuel's. On the way, we saw a dead guy lying in the street. It made us feel glad not to be dead. We felt terrible for that person, of course. The only place you can go after your show gets canceled and you lose your job and you see a dead guy lying in the street is Manuel's Tavern. That's a good recommendation to put on Yelp.

The best place to sit was always in the tall-backed wooden booths by the long wooden bar, with a dirty ashtray in front of you, and too many of your friends crammed in.

Was it my 40th? It was some big birthday. I just wanted to go to Manuel's. We had some beers and hamburgers with Caroline and Barry and Ward, and that was it. That's all you need. And sometimes a Dogzilla. It was always entertaining to see Theresa in another losing battle against the Dogzilla. What's a Dogzilla? It's exactly what you think it is.

I'm telling you these small personal things because you can read about Manuel's all over the Internet, its real history from 1956 on, with all the cops and politicians and crusty old-school reporters who made it their second home. It's worth researching. You can learn how to pronounce "Manuel's," for example, which is not the way you think. We used to see one of the original brothers who started the place. He had a lot of trouble walking by then. Everyone would be so pleased to see him and he'd painfully but

graciously, like a parade balloon with a slow leak, make the rounds of all his friends before taking his regular table by the window. Made you feel grounded to see him there, no matter how many pieces your J.J. Special was in.

I think there were famous people at Manuel's all the time but I never saw any of them. Once there was jolly light and noise coming from this kind of separate room up some steps, way in the back, and somebody said, "Jimmy Carter's in there." It was like when Jesus does a cameo in one of the old blockbusters, just his hand or maybe the back of his head, except there was even less of Jimmy Carter, like nothing.

I was around for one political thing. Senator Zell Miller, a Democrat and our former governor, spoke at the 2004 Republican convention, endorsing George W. Bush. Afterward he went on one of those cable news shows and turned all red and had frothy spit coming out of his mouth about something. Then this kooky painting of old Zell in a windbreaker disappeared from the main bar. We all went and looked at the spot where Zell used to be. He was over a toilet now, somebody said. Out in the dumpster was another guess. Zell and his leisurewear (was it a Members Only jacket, or am I romanticizing the past?) eventually turned up in the smoke-free room—a fate worse than we had imagined.

I guess the only time I didn't like being at Manuel's was during a presidential debate or on election night, although most people dug it. Easy to see why. The air was crackling. Serious, lively people called play-by-plays and sweated booze and laughed, smashed up against each other at the packed bar, row on row. But it knotted up my guts, all that potential heartbreak, volumes of it.

I wonder how many times in those fourteen years I said to somebody, "Let's meet at Manuel's." When I first had books coming out I'd invite interviewers, then I'd knock back one too many and make surly cracks that ended up in the paper.

Just before I left Atlanta, a guy wanted to take my picture for some article. I said, "Let's meet at Manuel's." He said, "It would be funny if you took off your shirt for the picture." I said, "No it wouldn't." And it wouldn't. And I didn't. But I did have three cold Guinesseses at ten in the morning on an empty stomach, which turns out to be highly advisable. It makes you feel like a king! I sat at the long, empty bar and the photographer kept encouraging me to have more beer for realism, but I kept my shirt on. That's when the bartender first seemed to recognize me, and asked my name, and after that he'd occasionally use it, and I'd feel like a million bucks. But before the thrill had even lost

its edge I moved to Oxford to begin the shameful life of a college teacher and I am sure I was soon forgotten.

They don't tell you when you start teaching that the students you love and advise to move away will move away, and you won't. I was unreasonably sad when the first batch graduated and split on me. Four of them, who had ended up in different parts of the country, congregated at Manuel's one night, though none of them lived in Atlanta. They emailed me a photo of themselves grinning in front of the sign. It killed me.

I don't know if Manuel's is the way I remember it. By coincidence, my sister lives across from there now. I could ask her, but I won't.

FAN THE SINKING FLAME OF HILARITY WITH
THE WING OF FRIENDSHIP; AND PASS THE
ROSY WINE.

—CHARLES DICKENS,
THE OLD CURIOSITY SHOP

Leila's Peugeot
Tehran, Iran
Azadeh Moaveni

Wine is the root of evils and the source of sins, whoever drinks wine loses his sanity . . . the spirit of faith and piety exits from his body and a defective spirit of devilishness . . . will remain in him . . .

—Ayatollah Ruhollah Khomeini

The punishment for intoxication is 80 lashes for both men and women.

—Article 174, Islamic Penal Code of
the Islamic Republic of Iran

Leila had picked us up at my aunt's house, gunning her car into the dead end and nearly running over the accordion player who roamed the back alleys of Elahieh singing "Sultan of Hearts" beneath people's open windows. Watching from my window I could see him step back startled as Leila bolted out of the car, her hand clenched around the neck of a plastic Sprite bottle of homemade vodka. She was our ride to the party that evening, and I had suggested to Simon, a Reuters colleague, that he come over for a drink before she picked us up. I hadn't thought to check whether my aunt had anything in her cupboards, and only once he'd arrived did I see she was out of everything, out of the vile bootleg Grant's whiskey that was smuggled over the border from Kurdistan, out of the sour wine made by an Armenian housewife in her bathtub, out of *aragh*, the homemade raisin liquor that everyone drank. We had exchanged glances, Simon and I, at that moment, the thought hanging unspoken between us: Should we drink the ethyl alcohol in the medicine cabinet? Simon shrugged. Worst comes to worst we'll go blind, but is there anything to mix it with?

When Leila arrived, her sandals clacking against the stairs, I mixed a bottle full of her homemade vodka with orange juice, and we set off into the warm Tehran night, into the Elahieh alley that smelled of jasmine. We never set out with the express purpose of drinking in the car, but there was something elusive in those moments of flushed transit that we wanted to prolong, such that we invented errands—a stop at the florist on Dibaji who wrapped flowers in burlap, or for fresh pomegranate juice to please the hostess—that would extend the journey, ideally taking us through the social routes of Vali Asr or Jordan Street. The streets where many young people, like us, drink in their cars, because Iran is a country with no bars, and there is no suppressing the human urge to drink publicly, in the unscripted company of both friends and strangers.

We were crawling up Jordan Street (its post-revolutionary name, Africa Street, universally spurned), one car amidst the many that circled up and down the boulevard in the arid summer heat, moving slowly enough to hold lane-to-lane conversations and toss cigarettes between car windows. I was tending our drinks, the homemade vodka mixed with juice in plastic cups, struggling with the awkward slant of the dashboard. Somewhere near the north end of the street, while at a light, a young man with winged eyebrows and full lips leaned out of the car next to us and said something to Leila. Someone always said something to Leila. We'd been friends for about a year and sometimes worked together reporting news stories, both of us too young to realize how precious it was, that carefree era of the Tehran press corps. I don't know if it was her sumac red hair, springing out from beneath her headscarf, her throaty voice and not-quite-but-almost prettiness, that had men jumping to help her, ask for her number, generally get in or out of her way. I couldn't hear exactly what he was saying—the music, Dire Straits I think, was on too loudly—but I could tell from the way she pushed her chest out and exhaled that she was provoked. When the light changed she slammed that little Peugeot's engine across the gears and we went spinning

down the street, already ahead of the other car, suddenly jolting left to avoid a motorbike, and then darting back into the lane. "My drink!" was all I could say, and Simon muttered "Fucking hell," from the back as he wiped his sleeve.

You may wonder at this point whether we were nervous about being stopped. Before that point, I had been stopped by police or some 15-year-old with an AK-47 a handful of times for various offenses like napping in the passenger seat, having a dog in the car, having a male colleague in the car. The latter resulted in a night spent on a dingy barracks floor, and it hadn't even involved being caught giggling with a plastic cup full of sin and a pale European in the back seat. If caught we might have been lashed in a public square for this drinking, like a few young men had been recently, their backs bared up to the sky and the militiamen foregoing the Koran they were meant to hold under their arm, to restrain the force of the whip. But there is nothing like a totalitarian theocracy to put irresponsibility in perspective. In the course of the evening, we had passed a giant mural of a woman suicide bomber cradling an infant, driven on a street named after an assassin, and stopped for gas near the hotel where the Hezbollah delegation usually stayed. With all that going on in the background, having a tiny sip of a cocktail while driving *slowly* around in evening traffic didn't seem all that stupid. I had faith also in

Leila's ability to extricate us from any mishap, and was convinced, with the reckless certainty of a young person and a journalist attuned to grander violence, that it just wouldn't come to that. Not that night anyway.

We eventually slowed down, and I felt for the grainy plastic of the door handle, looking out as a rosy dusk seeped into the city's skyline. We turned onto Vali Asr, where the corridor of plane trees led straight up to mountains, capped even in midsummer with white snow. Both sides of the boulevard swarmed with traffic, rickety powder blue buses, dilapidated cars and pickup trucks, driven by angry men and women in a hurry to get home, and the young ones, the ones like us, out just for the sake of it. We passed a narrow street that led towards an Asian restaurant, one of the few places where the city's moneyed intellectuals and old families mingled with the children of the revolutionary elite, its import-export businessmen and regime officials. It was said you could pass a bottle of wine to the hostess upon arrival, and that it would then be served in an opaque glass, posing as juice, in the same way that juice posed as wine in plays, with everyone pretending to know, or not know, what was going on, on the stage as in life.

But we rejected such subterfuge, felt ourselves to be above it. Like those housebound writers who refused to write novels after the revolution, refusing to appease the censor by making their characters drink juice, we refused to drink in restaurants that served mediocre sushi to the children of executioners. If Tehran couldn't have bars, then we would just wait it out. It was a city, after all, that had been littered with cabarets and nightclubs before the revolution, the names that I remembered hearing as I child: Key Club, Miami, Copacabana. *Hadn't one of them been around here?* I thought, peering up the boulevard toward Rumi Bridge.

A loud thump to the window made me jump, and I turned to see a girl with a hand pressed against the glass, waving furiously at Simon. Of all the sad things I can tell you about Tehran, the saddest is what girls will do if they spot a white guy in a car. This one, her eyes blazing above a scalpel-sharpened nose, was gesturing for Simon to put the window down, to make some kind of contact with him and his European passport. And Simon—I couldn't believe it—opened the door and pulled her in by her birdlike arm. They both started grinning at each other. She was wearing leopard print leggings and cartoon heels. Leila and I tried to behave politely until we realized neither of them was paying attention anyway. She turned sharply up toward Tajrish Square, toward where we had ostensibly been heading all along, the hillside home of Henri, a single Belgian diplomat, whose parties were minorly notorious among Tehran's demimonde.

By the time we got there our plastic Sprite bottle was empty, and as we headed up into the quieter streets of north Tehran, I began to relax. It was probably better for Leila to stop driving; she was on her third drink and how she would manage to get herself home I didn't know. She left the car near the bottom of the hill, and we walked up the steep lane to Henri's—Simon and the girl straggling behind. Henri lived in an

your own, night after night over successive years, is cloying in its intimacy, lacking in promise.

I saw some friends in the corner, near where the long-haired, Sufi musicians who Henri liked to bring in as entertainment were setting up. We laughed together about something, I don't remember now what, and heard shouting by the pool. Leila was standing on its edge, speaking angrily to her occasional lover, an economist. She had that glint in her eye, the same as when she'd cut off the guy on Jordan, the look you

THERE IS NO SUPPRESSING THE HUMAN URGE TO DRINK PUBLICLY, IN THE UNSCRIPTED COMPANY OF BOTH FRIENDS AND STRANGERS.

elegant villa that had probably been built by a mid-ranking official before the revolution, and flickering candles lined the pool outside, the water glistening in the dark. There were waiters roaming around with trays of drinks, proper imported wine and beer that would not endanger any guest of the European Union with blindness. But to be there, seeing the familiar faces around the house, holding familiar conversations about pet art projects and same-old politics, I wished we were still out on the streets in the Peugeot. To be perpetually drinking at home, someone else's or

get when circumstances propel you too close to an edge. Outside, in the dimly lit, moving interior of the car, she'd seemed still in control, but here it wasn't so clear. I watched as she stepped forward and brought her arms up as if to embrace him, only to grasp his shoulders and push him backward into the water, looking satisfied as he bobbed and spluttered to the surface.

"Quick, get a towel, he'll catch cold," I heard a woman in a beige sweater say to no one in particular, as the economist flailed in the water, coughing, trying to make his way to the rough stone edge. I walked over and steered Leila away from the pool, toward the room where the women's manteau and headscarves were heaped on a bed. The musicians were playing the *daf*, an old Khorasani lament about wasted youth and lost beauty, and as everyone moved toward the raised bed on which they were seated, I asked one of the waiters for two unopened beers and Leila and I scurried out into the street. Only once back inside the car, which smelled faintly of oranges and Leila's tuberose perfume, did we remember Simon and the girl.

"They can make their own way home," she said, steering the car down the hill, toward the lit street below. We drove around the rest of the night, stopping only for a quick *ghalyoon*, then back into the car, finishing the beers and gliding across the empty expressways, feeling ourselves a part of the city, so proud and unknowable in the darkness.

FAMILY

AN ONLY CHILD, ABANDONED BY MY
FATHER, I NEEDED A FAMILY, A HOME, AND
MEN. ESPECIALLY MEN. I NEEDED MEN AS
MENTORS, HEROES, ROLE MODELS, AND AS
A KIND OF MASCULINE COUNTERWEIGHT
TO MY MOTHER, GRANDMOTHER, AUNT
AND FIVE FEMALE COUSINS WITH WHOM
I LIVED. THE BAR PROVIDED ME WITH ALL
THE MEN I NEEDED, AND ONE OR TWO MEN
WHO WERE THE LAST THING I NEEDED.

—J.R. MOEHRINGER,
THE TENDER BAR

The Brass Elephant (closed)
924 N Charles Street
Baltimore, Maryland 21201
Laura Lippman

I stole my father's bar. I never meant to. It began as a joke, and not even mine.

It was 1989. I had recently joined the staff of the *Baltimore Evening Sun*, which was owned by the same company as *The Sun*, where my father had worked as an editorial writer for most of my life. I had landed my dream job in my dream city, Baltimore. (Don't scoff.) I was 30 and finding my way in the world. I needed a bar, my bar, in Baltimore — something a step up from the dives and ice houses of my twenties, a decade spent in Texas. I no longer remember what the other Baltimore contenders were. Midtown Yacht Club, with peanuts on the floor? The Calvert House, a mere two blocks from the *Sun* building? I did love Alonso's, a dim place that didn't take credit cards and served a dish called the Fish Thing, but it was way up on the north side.

My father preferred The Brass Elephant, a gracious townhouse in the city's Mount Vernon neighborhood, just five blocks from the *Sun*. His drink of choice was a gin martini, although my father would stipulate—as will I—that "gin martini" is redundant. The only true martini is made from gin and dry vermouth, with just the tiniest whiff of the latter. Olives or lemon peels are okay, but why would you want to displace even a drop of gin with those foreign objects?

My father was famous for drinking martinis—and for giving them up, usually for a week or so at the beginning of a new year. More than one photograph was taken of my father and the last martini of the year; the best showed him in a snowy backyard in hat and scarf, holding the quite chilly martini aloft. His colleagues poked gentle fun at his perennial, temporary temperance. "So Long, Lippman" was the headline on a column written by a friend who loved martinis so much that he once bribed a waiter at a favorite restaurant to pour them in his water glass so his family would not know he was drinking again.

That said, I don't think I ever saw my father inebriated except once, on a Christmas Eve at my home, where my sister noticed there was a slight waver to his walk and asked if he were ill. "I'm fine," he said. "Just not used to that expensive gin Laura buys." My father swore by cheap gin, Beefeater's, which he kept in the freezer. I think he was rather disappointed with my flirtations with Tanqueray and Hendrick's.

But that was later. In September 1989, not even a month after I started at the *Evening Sun*, a colleague of my father's thought it would be hilarious if I were sitting at the bar at the Brass Elephant when my father arrived for an after-work drink to celebrate his 60th birthday. He did think it was funny. Sort of. Like many fathers of daughters, mine did not want me to embrace all the things he loved—newsrooms and martinis among then. He offered to pay my way through graduate school if I would choose any other profession. "I'm afraid newspaper work

The Brass Elephant was hushed and civilized, a grown-up bar for proper grown-ups, something I wanted to be when I was 30. A quarter of a century later, I no longer remember why I was so anxious to be a grown-up. I bought my first house within a year of turning 30. (My father advised against it.) Within three years, I would marry a man who loved The Brass Elephant as much as I did. My father paid for the tent that covered my backyard for the reception. Within ten years, I would find myself lying to that same man, now a so-called house husband,

LIKE MANY FATHERS OF DAUGHTERS, MINE DID NOT WANT ME TO EMBRACE ALL THE THINGS HE LOVED— NEWSROOMS AND MARTINIS AMONG THEM.

coarsens a woman," he said once when I used a profanity mild enough to slide past standards and practices on a network sitcom.

After seeing me with a martini at The Brass Elephant, he went there less and less, while I went there more and more. It could have been a coincidence. He retired from the newspaper in 1995, lured by a generous buyout, and began spending most of his time in the small Delaware beach town where my parents would eventually settle. The bar was mine.

pretending that I had to work later than necessary so I could go to the bar with a female friend instead of coming straight home, as he expected me to. Instructed me to.

When, in 1993, I started writing crime novels set in Baltimore, I gave The Brass Elephant to my series character. Private investigator Tess Monaghan was never more my proxy than when sitting at The Brass Elephant bar, the light from the setting sun slanting through the pretty stained glass window, a plate of farfalle pasta or the divine *mozzarella en carrozza* in front of her. Eventually, the bar created an eponymous drink in her honor; a menu from the party celebrating that drink hangs in my office. The drink had peach schnapps in it. I don't much care for schnapps and—now it can be told—I didn't love the drink, although it wasn't quite as bad as I feared.

I can admit that now because The Brass Elephant closed in 2009. A new place opened in the same spot, but I didn't have the heart to go there. Because, in some ways, I don't want to be reminded of the young woman who used to climb the mahogany staircase to the second-floor bar, the woman who was in such a hurry to be a grown-up. I find it easier to romanticize the dives of my true youth, where the mistakes and stakes were smaller. The Brass Elephant, through no fault of its own, became the backdrop to a failed first marriage and a rollercoaster ride of a newspaper career. For even as my career as a novelist took off, my career as a reporter stalled—a crazy, sad story that no one really believes, so I've learned to stop telling it. My father worked at *The Sun* for 30 years and I set my goal at 31, having landed there at a much younger age than he did. We were somewhat competitive, my father and I. At any rate, I lasted only twelve years at the *Evening Sun*, which was swallowed by *The Sun* in 1995, the

year of my father's buyout, so I spent twenty in newspapers overall.

I last "visited" The Brass Elephant in 2012, for a novel I was writing. I made it the hangout for a band of devoted John B. Anderson volunteers who retreat there on election night to lick their wounds. A very young woman talks to the bartender who remembers her father, a man who disappeared four years earlier to evade federal charges for running a gambling operation. The bartender claims to know what her father would have thought about the 1980 presidential election and the young woman yearns to believe him. She knows surprisingly little about her father.

I wish I had asked the bartender of my day more questions about my father. Because while my father is still alive—and still enjoys a daily martini, just one, at which he nips off and on, while watching *Law & Order* reruns— he tells fewer and fewer stories. His memory is problematic. He's no longer quick, and my father was famously quick, an award-winning columnist who packed more in 600 words than others could in 1,500. The one thing he always asks me is if I know any gossip from our old workplace. I don't. In a way, the *Baltimore Sun* is like another Brass Elephant. A newspaper is still published in the building, but it's not the newspaper I knew and certainly not the one for which my father worked—a sober, well-regarded place with foreign bureaus and, back in the day, a policy that required my father to travel first-class when covering presidential elections. So long, Lippman.

I briefly aspired to find a new watering hole to replace The Brass Elephant—there's a cool, hipsterish place a block from my house—but the fifty-something self-employed writer requires much less watering than the thirty-something newspaper hack. I go to restaurant bars for lunch now—a ladylike salad, a glass of wine, never a martini. I had one at a steakhouse the other night and it was as if someone had slipped me a roofie; I fell asleep face-down on the sofa and could barely be roused to stumble into bed. I am only five years away from my own sixtieth birthday and I would prefer not to find my daughter sipping a martini anywhere on that celebratory day, given that she will be not quite nine at the time. I hope she won't be a writer, although she has shown some interest in what I do. She slaps her hands on keyboards, announcing that she is "doing my work." The other day, I showed her a prize I had won. Her eyes brightened at the shiny yet inexpensive object: "Can I have it?"

And although my father will probably not read this essay—he is reading less and less these days—it's as good a place as any to issue an apology for doing what children have always done and will always do when it comes to their parents' possessions and memories and lives.

Daddy, I'm sorry I stole your bar.

IS IT BAD TO SWEAR LOUDLY USING YOUR
MOTHER'S NAME? IT IS BAD. BUT HE DOES
IT. IS IT BAD TO DRINK MOONSHINE? IT IS
BAD. BUT HE DRINKS IT.

—MIKHAIL BULGAKOV,
DIABOLIAD AND OTHER STORIES

VFW Post 2950
195 W Highway 62
Corydon, Indiana 47112
Frank Bill

It was a huge cinder-block basement that had been built into a hillside with a dance hall above. It was a bar for members only, for those who'd served in a foreign war. It was a place I'd frequented as a young boy with my father, a man who'd given his time as a Marine in the Vietnam War from '68 to '69. It was VFW Post 2950.

From the time the weighted steel entrance door was tugged, the combined reek of stubbed out cigarettes and stale hops was glued to your skin and housed on the inner lining of your nostrils, while your eyes adjusted to the dim fluorescents that hummed down from the nicotine-yellow ceiling and led you over the scuffed tiled floor of green and ruby to the long rung of hardwood bar where middle-aged men sat, stained by Old Spice, Brute, and smokes, like Marlboro Red, Pall Mall, and Lucky Strikes. The Men wore T-shirts and unironic trucker caps. Some donned high and tight hair, others had Criscoed strands combed back over their skulls. The men held camp at their designated stools. The bartender always knew their names, what brand of beer or whiskey they'd be drinking and in what conflict they'd fought: WWII, the Korean War, the Vietnam War. The television recessed into the wood-paneled wall played a soundless ball game, the news, or a western. Daytime passed into the evening and more men came. Some with their wives and kids, others alone, firing one coffin nail after the next, swapping stories about the wars which they'd survived.

Most of my memories about the VFW start back in the late '70s to early '80s and trounce on into present day. Especially back when Carter was running for a second term and the economy took a big belch. My father found himself rebuilding his career, going from ten years of employment at a unionized job in a tobacco plant to attending night school to sell insurance like his older brother. Once he graduated, he landed an insurance gig that didn't pay enough to raise a family. Needing a second income, he got a bartending license, then bounced around from watering hole to watering hole, sharing shifts with others like him, slinging drinks for a demeaning hourly wage, relying on decent tips well into the a.m. until he landed the job of full-time evening bartender at the VFW for a decent hourly wage.

One of my father's duties—other than serving drinks, mopping floors, scouring tables, and scrubbing down the bathrooms—was keeping track of the inventory and resupplying it. Looking to save Post 2950 some money, he'd scan the weekly newspaper sale ads to find colas on the cheap, then take me around to all the grocery stores to help him load his truck bed with twelve-packs of Coke, Big Red, and Sprite. I'd then help unload the packs and restock the chromed coolers with the sliding doors. He'd always keep the weighted entrance door locked, not wanting someone to walk in and see a child behind the bar. I'd also help him haul the crushed cans—soda and beer both—to the recycling place and collect the coin for The Club. That's what everyone called the VFW.

When my mother worked third shift at the battery separator plant and I didn't go to the country to stay with her parents on their farm, I was left with my father's mother, Myrtle, a small raven-haired lady who wore cat-eye glasses and drank beer from a green coffee mug after lunch. She held a love for euchre and telling what she thought of a person regardless of how badly it might damage their feelings.

If nothing else, she was honest.

On Fridays she'd ready herself to socialize with her Noxzema-scented friends at The Club, where she'd seat herself at one of the blue Formica tables and crack open a can of Miller Lite or Natural Lite and pour the golden liquid into a chilled glass, sipping at it while she played cards.

When my grandmother drank, she paced herself. It'd take her most of twenty-four hours or better to get loaded. But there was one night when she'd been down at The Club and decided to cut out early as she'd not been feeling well, had drank maybe half a beer. On her way home she got pulled over by the town fuzz. She only lived a few minutes away—hang a left out of the Club onto 62, drive about one minute, hang a right onto Williar Ave., drive about another minute and hang left into her gravel driveway. She didn't drive much over twenty or thirty miles per hour regardless of where she was going. The cop had thought she was drunk for driving under the 45 mph speed limit and asked her to get out of the car for a sobriety test. She refused, arguing that she was okay. The cop called for backup, which included the county and state police. The town cop ended up opening her door, grabbing her arm, and pulling her out. That *really* pissed her off.

"Is that how you treat your own mother?" she yelled. "Pawing at a defenseless old lady with age in her bones?"

The cop took her to the station and gave her a breathalyzer. She was completely sober. Afterward, the cop drove her back to her car as she continued to give him the riot act.

It was a story she told with vigor down at The Club with her blue-haired friends, breaking everyone into hysterics with each telling while sipping her beer and saying if that cop ran for sheriff, there was no way she'd vote for that SOB. I'd tag along with her—beg for quarters to play Space Invaders, shoot pool, or plug in tunes at the jukebox: old country music like Waylon Jennings, Alabama, Johnny Cash, the Oakridge Boys, Kenny Rogers, Eddie Rabbit, Hank Williams Jr., or John Anderson. By this time I was around ten or eleven and I thought I could dance. My grandmother and her friends got a kick out of this, would sometimes load the jukebox with tunes and I'd give into the attention, knocking my knees together, twisting my arms, and shaking my head while gyrating my body with two left feet. A squirrel biting into a transformer and getting electrocuted could've done better.

To replenish my energy I'd gorge down bags of Munchos potato chips, drink cans of Coke, and consume copious amounts of beef jerky while my father stood behind the thick oak bar. At his back was a mirror and, lining the lower shelf, every brand of hard liquor. He served drinks and listened to members speak about their day, their family, their childhood, and of course their military service.

Two guys my father buddied up with were Mick, who was twelve years older than my father and Jones, who was about two years younger. Mick hadn't been in a war or served with the military; his wife, Dot, was a member through her brother who'd served in WWII, which gave them their membership privileges. Mick was an interstate truck driver who drove for Smith Transfer; he had vines of curly hair like Gene Wilder. He always wore slip-on shoes, nylon dress slacks, and a big-ass belt buckle to hold them up. He was a joke teller who was more of a weekender, drove his truck Monday through Friday and came in at the end of the workweek with Dot. She was a sweet dimple-faced gal who liked to slug booze, yap with my grandmother, and listen to country music. I'd always talk with one of their granddaughters, Beth, who stayed with her grandparents often, as her parents worked the county fairs and traveled all across the U.S. with their food trucks, selling anything from fish to hamburgers. Socializing with her normally meant listening to her gush over Duran Duran.

The other guy, Jones, looked dead-up like Hunter S. Thompson—balding, slender and tall—and smoked like a California wildfire. He'd flown choppers in 'Nam for the Army, did three tours. Then landed a job flying for the DEA, searching for pot being grown around the surrounding counties. Jones had a mouth that'd make a sailor blush, and an appetite for whiskey.

If memory serves, he was a Jack Daniels man. He was loud, crude, and what some would refer to as a hard drinker. He'd load up at the bar, tell story after story about pot busts or the war. I went to school with some of his kids—he had about six or seven of them—and each was sharp as a whip. Jones came in most evenings after work, wearing his aviator shades and a military-green jumpsuit that was honed from parachute material and tucked into shin-high black military boots.

Despite their difference in age, Jones and Mick were good buddies, real cut-ups. One year, they got a crazed idea to surprise my father on his fortieth birthday, seeing as he'd no special plans other than tending bar. These two shit birds got together over at Mick's place, started passing the bottle back and forth, and cooked up a big plan. They'd dress up like two prostitutes—lipstick, eyeliner, stuffed bras, pantyhose, garters, high heels, short silk dresses, the whole get-up. Then they'd go down to The Club, wish my father a happy birthday, flirt with him. Mick and Dot had a camcorder, and Dot would film the two of them all the way from Mick's house to The Club. After they were finished, they would give my father the VHS tape as a gift.

These two guys made for some gag-a-maggot hookers. When they came in, their loud voices bouncing like bullfrogs belching from bullhorns, everyone in the bar was overcome by whelped-eyes of laughter, especially my father. He couldn't quit crying as Mick and Jones approached him behind the bar—flirting, talking dirty, rubbing his back, goosing him, and wishing him a happy birthday, while the regulars giggled and drank in celebration.

My own most memorable night at The Club was a few years back, when my mother's father remarried. The reception was held in the upstairs hall above The Club. Everyone was there: my father and his new wife, my mother and her new husband, and my wife.

After the cake was cut, the food had been served, and the dancing was done, we all went downstairs to The Club, where one of Mick's sons was DJing karaoke and the place was packed with members enjoying their Friday night.

Getting slosh-eyed, my cousin whispered in my ear, "Dare you to sing the Dead Kennedys' 'Kill The Poor.'" I smiled, slugged down my Bud Light, and grabbed the songbook. Unsurprisingly, nothing by the Dead Kennedys.

I penciled out some other tune on a small piece of paper, passed it to the DJ, and waited my turn. When it came, I took the mic and blew into it, making sure it was working properly. Then—standing within the silence of The Club, everyone eagerly awaiting some old country or pop standard, the monitor not yet displaying the words to my song—I screamed, "KILL KILL KILL THE POOR! KILL KILL KILL THE POOR!" The DJ quickly ripped the microphone from my hand. The regulars sat for a moment or two with their faces clenched in horror. Then, in unison, they got up and left The Club. Meanwhile, my family was in tears. One of my uncles was laughing so hard he fell off his barstool.

I'd blown several of the speaker fuses. The DJ was fuming. But after I promised not to scream into the microphone again, he changed the fuses and kept the karaoke going. With The Club to ourselves, my family and I spent the rest of the night picking songs for each other to sing. I remember my cousin singing "Margaritaville." Then everything gets a bit foggy.

Years have passed, and so have plenty of The Club's regulars, including Mick's wife, Dot, and my father's mother, who died at 101. Sometimes I'll stop by for a drink and to catch up. The smoke no longer hovers overhead like cotton candy; air purifiers have been installed to remove it. The ceiling is no longer a dingy yellow; it has been replaced by new tiles inscribed with members' names, their branch of military service, the years they'd given, and what war they fought. Newer members from newer wars have joined. Jones gave up the

booze, yet he and Mick still come in regularly. My father still has their video. He'll break it out on special occasions to get a good laugh over a few drinks and some reminiscing.

Nelson's Landing
107 N Erpelding Street
Leonardville, Kansas 66449
Phil Hanrahan

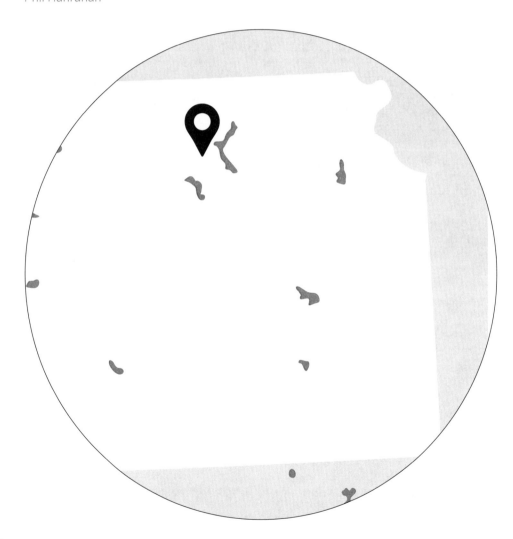

Having never been to a High Plains hamlet before, my references were literary and cinematic as I drove into Leonardville, Kansas, population 450, on a glorious Indian summer day in early November 2008. I thought of Willa Cather novels. And Terrence Malick films. And that opening to *In Cold Blood:* the white silos rising with temple elegance, the blue skies and livestock, the fields of town-bordering wheat. As in Capote's Holcomb, further west, here the old stone-built town bank was closed, and the signs on the weathered storefronts along the little main street faded.

My destination was Nelson's Landing, a year-old sports bar and restaurant opened by Alan and Kim Nelson, a farming couple whose middle child happened to be the Green Bay Packers' No. 1 draft choice that year. Six-foot-three with a buzzcut and blue eyes, Jordy Nelson had been an extraordinary athlete at the prep level, winning the AAU national 400 meters as a ten-year-old and later smashing records at nearby Riley County High School as a first-team, all-state football, basketball, and track star. Yet—overshadowed by kids from more populous regions and higher-profile programs—he ended up receiving not a single Division I college football offer. His route to joining the historic Packers and lining himself up to earn future millions included walking on at Kansas State, converting from defensive back to receiver in his second year, and going supernova as a senior, his 122 receptions making a mockery of the school's previous 75-catch record.

I drove the 850 miles from Green Bay to Leonardville, with a stop at the Dyersville, Iowa, farm where they filmed *Field of Dreams*, for a book I was writing on the 2008 Packers, the franchise's first season in seventeen without iron-man quarterback Brett Favre. That spring, Favre had tearily announced his retirement. After watching his press conference in my apartment in Los Angeles, I decided that a book about the first season with the new guy, Aaron Rodgers—the guy replacing the legend—might find some readers. A lifelong Packers fan raised in Wisconsin, I had lived in L.A. for seven years. Before that, New York City for six. Here was a chance to get back home, take up residence in Titletown, and follow my favorite team for a full season—a Cheesehead's dream. Along with being in the Packers' locker room, it would be my professional responsibility to attend all eight Lambeau Field pre-game tailgate parties, as covering the traditions and passionate fan behaviors of "Packer Nation" was part of my book's plan. That avocado tree four feet from my back door in L.A. was nice, but I remember feeling a certain nostalgia for snow at the time and told myself surely there would be no shortage of guacamole at rollicking Curly's Pub inside Lambeau Field.

I moved back to Wisconsin in July, ready to start reporting. Days later Brett Favre changed his mind, asked to rejoin the Packers, and a gigantic mess ensued, one culminating with the 38-year-old's bitter departure for the New York Jets in early August.

I had to cover the mess, of course, but my focus was on the performance of Rodgers—the Chico, California-raised, former Berkeley star who'd served as Favre's backup for three seasons—and his reception by Cheeseheads, many of them still loyal to the Ol' Gunslinger. The Packers were 4–3 on the day I arrived in Leonardville, the exact midpoint of the regular season. (The year before, with Favre, they went 13–3 and came within a win of going to the Super Bowl.) The Jets, too, were 4–3. Both quarterbacks were playing pretty well, though Favre loyalists were quick to point out that the grizzled Mississippi native, for anyone concerned about his age and skills, had thrown a career-best six touchdowns passes in a recent game against the Arizona Cardinals.

Yes, things were still a little tense in Packerland.

Originally, I'd had plans to drive to Kalamazoo, Michigan, to watch the Packers-Titans game on TV with the mother and minister father of the team's then No. 1 wide receiver, Greg Jennings. But when that fell through, I checked the forecast for the Great Plains, saw a weather map with a smiling sun, and that Thursday in the locker room after practice asked Jordy Nelson what he thought about me watching the game with his family and friends at his parents' sports bar. As low-key as they come, with a sneak-up-on-you wit and squinty grin, the sturdily-built receiver said that sounded okay to him. His parents should be there, he added, unless his dad was out cutting.

"Cutting what?" I asked.

"Corn," said Nelson. "And milo wheat. We got both."

•

There are other Packers-friendly bars outside Wisconsin, of course. In Chicago, there's rustic, Sconnie-themed Will's Northwoods Inn. In San Diego, there's the Australian Pub, run by a Sydney native who discovered catering to transplanted Cheeseheads on game days brought good business. My dad, brother, and I once visited the Rocky Flats Lounge, a no-frills roadhouse on a featureless stretch of highway between Boulder and Golden, Colorado, opposite the now-shuttered Rocky Flats nuclear bomb factory. Inside what was once the factory's payroll office there was for years a shrine to Brett Favre, and Friday nights at the Lounge you can enjoy a Wisconsin-style perch and walleye fish fry. Until it closed in 2011, there was a year-round Packers bar in Scottsdale, Arizona, Mabel Murphy's, incongruously situated on a palm-shaded, gallery-lined street in the affluent Old Town district. I was there just before Christmas of 2008 to watch the Packers play the Bears and dine on bratwurst with sauerkraut and fried cheese curds.

Gumbo, not Wisconsin cheese, is on the menu at the Broke Spoke in Kiln, Mississippi, Brett Favre's piney, Cajun town of some 2,000 residents. A weathered clapboard shack with a bullet-riddled sign painted to resemble a Confederate flag above its entrance, this former biker bar became a Cheesehead mecca during the 1997 Super Bowl, played in the New Orleans Superdome fifty miles west and won by the Packers. So strong is the bond forged between Green Bay's faithful and the Broke Spoke over the years, the bar proudly maintained its Cheesehead décor and identity even after Favre was traded to the Jets and later joined the Packers' division-rival Minnesota Vikings. *We're not painting it purple,* was the gist of owner Steve Haas's response after Favre became a Viking—Haas someone who liked to get on the horn during halftimes with Packers fans watching up in Green Bay bars. In addition to variously-colored brassieres hanging from the low ceiling,

the Broke Spoke greets visitors with green-and-gold barstools, a parking lot outhouse painted Packers colors, and the names and Wisconsin hometowns of hundreds of Cheesehead pilgrims scrawled in black Sharpie on the rough wood walls and ceiling. *Jerry from Sheboygan. Todd from Neenah. Becky from Little Chute.* (It was also here, in a Broke Spoke back room, where I sampled my first moonshine. "This stuff's the real deal. It'll knock your dick in the dirt!" sang the merry bartender, third cousin of Brett Favre's wife, dressed in a replica of the QB's crimson high school jersey, as he handed me a Dixie cup filled with clear liquor poured from a plastic milk jug.)

Arguably the most celebrated out-of-state Packers bar is Kettle of Fish in New York City's West Village. A one-time Beat poet hangout frequented by Jack Kerouac and Bob Dylan when in a different Village location, the bar moved to its present Christopher Street address in 1999 under the ownership of longtime Kettle bartender Patrick Daley, a hardcore Packers fan raised in Milwaukee. Daley decorates the place with team swag before games, cooks the bratwurst himself, and pretty much knows everyone he serves by name. Kettle of Fish is so popular on game days that Cheeseheads line up on the sidewalk outside two or three hours early to ensure entry, regardless of rain and snow.

I've been to these great Packers bars and a dozen others across the country and state of

Wisconsin, but only in one of them can you—so long as Jordy Ray Nelson keeps donning the green and gold—watch a game with the parents, siblings, and grandparents of a Green Bay player, eat a burger that comes from that player's family farm, and enjoy a slice of homemade pie baked by that player's grandmother—apple and cherry, gooseberry and banana cream—carried over fresh every morning by the pie-maker herself.

·

Named for Kansas Central Railway president Leonard Smith in 1882, the town of Leonardville is three blocks wide and five long. Nelson's Landing sits on broad, unshaded Erpelding Road, just off the corner with Barton Road, the town's main street. A compact, cinderblock-and-siding structure whose plate-glass windows were hung the day I visited with both a Packers flag and purple K-State banner, it shares a street with a cluster of silver grain elevators a block away in one direction and the town water tower in the other.

Slant-parking my car an hour before kickoff, I walked around the town in 70-degree sunshine. Nine red tractors stood before L & S Service, a farm machinery repair shop. Around the corner on Barton stood derelict, wood-framed Jim's Books, Carol's Secondhand Store (closed on Sundays), and Dr. Newman's Wonderful Emporium, the latter's facade painted once-bright colors, its front door thrown open to the day, and some of its stock, mostly used furniture, set out on the dusty sidewalk. I passed Auntie Em's Hair Shack in a gray shingled saltbox and turned around when I reached, on the outskirts of town, a nine-hole golf course with sand greens to save on water and maintenance.

Leonardville explored, I was ready to enter Nelson's Landing—a bright, airy two-room bar and grill with red banquettes, corner-mounted TVs, and vintage agricultural signs (INTERNATIONAL HARVESTER, KEY WORK CLOTHES) adorning paneled walls. Also framed on one wall was an official Jordy Nelson Packers jersey. The staff, some of them K-State students, wore forest-green T-shirts gold-lettered with Nelson's No. 87 in front and GO, PACK, GO! on the back. Display cases were filled with trophies, photos, and newspaper clippings, the earliest of which, a snapshot, showed 10-year-old Nelson on the winner's stand at the national AAU meet, blond and crewcut, in a blue tank top with a gold medal around his neck, still sporting his game face as he accepts a congratulatory handshake.

Nelson's parents, it turned out, were down in Manhattan watching their daughter Kelsey play point-guard for the Lady Wildcats, with Kim expected to return after the game. So weekend bartender and local builder Tom Fosha, who'd helped here renovating what a century ago was

B.L. Bredberg's Wallpaper, Books, and Paint store, showed me around, making introductions to a couple dozen people who'd known Jordy Nelson his whole life: friends, schoolmates, teachers. We all watched the game together, cheering Nelson as he returned a kickoff for 40 yards and later caught a pass, spun, broke a tackle, and gained 23 yards. In the end, the Packers lost 19–16 on a last-second field goal, but I was less bothered than I normally would have been. Nelson had played well, even trusted to be in there and thrown to with the game on the line. I'd eaten what I still consider the greatest cheeseburger I have ever had, made from never-frozen Nelson beef. And I'd wandered from table to table, Budweiser in hand, hearing stories about Jordy Nelson, quite possibly the least onerous interview situation I'll ever experience.

Kim Nelson—attractive, quick-witted, no non-sense, with short blonde hair and wire-rim glasses—arrived after the game and spoke to me about her son while looking through the day's receipts, proud of the way he ignored doubters on his way to the NFL, remembering that some Packers fans had booed her son's selection at the team draft party, not believing the team needed another wide receiver, especially a Corn Belt kid.

He'd been home the previous week, she said—the team's bye week—and she spoke of joking with him about the way he, a top NFL team's first pick, was spending his break, busing tables here at the Landing and getting cow manure on his boots at the farm.

She then took me on a tour of two adjacent abandoned structures she and Alan had also purchased, with plans to renovate. The bigger one was a former department store on the corner of Barton and Erpelding with marvelous views out large second-story windows. Given all their obligations at the farm, I asked Kim why they'd opened Nelson's Landing.

"Leonardville didn't have a place to eat or drink anymore," she said as we gazed out high windows to the horizon. "This is our town; we grew up here. These buildings had been empty for a while. Now instead of having to drive out of town for a meal, people come here, as do people from across Riley County."

The renovations are complete now, Kim Nelson told me early in 2014. They rent out the middle building to a vintage clothing store, and use the historic corner building for entertainment, including the popular Dueling Pianos. There have been a few changes inside Nelson's Landing, too, though not many. Photos, press clippings, and a wall poster commemorate the Packers 2011 Super Bowl victory, with a focus on the contributions of a certain Leonardville native, whose nine receptions for 140 yards set a new team Super Bowl record. The additions include a framed *Sports Illustrated* magazine cover featuring Nelson and Aaron Rodgers in mid-air, high off the ground, shoulder-bumping to celebrate a Nelson touchdown catch.

Kim and the whole clan were in Dallas Stadium for the game, but the rest of Leonardville was in Nelson's Landing, the same place where Jordy Nelson had received his draft-day call from Green Bay. "His eyes got huge," Tom Fosha had told me, "and he started pumping his fist. Then he mouthed the word 'Packers.'"

But on the day I visited, that Super Bowl record, and that magazine cover, and the declaration of "Jordy Nelson Day" in Kansas were all in the future—and honestly, more than I ever would have imagined during that balmy autumn afternoon. I said goodbye to Kim, headed out to Erpelding Road, and with shadows lengthening across town, drove to the high-school football field and running track where Nelson had excelled. I was alone. Late sun lit fields stretching beyond windbreak pines to the south. Birds sang from the tops of the stadium light-standards. I stood there a while, thinking about the season, thinking about the town, thinking about my life. Then I crossed over to an old pioneer cemetery opposite the high-school, a stone's throw from a windswept, white-steepled Presbyterian church. The name "Fosha" was on one of the weathered, nineteenth-century headstones. As was the name "Nelson." I took a last look out at the wheat fields. Then I got in my car and started home.

THREE GLASSES OF WINE END A HUNDRED QUARRELS.

—CHINESE PROVERB

La Cabañita
3445 N Verdugo Road
Glendale, California 91208
Heather Havrilesky

In San Sebastian, Spain, my soon-to-be husband and I drank cold beers at an outdoor cafe, watching children speed through an open city square on scooters and bicycles, yelling and laughing as their parents drank nearby. "This is what it'll be like when we have kids," I thought.

I was wrong—so very, very wrong. Because in Los Angeles, and in the States in general, we don't have gorgeous town squares where parents sip beer and nibble on manchego and *jamon iberico* while their offspring frolic nearby. We have Gymboree and Jump 'n Jammin, corporate kiddie warehouses designed to amuse screeching, pushing, crying children and to incite suicidal ideation in their parents. That's what you see clouding the faces of those parents at The Little Gym and Pump It Up, standing around awkwardly in their fucking socks with their hands stuffed into their pockets. They're thinking about death's sweet embrace, and the alternative: spending the balance of their days on Earth watching kids shove each other in some padded, primary-colored purgatory.

And what protects most of us from such dark thoughts? Lager. Vodka. Pilsner. Tequila. But do they dispense alcohol at these godforsaken amusement centers? Of course not.

Because just as American children are not meant to cartwheel through non-commercial public spaces paved with unfriendly cobblestones, troublingly devoid of Apple stores and Panda Expresses, American parents are not meant to pour alcohol down their throats in the company of their children. As a result, American parents rarely have the chance to enjoy themselves in adult ways, away from home, with loose talk and salty cured meats and booze in the mix. If your kids are there and you don't feel demeaned and edgy, there's something wrong. If you're not agitated and overwhelmed by the pointlessness of human existence, if your hair looks combed and you're still wearing your shoes and you're making eye contact with another adult who isn't talking about bad teachers and potty mishaps, if your ears aren't ringing and you don't have an urge to strangle someone? You're a shitty parent, basically.

Meanwhile, Europeans essentially go bar hopping with their kids in tow.

Bars. Remember those? As impossible as it is to believe, there are still places where adults hang out and talk loudly with other adults about adult things, and no one wets their pants or cries for no reason (unless it's after 2 a.m.). Just thinking about the continuing existence of bars is enough to render the average American parent despondent. Yet the bars just keep humming along without us. Sweet hoppy nectars pour from cold taps, hour upon hour, while we wipe bare butts or stuff dirty laundry into washing machines. We disappeared and all of those bartenders just kept clinking ice into glasses and shaking up cocktails and putting little orange wedges into whiskey sours. It's like we were never there in the first place.

•

Yet, at the very moment I gave up on communal drinking and resigned myself to haunt those purgatorial warehouses with the other bewildered parents for the rest of my days, my husband and I took our baby and our toddler out to an early dinner at La Cabañita, a Mexican restaurant nestled in the hills just north of Los Angeles. After just one of their very strong house margaritas on the rocks with salt, consumed along with a plate of *puerco en salsa verde* and homemade corn tortillas, I found myself gazing contentedly at my family for the first time in what seemed like many moons. Our three-year-old, Claire, was coloring happily between spoonfuls of carrot soup. Our one-year-old, Ivy, was quietly smearing black beans and rice all over her face. My husband was chatting aimlessly about personality clashes at his job. Instead of growing impatient with the

work talk or wiping beans off the baby's face or telling my oldest to put down the crayons and eat, I thought, "This is really nice."

Then my mind was seized by panic. *Why? Why am I not agitated and consumed by thoughts of death, like I usually am when I leave the house with my kids? Why does the late-summer sunlight filtering into the windows have such a golden tint to it, making the blue-flowered tile tables and the Mexico flags look so glowing and special? Why don't I care about the food being spilled all over the floor? Shouldn't I clean that up or something? But look how relaxed our waiter, Angel, is about it, so upbeat, fetching extra black olives for the kids. Angel is amazing at his job. Didn't he say that I looked just like Jennifer Garner when we first came in?* I really do *look like Jennifer Garner.*

That's when I remembered: *I am drinking tequila.*

At first, the injustice of it all hit me hard. How many years had the blood in my veins cried out for tequila, never to be heard? What a travesty, what an injustice, that I had been deprived of this sweet elixir for lo these many years, filling my days with the relative trivialities of work and children and keeping the domestic factory chugging along! Because what could be more important in life than pouring tequila into my face? My priorities had gotten all mixed up, and I hadn't even noticed!

But then, because I am an American and a parent, and the modern American parent is not supposed to have fun drinking booze with her shoes on and her children present, I immediately felt guilty.

Then something funny happened. I looked around the room. It was just like one of those scenes in a movie when the camera pulls back to a crane shot of miles and miles of people in the same predicament as our hero. But instead of miles of zombies or bad traffic or people in line for Soylent Green, what I saw was an entire restaurant filled with babies and toddlers and happy parents with margaritas in their hands.

That's when I understood the truth: *This* is where the wisest parents of greater Los Angeles go to beat back their existential dread! The Mexican restaurant, with its child-friendly foods and its giant tequila-infused drinks. This is a natural haven, a tequila-spewing oasis, for my fellow weary travelers.

After this epiphany, we went to La Cabañita at least once a week. We tried everything on the menu. We were on a first-name basis with most of the waiters—all of them just as capable and as tolerant as Angel. We brought all of our friends there. Anytime someone suggested that we meet for dinner, we pushed La Cabañita. When friends or family came to town, we went to La Cabañita. It was as if happiness and contentment had a location

on the map, and we'd finally found it. A year later, we moved to the neighborhood, ostensibly for the good schools, but those golden hours of peaceable bean-smearing and tequila-sipping had more than a little to do with it.

•

Drinking in restaurants is different from drinking in bars. Restaurant boozing is a limited engagement. The aim is not longevity. You are looking for a discrete buzz, not one that lasts until two in the morning. As a result, you definitely want to feel the booze. With kids present, you don't have time to ease into it slowly. One strong drink, maybe two, and then the kids get impatient or need to be bathed and read to and all of that other stuff (all of which goes pretty smoothly after two drinks, let me just add). At a restaurant, you are drinking on a deadline. You've got to make those two drinks count.

Now, if you had two strong margaritas within an hour at a bar, you'd be in danger of either getting way too drunk over the course of the night, or being forced to sip ice water from that point forward. At a restaurant, though, you have the luxury of drinking a little too much too fast. (Especially if your spouse is driving. Mine always is.) Once the kids are done eating, and have nothing left to color, Drunky Hour is over.

La Cabañita, with its welcoming, relaxed waiters and its hand-blown margarita glasses and its likable clientele and its unerring climate control, not only allowed me to drink outside the home as a parent, but it also taught me *how* to do this. When you're a parent, you don't drink to get drunk. You assiduously avoid drunkenness, for obvious reasons. Do you want your small child to know what "drunk" means? No way.

Having a hangover with two loud children in the house cured me of that impulse pretty quickly. And La Cabañita taught me that you can have a strong buzz and then stop drinking completely, as totally outlandish as that concept seemed to me at first. You can have two great drinks, and (bonus) if it's the right tequila, you won't get a hangover.

SWEET HOPPY NECTARS POUR FROM COLD TAPS, HOUR UPON HOUR, WHILE WE WIPE BARE BUTTS OR STUFF DIRTY LAUNDRY INTO WASHING MACHINES. WE DISAPPEARED AND ALL OF THOSE BARTENDERS JUST KEPT CLINKING ICE INTO GLASSES AND SHAKING UP COCKTAILS AND PUTTING LITTLE ORANGE WEDGES INTO WHISKEY SOURS.

As something of a booze hound, this wasn't the easiest adjustment for me. I didn't want to give up that precipitous slide into obnoxiousness that I'd embraced for so much of my adult life, somehow without ever tumbling into full-time drunk status. I was oldish and I had kids, but some small, sick part of me still wanted to act like an asshole every now and then.

Notice I didn't say "good tequila." La Cabañita puts Montezuma tequila in their house margarita. I don't think that qualifies as the good stuff. All I know is that it doesn't give me a headache. Once, my brother-in-law upgraded to some more expensive top-shelf stuff. His margarita tasted completely wrong. Why mess with a good thing?

But let's just be honest: I have no idea how much tequila I'm drinking. That's the beauty of it. If I knew, I might be appalled and ashamed. I'm *grateful* not to know. I am blissfully ignorant of the dosage of my elixir. I am only aware of the sheer joy I feel after just a few sips. Suddenly the light looks just right, I have important stories to tell, and the kids' interruptions are just adorable way stations on the road to the incredibly weighty and significant point I'm about to make about something at once lighthearted and complicated and hilarious.

Yet, like a benevolent but watchful God, La Cabañita's margaritas will punish you for having more than two of them. Once we took some out of town guests there and left the kids at home with a babysitter. I had three margaritas, which I figured would be even better than two. False. It was terrible. I said stupid things. I slurred. When I went to bed, the room was spinning. The next day, I felt awful. I've never ordered a third margarita again.

La Cabañita protects its flock, so many of whom are drawn to liquor like dysfunctional sheep to an overbearing shepherd. La Cabañita keeps us safe. So for months, my husband and I returned again and again. We drank. The kids ate without complaint. They laughed and behaved and made giant messes that we were urged, over and over, not to attempt to clean up. They colored and chatted happily. *We* chatted happily. We almost never had a bad time.

•

Which is maybe why we started to cheat on La Cabañita after about a year. Like a happy marriage between kind and loving partners, eventually the lack of rancor seems to suggest a need for a little cathartic drama, a little extracurricular stress, a little challenge to the status quo.

Our eyes started to wander. It's shameful, but I'll admit it. We started to notice that our new neighborhood was absolutely filled with Mexican restaurants that served giant margaritas. It's a pretty small area, but somehow there are five other Mexican places within two square miles. One of them had to be good, right? Our rationalizations seemed sound enough: *What harm would be done? If we had such a great time at La Cabañita, surely we'd have fun at a few of these other places. Why not switch up the scenery a little?*

One by one, we discovered that the other Mexican restaurants weren't just bad, they were fucking terrible. Yes, occasionally the margaritas were ok. Too sugary, but fine. Sometimes they were really big, which is tough to resist. Other times, there was a guy who made guacamole in a cart by your table. That was important, since everything else on the menu was inedible. For months, we sampled tasteless refried beans. We tolerated store-bought corn tortillas. We choked down charred, gristly meats and jarred-tasting salsas and stale chips.

But it wasn't *just* the food. The waiters and managers at the other places were all wrong. They were too fake, or too grumpy. They were too inattentive, or too attentive. They seemed to be aware that their food sucked, and that appeared to depress them. They didn't like their jobs. They secretly hated our kids (not that we would necessarily blame them for that).

It was the other patrons who bothered me the most, though. Who *were* these people? Who could order charred knuckle tacos with a straight face? How could they even digest this stuff? Why weren't they embarrassed to be here, among the giant plates of soupy, soot-colored beans and yellow cheese?

Even our kids knew the difference. They never liked any of those other places. "I hate Mr. Mexico!" Ivy would say. "I hate El Gringos Estupidos! I want Cabañita!" They knew what we didn't: We belonged at La Cabañita, and nowhere else.

But then, we weren't *just* looking for a restaurant. We had to admit that to ourselves eventually. We wanted to feel right at home, the way you feel at your favorite bar. That feeling is what makes a bar tick. Not the sweet hoppy nectars, not the décor, not the bartender's easy, rambling acceptance, but some strange blend of all of the above. At La Cabañita, the music, the flowered tiles, the wooden chairs, the paper flags: they form a weird kind of poetry, a familiar landing spot for the senses.

Maybe it's faintly Pavlovian. The familiar sights and the hum of background chatter and the look on our favorite waiters' faces signal that alcohol is about to enter the bloodstream. But I like to think there's some magic in the mix. Somehow, all of the sights and smells blend and make the heart feel at ease.

When you look around, you see other people who, unlike most people on the planet (or maybe just in America), know the difference between good and bad. Why does that feel so personal sometimes? Going to those other places was like sitting through a terrible movie, listening to other people laugh at painfully bad jokes. At La Cabañita, you look around and you know: These people would NEVER eat at Mr. Mexico. They're not idiots!

La Cabañita is where we escape death, among giant margaritas, the perfect blend of sweet and sour, and giant plates of really great mole and *albondigas* and tomatillo salsa. Thanks to La Cabañita, I said goodbye to purgatorial primary-colored warehouses forever. I refuse to eat bad cheese pizza in my socks, ever again. Instead, I have joined the heroes who stream through those doors with their babies and toddlers and young kids and teenagers in tow, to sip that yellow ambrosia flowing over ice. La Cabañita bends the arc of the parental universe toward justice. This is our place. This is where everybody knows our names. Or at least knows the names of the most attractive actors we loosely resemble.

I DRINK TO MAKE OTHER PEOPLE MORE
INTERESTING.

—GEORGE JEAN NATHAN

The Bena Bar (closed)
County Road 8
Bena, Minnesota 56626
David Treuer

Hey, bro. Hear about The Bena Bar? Actually, I don't even think they call it that anymore. Now it's the Winnie Café or something like that. Fuck it. Back in the day, back when Grandpa Harris owned it they called it The Wigwam. Before that he owned the Gitigan right there across the street. Though that was burned down long before we came around. So was The Wigwam, before it was called the Bena Bar. It might have burned twice, but it'll always be a rez bar. Maybe the oldest and baddest on the whole Leech Lake Reservation. Who knows?

Remember the first time we went there? I was seven or something. But we went there. Remember? It was you and me and Del and we were parked at Del's house. Uncle Ditty and Aunt Shirley were heading out "on the town"—though since the town was only the few dozen houses, the gas station, the Catholic Church, Senior Center/ Post Office, and the Bena Grocery, "on the town" only meant one thing. It meant the Bena Fucking Bar, Baby! Anyway, they were headed out over there and we were supposed to stay put. They even got us, like, two Tombstone pizzas and made sure we knew how to work the TV, and then they left up out the house and headed on down the road along with the rest of the grown-ups in the village, sucked into the mouth of the bar and spit back out, chewed up and wet with sweat, at closing time. So there we were. We were hungry as shit and so took the Tombstones out of the oven too soon and they were still cold and Del thought it'd be funny to have a "pizza war" and so we did and one piece actually stuck on the TV, right on the screen! Good times. And then we got antsy and so Del said, "Why don't we egg the fuck out of the Bena Bar?" And we said, "Sure." Del always did have good ideas. So we grabbed up the eggs, I think we only had eight. You were always the brave one, bro, and so you egged the bar but since it's made out of cinder block there was no real good effect, no explosion or whatever. So Del says, "Dave, grab the door and when I say 'Go,' open it up!" I grabbed it and he says "Go!" and I opened it up, yellow light and voices spilling out into the summer air. Del lobbed, like, four eggs inside the bar! Like I said: he was always a thinker. Everyone started yelling and shouting inside the bar and Del says, "Run!" and so we ran. We tore ass through the village and since I was still holding an egg and hadn't done my part I chucked it at the rectory and *BAM!* it smashed through the storm and the regular window. Either that means something about the eggs from Red Owl or it means something about the Catholic Church.

We made it back to Del's but got depressed and shit. Remember? After an escapade like that everything else is kind of a downer. But then. But then we saw some vacant house across the village burst into flames. Someone burning the vacants for shits and giggles. So we watched the flames leap up toward the jack pine through the window. But then! And this is the best part, remember? But then the phone rang. Remember the look on Del's face? How his face kind of sunk and it got that quivery serious look to it, like when Ditty or Shirley was yelling at him? He handed the phone to you cause you were the oldest. And so you took the phone and you got the same look on your face! You hung up and said, "Some lady said they know we started that house on fire and they're coming over here to burn *this* house down. With *us* in it." Holy fuck. Grade school doesn't prepare you for that shit, right? And we didn't know what to do. We couldn't go to the Bena Bar cause we just egged it. And suddenly we remembered we weren't supposed to leave the house. Del thinks for a minute then says, "We got a shotgun." So we found the 20 gauge and then found the shells and we broke the action open and loaded a shell into it and snapped it shut. Then we sat on the couch facing the door. You got to hold the gun cause you were the oldest. I was on your right side. Del was on your left side. You had your knees drawn up and you had the gun resting, pointing at the door, over one of your knees. Del fell asleep after awhile. I couldn't. Then, a long time gone, we saw headlights and they turned in and sprayed the house and grew real bright and we heard the sound of tires on gravel. The car stopped. The headlights went off. Two doors slammed. I could feel your body tense up and you used your thumb to raise the hammer. I heard it click. The front door opened. I was thinking, "Shoot! Shoot!" Because whoever it is is gonna burn the house down with us in it. You settled the stock down into your shoulder like Dad taught us to and lowered your head along the barrel. And then Uncle Ditty walked in, with Shirley behind him. "What the fuck you doing with my gun?" He growled and he snatched it away and dropped the hammer and broke it open and the shell popped out and fell to the floor. He couldn't bend down and grab it. He was too drunk to do it. "Fuck it," he said. And then him and Shirley went back to their bedroom. We woke Del up and the three of us went into his room and all got into bed. You guys fell asleep pretty quick but I still couldn't sleep. I could hear Ditty and Shirley going at it for awhile—*creak creak creak creak creak creak*—and then Shirley said, "For fuck sake," and then I heard Ditty snoring. Good times. Good fucking times.

And remember the time we went there when were back from college for Christmas? You and me and Mom and your buddy from Japan, Sumio. It was kind of cruel to bring Sumio there in a way. I mean—he comes all the way from Japan and we bring him to the rezziest rez bar there ever was, packed to the rafters with Indians and white guys so fucked up they might as well be family. But it was Christmas and they were serving Tom and Jerrys and so everyone was there and we were only home for a short trip so if we wanted to see everyone there was no better place to go. Everyone was there. Davey and Lanny and Sonny and Barb and Jerry and Ditty and Kay and JoAnne and Grandma. It was packed and everyone was drinking their Tom and Jerrys and having a good old time. Ditty was pretty well drunk. He had a right to be. Shirley had just passed away. Del was sitting in jail for a year. He was feeling pretty sad. So he sees me and he says, "That's my goddamn nephew! I love my goddamn fucking nephew!" Then he sees you. "And this one! He's my fucking nephew, too!" Pretty soon he had us both in headlocks and the tattoos on his arms were fuzzy and the light was fuzzy and his voice was fuzzy and thick—with booze, with grief, with love. And then he sees Sumio. He let's us go and stands tall and comes over and stands right in front of Sumio. And he says, "You Japanese?" And Sumio says, "Yes. Yes, I am Japanese." And Ditty starts talking to him. IN JAPANESE. They go on for a few minutes in Japanese and I'm like, What the fuck? Then it's more headlocks and more I love yous and he's off to the bar for a refill. On the ride home I asked Mom where Ditty learned Japanese. She said, "Oh, he was stationed there after Korea. Didn't you know? He had a girlfriend, a Japanese girl. He was in love with her. She got pregnant and he wanted to marry her but your grandma said, 'You marry her don't

bother coming home.' Pearl Harbor, you know." All the while I'm wondering: *He chose this village and this family? Over love? Over true love?* What a world. What a goddamn world it is.

Anyway, the reason I bring all this up is the Bena Bar—or whatever they call it now—is for SALE. Sure as shit. I think they're asking too much. But what if we bought it? Wouldn't it be great? Buy the place and fix it up a bit and then throw the doors open wide, as wide as our arms, as our hearts. As wide as can be. We'd throw them open and everyone would come. All the cousins and nephews and nieces and what uncles and aunts are left. Shit, our kids, too. Why not? With the doors wide open and the lights on and the place looking all nice and with some choice taxidermy, the light would spill out onto the street, like gold spilling from a purse. The beer would flow from the tap all day and night, slopping and spreading, covering the whole town, licking right up to everyone's doorsteps. No one would have to even stagger home, they could just lie down in the beer, in that golden dew, and mouths open, drink their way to the bar and drink their way back. Or even better: they could paddle there in their canoes and raise their paddles and let the beer run down the shafts and into their mouths like voyageurs of old. Isn't that a grand thought? The place would be warm and safe and the village warm and safe and everyone would be warm and safe. Just like in the old days. Right, bro? Right?

IDENTITY

THERE ARE, BROADLY SPEAKING, TWO TYPES OF DRINKERS. THERE IS THE MAN WHOM WE ALL KNOW, STUPID, UNIMAGINATIVE, WHOSE BRAIN IS BITTEN NUMBLY BY NUMB MAGGOTS; WHO WALKS GENEROUSLY WITH WIDE-SPREAD, TENTATIVE LEGS, FALLS FREQUENTLY IN THE GUTTER, AND WHO SEES, IN THE EXTREMITY OF HIS ECSTASY, BLUE MICE AND PINK ELEPHANTS . . . THE OTHER TYPE OF DRINKER HAS IMAGINATION, VISION. EVEN WHEN MOST PLEASANTLY JINGLED HE WALKS STRAIGHT AND NATURALLY, NEVER STAGGERS NOR FALLS, AND KNOWS JUST WHERE HE IS AND WHAT HE IS DOING. IT IS NOT HIS BODY BUT HIS BRAIN THAT IS DRUNKEN.

—JACK LONDON,
JOHN BARLEYCORN

Deep Eddy Cabaret
2315 Lake Austin Boulevard
Austin, Texas 78703
Oscar Cásares

Back then, my family and friends knew the best way to get ahold of me was to call me at the bar. At the time, in my late twenties, I could not have told you what I was doing night after night at Deep Eddy—sometimes sitting with three or four friends telling stories at the big round table near the front door, other times sitting alone at the end of the bar. If you had asked me why I was there so often, I might have said that I was just hanging out, which would have been my way of answering and not answering, a skill I had picked up since moving to Austin in 1989 to work at an ad agency. Because the truth is, I had a strong suspicion that I was doing nothing more than killing time. And after growing up in Brownsville, Texas, a town as far south as you can drive and still be in this country, where it always seemed there was little to do or see, I was familiar with the idea of killing time. Then again, this was why I had moved to Austin. Another part of me sensed that I wasn't killing time as much as I was waiting for something big to come along. I didn't have a clue what that something might be, though. I was drinking, sure, some nights too much, but most nights just enough to justify taking up a seat at the bar.

The regulars—guys like Scotty and JT—will tell you what makes Deep Eddy special is that it hasn't changed, or hardly changed, since it opened in 1951. I suppose there is a certain charm to this, especially in the self-proclaimed "Live Music Capital of the World," where it seems a hip new club is popping up every weekend. You would think I might have found a more interesting place to hang out than a neighborhood bar where the music selection was limited to The Temptations and Bobby Darin or whoever else happened to be playing on the jukebox. Deep Eddy was less than five minutes from my apartment, making it easy enough to swing by most nights. They had only four or five beers on tap, all domestic, and the wine came out of a jug kept under the bar. The drinks weren't expensive, but they only took cash, and back then I don't recall there being an ATM nearby. But it was the smoke that really turned people off. It was bad enough when you were there breathing it, but then you would wake up in bed the next morning smelling like someone had emptied an ashtray onto your pillow. The only way to get the smell out of your hair was to stand under the shower and let the smoke rise from your scalp. There were also a couple of pool tables in the back, but it wasn't easy to hear over the noise, so when my friends from work showed up we spent time at the bar or at one of the tables where we could talk and tell stories.

Most of my stories were about the border town I had escaped from the first chance I had. All of this was new to my Austin friends, who had only seen Brownsville on the map. One of the stories might be about how as a child my great-great grandfather was living in northern Mexico in 1850, and had been kidnapped by Indians and brought to the U.S. And the next story might be about the time my uncle, tío Nico, had been working on his Toyota in the backyard and it rolled off its blocks, pinning him to the ground until three of his grown daughters managed to lift the car and then his fourth daughter dragged him out by the ankles. And so on. One night, after talking for more than an hour, a friend who had been buying the beer asked if I was ever going to use these stories to write a book. I remember laughing and saying that I wasn't a writer. Then after a while I moved on to the next story.

As far as I knew, a writer was someone who grew up in a house with books. My parents' house had no books. A writer was someone who had been reading from an early age. I never read as a kid and only rarely as an adult. A writer was someone who loved books. I could never find any that kept my interest. A writer was someone

who had been writing from an early age. I had taken one creative writing class that I had barely passed. I could sit in a bar and tell stories all night, but I was no writer.

Telling these stories to friends at the Eddy had started off as a way of passing the time, but after a while it seemed to be the only thing I could do with myself, as if I had forgotten some critical detail having to do with my life and the only way it might come back to me was if I kept telling people about the place I was from. Sometimes I'd tell the same story to a different group of people on the same night, trying to figure out how best to set it up or foreshadow some major event or pause at the right moment before reaching the end. The stories were about things I'd seen and done in Brownsville, but many of these stories were ones that my uncles had told me when I was growing up. My tío Hector lived on the next block and stopped by my parents' house to tell stories two or three nights a week, each time showing up with his six-pack of Falstaff and sitting at the far end of the sofa, next to the screen door, where he could smoke and use his first empty can as an ashtray. This was where and how I first learned to tell a story, not from reading and not from any workshop.

Now that I was older I sensed that there was a huge difference between telling a story and writing one. I was curious to know more about this difference, though not quite curious enough to leave my barstool. By this point I was thirty-two and had been working in advertising for almost ten years. This storytelling thing was something I could mess around with at the bar, but I wasn't about to take it too seriously and think of myself as a writer. I had long ago missed that train and, for that matter, doubted I even knew where the station might be.

But it was precisely because I didn't take it too seriously that one day while I was sitting at a coffee shop I tried to write the story I had told the night before. It was a crazy story, the kind that involves bodily fluids and that you only attempt to tell after a few drinks—just a dumb bar story. I already knew the beginning, middle, and end; now all I had to do was get it down on paper. If it was terrible, no one else had to know I had even tried. It was my little secret.

Though on paper the story turned out not as funny as it had been at the bar, it was just as much fun to write as it had been to tell. So I tried another one. I had dozens of these that I had been telling the last few years and so it felt like I had already done most of the work. As the weeks went by, I was writing more and more and spending fewer nights at the bar. I was also reading all those books I had avoided, ones that hadn't interested me before but were now teaching me how to write.

In late 1996, five months after I wrote that first story, I walked into my boss's office and quit so that I could write full time. I had a little money saved up. I told myself that if things didn't work out I could always find another job in advertising. Anything seemed possible.

That night I celebrated with some friends at the Eddy. It was a busy Friday night and we crammed around a small table and talked about my big step like it was only a matter of time before things started falling into place. Of course, I knew next to nothing about writing or publishing. I had no idea what I was getting myself into and how much harder my life would get. So for that one night I could let myself imagine that soon I might make a living off my writing and be paid for what I loved to do and would have been doing anyway. And who knows, I told myself, someday a publisher might want to buy my collection of stories and that might lead to a second book and then maybe years later I might even write and publish something about all that time I used to spend in a bar called Deep Eddy. Wouldn't that be something?

The Napoleon House
500 Chartres Street
New Orleans, Louisiana 70130
James Sallis

My band Three-Legged Dog is playing, on guitar, fiddle, and cello, a medley we came up with, "Bonaparte's Retreat" followed by "Napoleon Crossing the Rhine." As I break out of straight time to a hard downbow for the start of the second part, I smile. Memory, part-time reporter, part-time poet, sometime grifter, steps up beside me on stage.

Late afternoons, as day's weary head began to nod, we'd sit there, doors open as a mummer's parade of local characters passed by, close enough to reach out and touch hands, on the sidewalk outside. Condensation ran down our drinks, sweat ran down our backs. We'd hear Nep as he emerged from the back room or patio towards the bar reciting, "Two Jax, two Jax." Legend had it that, were he interrupted, he'd have to return to the table to retake the order. In an earlier life he'd been a fighter, a boxer.

We'd all been something else in earlier lives.

Bill, as willowy and lank as Nep was squat, supposedly had a Ph.D. from the University of North Carolina, came to New Orleans on a visit and never left. Once a friend sat reading the first volume of Durrell's *Alexandria Quartet*. Bill took

his order, brought it and, before stepping away, quietly said how much he envied my friend just to be *beginning* to read the novels.

So the story went, anyway. And we all had stories.

We were patching our lives together, understand, creating them pretty much ex nihilo—from bits of where we'd been, what we'd read, from scraps and tatters of what we imagined the world might be. From the way in which darkness came through the open doors and moved slowly across the tables . . .

I was a student at Tulane, there only by grace of a scholarship I needed to retain, so by definition an uptown boy, but one who at every opportunity traversed the campus, from the dorms off Freret to that world's opposite edge, and swung aboard the streetcar for the lurching, bell-clang ride down St. Charles, around Lee Circle to Canal Street, there to climb down and continue on foot, past the 24-hour newspaper and magazine kiosk, past the antique shops, one of which displayed in its window a glistening Gibson harp guitar, into the Quarter, to Chartres.

Dialing back now to the early '60s. On the day I learned of Kennedy's assassination, this is where I wound up, sitting without words watching the stunned faces around me. No one was speaking. Even the trademark classical music, often so regal and restorative, took on a funereal air. Then and now many of the regulars, many in the mummer's parade, reminded me of Robert Lowell's Czar Lepke, future and past run together in a temporal tie-dye,

with the river's, an unmistakable part of the Quarter.

When warm sun came back after afternoon rains, moisture rose in waves from the pavement and that smell joined hops, river, car exhaust, and the droppings of carriage horses. The entire city reared up mirage-like about us, a promise, an illusion.

Dissolving?

WE WERE PATCHING OUR LIVES TOGETHER, UNDERSTAND, CREATING THEM PRETTY MUCH EX NIHILO—FROM BITS OF WHERE WE'D BEEN, WHAT WE'D READ, FROM SCRAPS AND TATTERS OF WHAT WE IMAGINED THE WORLD MIGHT BE.

hanging like an oasis in his air
of lost connections . . .

No food back then, just drinks. Drinks and classical music. You rummaged through the LPs, put what you wanted to hear at the bottom of the stack. There was the Pimm's Cup, of course, for which the Napoleon House was famous, and the Sazerac, for which the entire city was famous. And lots and loads of Jax beer. The brewery stood blocks away, its smell, along

Becoming?

For me a great attraction of New Orleans has always been its inescapable sense of history. Standing on the levee I could gaze across the river to where slaves were quartered before being brought to the Quarter and put up for sale. Looking out at the cathedral from Jackson Square I couldn't help but recall those hung there. Or fail to think of Congo Square and the blacks with their banned drums. *French*

Quarter, yet much of the architecture was clearly Spanish, its accents from island and Caribbean cultures. ("We're in a third-world country," my wife Karyn would say upon first going back with me decades later.) You could still see the layers, sense the floods, storms and fires that ravaged the Quarter, see the patchwork, the rebuilds, the coverings-over, everywhere.

And so it was with the timeless patchwork of The Napoleon House. The doors, cracked and dried like the wood of ancient stringed instruments, looked to have been around even as carpetbaggers streamed into the city. The courtyard well might have become a favored retreat for Napoleon had he been able to accept Mayor Girod's offer of refuge in 1821. And was that—it certainly seemed possible— the original paint scaling from the walls?

Both places, city and the bar, became templates for my own history. My brother was doing graduate work at Tulane as well, and often, after a weekend meal of sauerbraten at Kolb's, we'd end up at The Napoleon House talking about the classical music we both loved, about writing (which had claimed me), and about philosophy (which, after something of a false start with math, had claimed John). He has, he says now, many fine memories.

New Orleans was my first city, the first of many— Manhattan, Brooklyn, Boston, London, Dallas— and one I'd find myself circling back to again and again. It was where I began writing. Where I first performed in public, with native New Orleanian Chris Smither, at a folk club on Bourbon Street. Where I wound up yet again just after my first book was published. Where I went to revise my first novel, *The Long-Legged Fly*. Where I'd set that and five subsequent novels about a black detective named Lew Griffin.

And where I'd once lived in an apartment above—yes—The Napoleon House. You went in through an open hallway with street access, along the far edge of the bar's courtyard, and up its hugely romantic swayback staircase to the third floor. You stepped into history, into a place where the stories of a new and often troubled nation reared up everywhere around you and would never leave, becoming forever, inescapably, a part of you.

Two Jax please, Nep. For old time's sake.

McHale's (closed)
251 W 51st Street
New York, New York 10019
Susan Choi

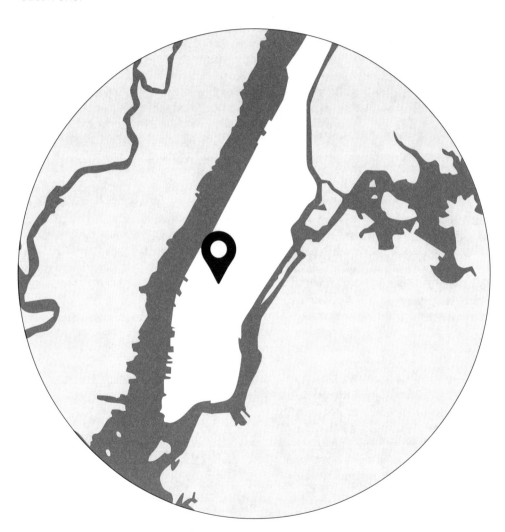

Once upon a time there were bars that were simply for drinking, in much the way there were coffee shops simply for eating. Apart from a difference in lighting, their spirit and aesthetics were largely the same. That you knew what to expect, walking in, was an asset. Affordability was assumed, not considered a signal of dubious quality. Those items on offer were as familiar and iconic as the neon sign outside, as the chrome stools lining the counter or bar. There might be powdered donuts on display, or a wire rack of chips. The printed menu, whether coffee shop or bar, was wholly unnecessary. Only a time traveler or a Martian might not know how to order: grilled cheese sandwich or Manhattan, two eggs over easy or a bottle of beer. Coffee shops and bars were for people, they weren't for themselves. They comforted us and served us, they enabled our communion or our solitude. They didn't demand recognition for artistry, or purity, or irony. They didn't grow their own mint for mojitos. They didn't try to outdress or abash their patrons as if they were the first punk-rock kid in sixth grade. They were brisk, adult places, far more about the working lives of their patrons than they were about leisure. They fit themselves in—to available time and available budget.

I think of them longingly now, deep into my adulthood, when, bewilderingly, they're as rare as they once were ubiquitous. Every place to eat and to drink now—of course I mean in New York, perhaps elsewhere things are still as they were— is some sort of performance. When I want to just have a drink with a friend, I have to sort through the whole range of potential experiences in an effort to choose the right one. With the sorts of extinct bars I'm talking about, you simply chose the nearest, most comfortable one. For me, for a long, happy time, that bar was McHale's.

Oh, how unexpected to be one of those middle-aged cranks who extols the superior past! Get a load of the antiquity of my remembered scene: when I first started going to McHale's, sometimes I'd leave my magazine fact-checking job so late they'd already be loading the next morning's paper, damp off the presses, into the big idling New York Times trucks all along 44th Street. The quality of the light in Times Square was different then, and not just because of the haze of nostalgia. There really was quantitatively less light, and qualitatively different light, most of it incandescent, with a palpable, bodily warmth. It was still the same light Hopper painted, fifty years earlier, in "Nighthawks," and it was the same light you glimpsed through the windows, approaching McHale's. The neon sign projected from the deco-style corner entrance like the bowsprit from a prow; and once inside there was the pleasure of everyone else looking hale and glad, the way everyone does in the light of a campfire.

At that time of my life there were a lot of through-the-looking-glass bars, where after a certain

the blink of an eye, or the well of a shot glass. I never sang "Cats" with the bartender, or drank for free from 2 a.m. until dawn, or had my shoes pissed on because the man next to me at the bar didn't want to waste time meant for drinking locating the bathroom. There was no dying parrot nor oracular crazy old woman. I never fell in love there, or did coke off the toilet seat, or even so much as danced to the jukebox. For all those reasons, for a long time I undervalued

I NEVER SANG "CATS" WITH THE BARTENDER, OR DRANK FOR FREE FROM 2 A.M. UNTIL DAWN, OR HAD MY SHOES PISSED ON BECAUSE THE MAN NEXT TO ME AT THE BAR DIDN'T WANT TO WASTE TIME MEANT FOR DRINKING LOCATING THE BATHROOM.

hour the laws of nature and even of gravity seemed not to hold, and adventures were had that were thrilling but squalid, that you retold like exhibiting scars. McHale's wasn't like that. It was, after all, equal part restaurant, renowned for its burger, although in my experience most meals there occurred hours into a night of convivial drinking, to enable the drinking to last that much longer. Yet I never had a binge night at McHale's. I never lost two or ten hours in

McHale's—the Wayne Gretzky hockey stick over the bar, the unremarkable after-work crowd, the squeeze bottle of French's mustard. It was equally close to my office as it was to the subway I took to get home, so that I didn't realize it was worth traveling for because I'd never had to. It didn't occur to me that the seeming ordinariness of its ability to meet my every need, to be just the place that I wanted, one evening after another, was in fact painfully rare, so rare I've never found it anywhere since.

In the late '90s I left my job in midtown, and not long after that I left Manhattan entirely and joined the exodus to Brooklyn. I don't remember the last time I went to McHale's. It wasn't the bar that I sat in the day the Twin Towers came down, or the bar to which my husband and I lugged our newborn son straight from the hospital, tinily strapped in his bulky car seat, so I could have my first postpartum beer. As easily as it entered my life, McHale's—that welcoming ship on calm water and strung with warm lights—slid away.

It was years before I passed by that corner again and realized where I was, facing the cold gray façade of a steel and glass high rise almost laughable in its total adherence to the Death Star architectural style. Before the McHale's building was sold by its landlord to New Jersey developers, who tore it down in 2006 to build luxury condos, McHale's had been run by the McHale family since 1953. The same cook, Italo Huaringa, had been making those mythical burgers for thirty-five years. The bar had come from the 1939 World's Fair. These were facts I hadn't known when I drank there—but no sum of the facts can explain why that place felt like home. Standing there on that sanitized corner, I was sick to my stomach with loss. McHale's had been a club for all of us, and now not just

the physical place, but that very idea, seemed by some selfish power destroyed. I didn't realize how much McHale's mattered until it was gone.

Harry's Bar & Tables
501 Westport Road
Kansas City, Missouri 64111
Paul Shirley

As a kid growing up in small-town Kansas, I loved to read biographies of sportsmen, devouring books about Lou Gehrig and Ted Williams and Jim Brown and Bill Russell. What I gleaned from those pages was that being a professional athlete was a) an attainable goal, if one could throw a baseball 90 miles an hour or dunk a basketball, and b) pretty much the best thing in the world, next to having an entire two-pack of Nutty Bars to oneself. To my young eyes, it appeared that professional sportsmen's lives consisted of playing on the field together, going to dinner together, going for drinks and woman-chasing together, and then doing it all again the next day.

I pretty much expected something similar, if I got to the pros. And then, by some combination of luck and hard work and the right guys tearing the right ligaments at the right times, I did. I played professional basketball for ten years, even clawing my way onto three different NBA teams along the way.

What I saw when I got there was far different from what I'd learned to expect from the Biography section at the Topeka Public Library. Professional athletes turned out to be far more boring than I had hoped. The players knew how important their images were, and they did everything they could to protect those images. The modern professional athlete knows that there are a whole bunch of guys just as talented as he is, so he'd better not fuck up and give them anything like an advantage by appearing in a police blotter or Twitpic. So while you're no doubt hoping I'll say my favorite bar is some club in Los Angeles called Pure or Smoke or Sweat where I went and did some drug you've never even heard of with LeBron James and two members of the Dallas Mavericks dance team, the truth is that my favorite spot to get a beer was a slow, quiet bar in the place I spent my offseasons: Harry's Bar & Tables in Kansas City, Missouri.

Harry's gets my nod because, in a crowded field of contenders—Kansas City is a far better place than most people realize, in part because of its bars and restaurants—it does what I like best about a bar: it makes its patrons feel that, while they are inside the bar, they are a part of a group of like-minded souls who came there to get out of the cold (or the heat, because jeesh it can get hot in Kansas City) and who have now, because of chance or destiny, created an Us that is united against the Them that remains outside. Not because They are worse than We are, because They are not with Us right now. And to be with Us right now is to feel that you will always be with Us, because We are right to be here.

I've always searched for this sense of togetherness—in professional basketball, in the grocery store, in a bar. Nothing makes me feel like an outsider more than being reminded that I am perceived as different, strange, beyond the norm. Maybe because half the population in the Midwest has at least some Nordic blood, at Harry's it is rare that someone pulls me away from the illusion I have about myself, which is that I am just like you, just like her, just like everyone.

To put it more succinctly, at Harry's no one ever asks me how tall I am.

I am six feet, nine inches tall. The fact that I am only three inches shy of seven feet features prominently in approximately 60% of the conversations I have with strangers. People cannot escape from my height. Height is not like claustrophobia or a love for the film oeuvre of Dolph Lundgren. When you see me, you will notice that I am tall. And you will likely say something.

There's the guy in the pasta aisle at my local grocery store who says, "Man, you're tall, how tall are you?"

I answer, "Well, hi, I'm six-foot-nine!" thinking, *OK, good, we've settled THAT.*

But then it happens again the next day, or the next hour, or maybe even over at the deli counter and we're right back to talking about my height.

If my height has this pervasive way of intruding on normal, everyday encounters in sober places like the grocery store, imagine how often people bring it up when they're shitfaced.

Like, let's say I was in a bar back in my playing days. (Which ended all of three years ago; I speak of them like they happened in the Hayes administration.)

A group of people says, "Hey, you're tall. How tall are you?"

I tell them.

They ask the next question, which, more often than not, is "SOOOO, do you play professional basketball?"

I have a choice here. I can say that, yes, I do play professional basketball, and deal with the subsequent conversation, which will feature the person saying, "That must be awesome!" or something similarly profound. But then I will have to give my name, noting in the process that no, they haven't ever heard of me. Or I will have to explain that yes, I know, playing professional basketball sounds fun, but then again you, sir, have never ridden on an overnight bus between Bismarck and Sioux Falls for $700 a week.

Here's where things gets tricky. I spent the bulk of my adult professional life playing basketball for money. I identified with what I did, because that's the only way I knew how to be even reasonably good at it; I had to care deeply about basketball to have a chance of competing with the Kobe Bryants, the Amar'e Stoudemires, even the Brian Scalabrines. But my professional basketball career could only be considered successful like the consummation of an extramarital affair can be considered successful. I did what I set out to do, but I wasn't 100% proud of it. Sure, I was proud I made it to the NBA. I was proud that I'd set out for myself this goal of making money putting a ball in a hoop and then later actually did make money putting a ball in a hoop. But I wasn't a star; usually, I couldn't even hold down a contract for longer than a few months. That caused a fair amount of cognitive dissonance. I wanted to talk to people, but I didn't want to explain my life, because they had preconceptions of what that life was like, and I was going to ruin those preconceptions (much as I've done here), and probably I was just going to end up feeling weird or silly or like I was never going to meet anyone in the world who understood me.

There was, of course, the option to simply lie and say that no, I did not play professional basketball. But then I'd have to suffer some inspired riposte like, "Well, you probably should think about it!"

That would just make me want to set someone's head on fire.

I know what you're thinking: What if she was cute?

To my great chagrin, I learned (after about 100 test cases) that if a girl walked up on me at the bar like I was a microphone and she was Steven Tyler, saying as she did, "Hey, how tall are you?" it usually was not a pickup line. Most of the time, the height question arose from pure curiosity, or because the girl's boyfriend had sent her over to ask. Let me tell you, nothing—I mean NOTHING— is as unsettling in a bar as finding out that the private-school-looking assholes two tables over have been guessing your height for the past twenty minutes.

Even if it was a genuine pickup line and even if she was cute and even if she wasn't falling-down drunk, the sorts of girls who are impressed that one plays professional sports are not usually the girls one wants to impress. In fact, most of the women I met in my playing days were actively turned off by the fact that I played sports for money, because they assumed I had A) herpes, B) an IQ of 85, C) at least four (likely illegitimate) kids, or D) all of the above. This was a particularly devastating realization. I mean, half the reason I started playing basketball in the first place was to get girls!

There are a lot more athletes like me than you might think—guys for whom explaining their life is complicated and confusing and not all that fun and who therefore when asked to choose their favorite bar would, like me, pick a place that was quiet, familiar, and comforting.

A place like Harry's Bar & Tables. A place that's all wood, brass, and understated class, smack dab in the middle of a city no one associates with any of those things. But the thing I love most about Harry's is that I don't have to suffer inquiries about my stature or ruin anyone's day by explaining why being a basketball player wasn't anything like those biographies I read so long ago. At Harry's, people leave me alone. At Harry's, I can create an illusion. At Harry's, I am normal, which is all I ever wanted to be.

WHEN ONE LONGS FOR A DRINK, IT SEEMS
AS THOUGH ONE COULD DRINK A WHOLE
OCEAN—THAT IS FAITH; BUT WHEN ONE
BEGINS TO DRINK, ONE CAN ONLY DRINK
ALTOGETHER TWO GLASSES—THAT IS SCIENCE.

—ANTON CHEKHOV

The Beagle Tavern
1003 E Main Street
Norristown, Pennsylvania 19401
Jennifer Finney Boylan

So there I was in the Beagle, on Drag Trivia night. I forget the names of our hostesses, but it was something like Miss Begotten and Miss Steak. One of them was a professor in the theatre department at Ursinus College, where I was teaching English that semester. His name was Dominick, but he was unrecognizable as Miss Begotten—the wig went up to the ceiling, the sequined hemline went down to the floor.

I sat there with a nice pint of Guinness, doing my best to answer the trivia questions, many of which concerned the lyrics to Broadway musicals I'd never heard of, or involved the details of sex acts I'd never committed.

"And now some questions about rimming!" shouted Miss Begotten. Everyone cheered.

"Uh-oh," said Janet.

I drank my drink.

"Are you okay with this?" Janet asked nervously. I adored Janet, who was married to another one of the Ursinus professors, a guy named Jon whom I also loved. Jon had a single potted ivy plant in his office at the college that, over time,

had grown all around the perimeter of the room and back again. It was a ponderous plant.

As for his wife, she had a beagle that liked to crawl on my head.

"Why wouldn't I be okay with it?" I said, as Miss Begotten and Miss Steak engaged in pornographic banter.

"I don't know," said Janet. "I just want to make sure you're not insulted."

That she was concerned with my feelings at all showed what a kind person she was, to be sure. But it's also true that, if I didn't know Dominick and Janet, I might well have been a little bit antsy. The fact is that, in spite of casting a pretty long shadow as an out transsexual woman, I hadn't spent much time in gay bars over the years. I didn't like the kind of music that got played in such places. I didn't like being in places where the music was so loud you couldn't talk. When I did want to hear tunes, my tastes, I am so sorry to say, run pretty much to the Grateful Dead.

Which, basically, is another way of saying that as a gay person I am something of a failure. It was entirely typical of me that, as Yukon Cornelius said, "Even among misfits, you're misfits."

The fact that I was the only woman in this room of men dressed as women who'd actually gone through transition and become female made things even more complicated.

"Okay," said Miss Begotten. "Now it's time for the parade."

"Uh-oh," said Janet.

The two hostesses handed out plastic trash bags and duct tape, and instructed everyone in the bar to make a costume out of them. The prize for first place was a CD of show tunes.

"What's uh-oh?" I said.

"Just tell me if you're okay with this. I don't want you being embarrassed."

"Why would I be embarrassed?" I asked, and began to make a mini-dress out of the Hefty bag.

The thing is, there's a strange tension between gay men doing drag and actual transsexual women. You don't have to be Einstein to figure it out. On the one hand, you have gay men imitating women, doing the whole performance and social commentary that's the delightful thing about drag. On the other, you have people born into male bodies, who identify as women on a fundamental level, who go through the whole transition in order to be seen as "normal" women, whose identity as females is not about performance or irony. It might have been possible for a stranger to look at Miss Steak and me, and see two people both transgressing gender. But our dreams couldn't have been more different.

"Okay," said Miss Begotten, once our costumes were complete. "Let's start the parade!"

I'd had a couple Guinnesses, but that probably doesn't fully explain what happened next. I had to take off my pants in order to make the trash-bag dress fit. Which I did. And so it came to pass that I found myself marching around The Beagle without any pants, wearing a trash-bag dress and a duct-tape belt as the stereo played Gloria Gaynor.

First I was afraid. I was petrified.

There was another woman behind me in the parade. I don't know what her story was, but offhand she seemed kind of like another soccer mom like me. She was wearing a trash bag, too. She looked at me and smiled and shrugged. "What are you going to do?" she said to me with an air of sweet inevitability, as if marching in a parade wearing a trash bag in a gay bar after your sex change is just one of those things that happens, and you might as well make the best of it.

She looked over at Miss Begotten and Miss Steak. They looked fabulous, in their false eyelashes and sequins.

"They're kind of amazing, aren't they?" she said, and the way she said this to me made it clear that she had no idea that I'd once been a man my own self. In that moment I realized that the reason I felt uneasy was that people might mistake me for a drag performer, and that my identity as a woman might somehow be called into question. But the difference between us was very clear now. Those two men were the beautiful women. I was just some character wearing a trash bag.

"Wouldn't it be nice," the stranger said to me. "To be that beautiful?"

"I guess," I said. "But it would take so much work."

We marched around to Gloria Gaynor. *Oh no, not I. I will survive.* Everyone cheered.

When I got back to the table, Janet had bought me another Guinness. I sat down and took a sip.

"You're sure you're okay with this, Jenny?" she asked me.

"Of course," I said. I was putting my pants back on. Plastic really wasn't the best fabric for me. I thought about the whole ridiculous situation and laughed.

I think it was while I was laughing that I realized that, ten years after first coming out as trans, my transition was finally over. There'd been a time once when I was young that I might well have been mistaken for a gay man doing drag—although my idea of drag back in the 1970s had been peasant skirts and Jerry Garcia T-shirts. It had been a long, strange trip, featuring hormones and a surgeon and a trip to the large-size shoe store, but at last my womanhood was a well-established fact, and nothing could take it away from me—not even a plastic trash-bag dress, not even a beagle on my head.

Miss Begotten came over to our table and kissed Janet, leaving a big pink lipstick mark on her cheek.

"Well, well, well," she said to us. "And how are you ladies doing?"

Stanley's (closed)
551 E 12th Street
New York, New York 10009
Ishmael Reed

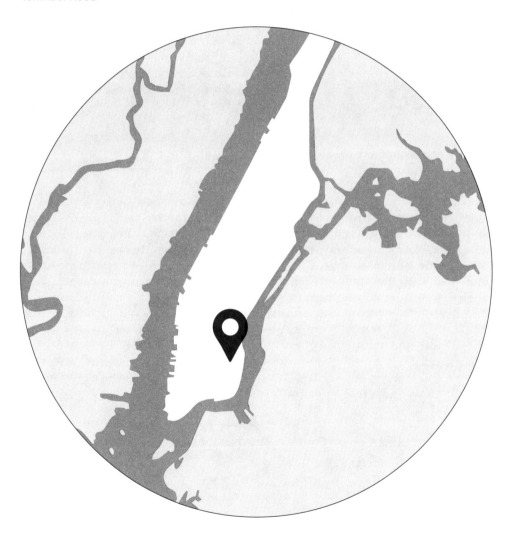

About six months after arriving in New York City from Buffalo, I got an apartment on 6th Street near Avenue B. My friend Harvey Peace III had been one of those students who came to Buffalo, where I grew up, to supplement their income by working at manufacturing jobs during the summer. He was attending Shaw University in Raleigh, North Carolina, a historically black college. He'd later author one of the first books about the civil rights struggle, *The Angry Black South*, published by Ted Wilentz's Corinth Press, which also published Amiri Baraka's *The Dead Lecturer*. Harvey was living a few blocks from my apartment. He introduced me to Stanley's, which became my hangout from that time in 1963 to the time I left New York for Los Angeles in 1967.

It was a watering hole for poets, actors, painters and musicians. The scene was interracial and at the time, integration seemed possible. Southern terrorism soon destroyed that hope and eventually the Lower East Side became polarized, but for the brief moment while it lasted, a collaboration between blacks, whites and Puerto Ricans led to what I have called "a mini Renaissance."

Stanley's was the scene of great highs and lows for me. Highs because I attended Stanley's in the company of two smart and beautiful women, who steered me through a tough time in my life. One was a young Doubleday editor, whom I met during our Umbra Writers Workshop meetings held in the home of poet Tom Dent. The other was an art history major who was completing her studies at NYU. I lived with her for nearly two years. She became an art broker and now lives in Seattle.

After the Umbra meetings, we'd usually go over to Stanley's. Since Tom was working for the NAACP, celebrities would sometimes accompany us. One night, A.D. King, brother of Martin, went drinking with some Umbra members. While I spent a lot of time at Stanley's, I wasn't aware of its history. A 1965 guide to Greenwich Village had this to say about the place:

Stanley's, Avenue B cor 12th St. The grand-daddy of the East Side "in" bars, it's as friendly and warm as Stanley himself. This bar operated wide-open during Depression days. In fact, when Teddy Roosevelt was New York's Police Commissioner, he used to tear up this street in his horse and buggy to rout out his Irish-Democrat cops who had stopped in here for a nip. Stanley unlocks the door to you personally. Downstairs a converted wine cellar is for couples only. Hot sandwiches, 50 cents; beer from 15 cents. 4 p.m.- 4 a.m.

Stanley's was where I met Walter Bowart, who was a bartender at the time. He and I would co-found *The East Village Other,* which I named. It would be one of the first underground newspapers in the country and carried articles by Allen Katzman and myself and cartoons by Spain Rodriguez and Robert Crumb.

In 1977, Ron Sukenick and I founded *The American Book Review,* which I also named. Ron lived across the street from Stanley's. Later in the 1970s, Sukenick and I, while officers of the Coordinating Council of Literary Magazines, helped to launch a multicultural revolution in the small press and literary magazines. Ron was also a chronicler of the Lower East Side. In his book *Down and In: Life in the Underground*, he paints an accurate portrait of Stanley Tolkin, Stanley's proprietor.

> . . . a nervous, modern version of Chaucer's canny host, had cultivated a lumpenintelligentsia clientele whose beards had totally displaced the red noses of indigenous Polack rummies. His name, an arc of small gilt letters, vowels obliterated, smiled from plate glass like the gold teeth of an impoverished immigrant. The bar was an old establishment, and he had taken care to preserve the woodwork and glasswork of the manly, mustachioed nineties. I moved through the beer-laced mist of tobacco smoke to find a place at the bar and asked for an ale . . . one foot on the brass rail and my elbow resting on the bar . . . filled with a comforting sense of assurance that seemed to inhere through the long mass of the bar by virtue of its solidity, by virtue of its age, by the beauty of its wood, by its sheen of long use . . . Stanley liked us.That wasn't why every third beer was free at the beginning. The frequency went down as business went up, but he was still occasionally generous with the regulars. He liked having interesting, educated people as customers. He liked the girls with their new sexy styles.

One night, during one of the worst weeks in my life, I was approached by an angry regular named Mike. He and I had a personal rift about politics; mine were stupid during that period. I remember we had an argument about General Douglas MacArthur, whom he saw as a hero—Mike was a veteran—and whom I saw as a jerk. He approached me while I was sitting with the Doubleday editor and grabbed me by the collar. I hit him on the head with a stein of beer. A German friend of mine, a Trotskyite, who taught me the art of investigative journalism, had told me that beer steins were used as weapons during beer fests, but if it hadn't been the intervention of Ray Johnson, one of those members of the Lower East Side black avant-garde, we might have murdered each other. We ended up in Bellevue Hospital, both bleeding profusely. I had to go to Buffalo that weekend and when I returned I learned that he was looking for me, armed with a lead pipe. The night of my return the Doubleday editor came to my apartment. She had negotiated a truce. I met with Mike at The Annex, a bar that Mickey Ruskin had opened. We became friends after that and when I returned to New York from Berkeley, where I had been teaching at the University of California at Berkeley, he helped me move into an apartment—on Saint Mark's Place.

That was 1970. By then, Stanley's had been replaced by Pee Wee's, which was run by a black proprietor named Emmit C. Walthall. It was a black bar, indicating the breakup of the multiracial coalition downtown. Jazz artist Albert Ayler was a regular and so was novelist Toni Cade Bambara, actress and NPR commentator Verta Mae Grosvenor, actor Walter Cotton and painters Ellsworth Ausby and Algernon Miller. One of the bartenders was Marcus Gorden, founder of the *San Francisco Carnival*. When

Walthall was murdered in his bar in December 1976, I wrote a eulogy that was published in *The New York Times*:

> I used to kid him about being a "capitalist," and he used to kid back. That was before I found out that an independent black businessman or worker threatens the status quo more than those who spend a lot of time saying that they do . . . That's why Pee Wee had to struggle to stay in business. . . . He had to do battle with cops and "inspectors" who pulled every technicality in an attempt to close him down. . . . He had to take it from his own people who'd pull stunts in his bar they'd never attempt in the Plaza Hotel, like this pile of mildewed ---- who went into Pee Wee's that night and shotgunned Pee Wee because he insisted that they pay for their drinks. "I don't give beer away, I sell it," Pee Wee said. I can just see Pee Wee now, saying those words, inhaling from one of those cigars, smiling squint-eyed. That robust frame, big neck filling out his collar. . . . The creeps who did it probably won't serve a year. Pee Wee got life. All the black Pee Wees we keep losing. They get life in a pool of blood.

Some of the Umbra people—writers Charles Patterson, Askia Toure and William Patterson—had moved to Harlem with Amiri Baraka, who before this move had been dubbed

"The Emperor of the Lower East Side" by *The Herald Tribune*. They formed the black separatist Black Repertory Theater in Harlem, which was supported with funds from some of Baraka's downtown white friends and government funds. I returned to California after that final summer and never returned to New York to live.

It took the late Bill Amidon, one of the Stanley regulars, to write a requiem for that time in an essay that has become a classic. Published in *The Village Voice* in August 1972, it was entitled "Where Have All The Hipsters Gone?":

> Talent in New York does have an abstruse way of coming together like that. In '63-'64 at Stanley's (before anybody knew who most of them were) you might have walked in on any given afternoon or evening and encountered writers such as Ishmael Reed, Calvin Hernton, David Henderson, Ron Sukenick, Allen Ginsberg, Tuli Kupferberg, Ed Sanders, and Lennox Raphael; actors like Moses Gunn, Mitch Ryan, Lou Gossett, and Cicely Tyson; musicians such as Odetta, Marion Brown, and Richard Andrews; Khadeja the fashion designer who was Afro before people knew what that meant; Tom Dent, one of the founders of the Free Southern Theatre; Walter Bowart, who tended bar there and later was the original publisher of EVO—and Clark Squire, one of the Panther 21.

Lennox Raphael's play *Che!*, one of the first that included simulated sex, landed him in court. Amidon might have also mentioned such painters as Joe Overstreet, Jack Whitten, Gerald Jackson, Algernon Miller, and Ellsworth Ausby, and the writer Steve Cannon. Amidon also wrote the best book about the Stanley's culture, a novel called *Change*. In it, I'm represented as the character Joshua Woodwind.

I entered New York in 1962 with very little money. I left in 1967 with a contract from Doubleday books, which feted me in French restaurants and geared up the publicity machine that would have made me a token in waiting. Instead, I relocated to Los Angeles and spent a lonely summer working on my second novel, *Yellow Back Radio Broke-Down*, which landed me a thirty-five-year teaching job at the University of California at Berkeley.

Whatever success I've had in the arts, I owe to those five years living in New York. They were hard years, but they were also joyous years. The rents and food were cheap, the men were brilliant, and the women were both brilliant and beautiful. And among our patrons was Stanley Tolkin, who is probably closing a Stanley's in heaven with his famous call, "Time, Gentlemen!"

HUMANITY I LOVE YOU BECAUSE
WHEN YOU'RE HARD UP YOU PAWN YOUR
INTELLIGENCE TO BUY A DRINK

—E.E. CUMMINGS

Raccoon's
3240 Lithia Pinecrest Road
Valrico, Florida
Alissa Nutting

On any given week, I usually visit one or two of what I refer to as "lowercase-b bars." These are bars where I do not consume much alcohol. Sometimes it's business when I'm traveling, other times it's part of an evening and it feels more like a fine-dining experience than anything else. Craft cocktails with lavender. Microbrew IPAs so deliciously hoppy they numb your tongue. Such bars feel like extramarital affairs to me: they're pretty to look at and always hold new offerings, something I haven't tried before, but I could never settle down with them. When I go to these bars, I'm a particular version of me: I have on an opaque professional exoskeleton that (hopefully) somewhat conceals my dog-hair-covered-bath-robe-wearing proclivities, my preference for cursing when it's least required ("I fucking love this new toothpaste"), my ungovernable passion for fast food. At lowercase-b bars, I'm dressed up. I am likely wearing a Spanx bodysuit. I'm not going to be getting intoxicated—undergarments with enthusiastic spandex and frequent urination do not mix. While it's fun to have a drink or two there, it's clear no deeper bond is going to form between us. For one, there's no room for an unhealthy codependence to form, because *they don't need me.* They are sleek and flashy and classier than I ever could be, even with Spanx pulling my gut in and my sailor mouth censored. They don't need me? Well, I don't need them. I will drink their cocktails because they are tasty and I will pay more than I wish I had to pay for the privilege of doing so. Need, though, doesn't factor into it.

Here's what I do need, in a "capital-B Bar" and in all things really: openness. I want it to feel like it's okay with the establishment that I'm not trying to look like a woman on the cover of a magazine when I walk inside. Actually, you know, let's dial it down a little further: I want it to feel okay that I didn't brush my hair. I think I've always had my hair brushed when I've gone to Raccoon's, but that's not the point. They would serve me with non-brushed hair. They would serve me with day-old mascara that is smudged all over my eyes. In fact, this would allow me to make a joke about the affinity of my own appearance and that of their namesake animal mascot, allow me to bond with Raccoon's even further. I should add that their karaoke experience is unafraid of the tambourine—there's usually one there for you to shake the hell out of. It's just another indicator that you don't have to hold back when you're inside.

Raccoon's is located in a suburban stucco strip mall in sunny Florida. You can look out its tinted windows and see families going to get ice cream after little-league games. The plaza holds a dentist, a hairstyling academy, a Chinese restaurant, a gym, a realtor, and a pet groomer, amongst other businesses. Raccoon's does not announce itself. You know where to find it, and you do, and if you want to visit a pool supply store before or after, there is one in the plaza for your convenience. Visiting it is not an event you must prepare for. You don't have to change out of your sweatpants. You just enter.

Oftentimes, you stay. Their beer menu prioritizes being able to drink cheaply for hours over taste. Raccoon's has beer-bucket specials starting at 9:30 am. I mean, on a Tuesday morning. This singular fact would qualify it as my favorite bar all on its own. I don't know the average stay of a typical Raccoon's customer; I haven't performed any type of quantitative study, but I would clock mine in at about four-and-a-half hours. I don't go to have a top-shelf experience; I go to have a human experience.

I officially dubbed Raccoon's my favorite bar in the world one Christmas Eve in my early twenties. First of all, it was really late Christmas Eve, I guess Christmas morning, and yet they were still open. People inside were in all kinds of shape—the holidays can be pretty rough. Some were deliriously giddy; others were clearly just trying to hold on. (Suburban misery is one of the darkest forces on earth, which is another reason Raccoon's does so much good in its location.) But we were *together*, we were a group, and here was Christmas again, and we'd made it. Raccoon's promotes community and provides freedom of expression: you can begin crying or singing at any time, at nearly any volume, and rather than being asked to leave others will come join you, and vice versa. That's the bargain you make when you enter Raccoon's, the gift you give to others and receive in return: *I will engage with you in a friendly and affable manner, because we are both here to find a more accepting place than the world beyond these doors.*

It was a really odd feeling to know that I could say or do almost anything, and as long as I wasn't hurting myself or others, it would be accepted. Say you're twenty-two and you're a female and you're not so sure about your worth in the world. You're getting messages from the media and television telling you that if you want to be successful you need to look like *this*, but you don't look like *this*. Messages saying that you need to act like *this*, and you don't want to act like *this*. What you don't see a lot of in the media are kind women in their forties and fifties who haven't been worried about looking like *this* or acting like *this* for a long time, because they've been living their lives and didn't have the time or interest, and guess what: they are spunky and amazing and exactly the type of woman I wanted to know I could grow into. You don't see much of the other paths. You have no idea—I had no idea, at least—the freedoms you can have to go your own way if you can summon the strength to not care what the wrong people think.

When you're twenty-two, it can be hard to meet a broad range of forty- and fifty-year-old women who are open to having long and very confessional conversations with you. Our society is big on mentorship when it comes to children, even teens, but suddenly you're twenty-two and you're beginning to notice how limited the characters and roles given to fifty-year-old women in the movies and on television are. It seems like the best you can hope for is to be a tastefully dressed woman who spends a lot of time in the Botox chair and is careful not to flaunt her sexuality. I didn't want this. I *don't* want this. I want my roar to grow louder as I age. I want to age into audacity. (I don't wear bikinis now, but I plan on never taking them off the moment I hit seventy.) I want to get older and wear way too much eye makeup, go the powder-blue monochromatic full-lid route, occasionally adding some clumping mascara. I don't want to have a lot of need for the beauty tips in magazines. I want to know how to gracefully smoke on crutches.

Where do you find these women who can show you a different model for yourself? Who wear lace leopard-print shirts and place kind hands on your shoulder? Who remind you that, "Those bastards can only break your spirit if you let them?"

At Raccoon's. That's where.

Raccoon's is like an alcohol-infused Big Brothers/ Big Sisters program, except the kids are adults and the adults are older adults. That Christmas Eve night and over the years that followed, I found surrogate mothers there, women who didn't judge the jagged path I was taking toward becoming a writer. Who didn't care how much I dropped the f-bomb because they dropped it even more. Who affirmed I was okay when I really needed it most.

I'm thirty-two now. It's been a decade since I first fell in love with Raccoon's. I make it a point to go there whenever I'm visiting "home" in central Florida. As I move toward forty, then fifty, I hope I can be one of the women in the bar who are in the business of encouraging and saving the spirits of younger women, who will talk with them openly, and who will listen, usually completely anonymously. I don't know the names of any of the kind women who inspired me and listened to me and gave me real-world advice, but I'll never forget their words. There's the famous line from the theme song of *Cheers*: "Sometimes you wanna go where everybody knows your name." Well, no. I don't, really. I want to go where my name isn't important, and neither is anyone else's. For me, that place is my beloved Raccoon's.

MIKE ALBO is a writer and performer living and loving in Brooklyn. He is the author of the novels *Hornito* and *The Underminer: The Best Friend Who Casually Destroys Your Life* (co-written with Virginia Heffernan), as well as the novella *The Junket*. He's performed all over the U.S. and Canada as well as in London, Copenhagen and on top of a bar in Paris. Solo shows include *Mike Albo, Mike Albo: Spray, Please Everything Burst, My Price Point,* and *The Junket*. His essays, fiction, poetry, nonfiction, plays, and humor appear in numerous magazines, anthologies and websites, including *The Show I'll Never Forget*, also edited by Sean Manning. Twitter and Instagram: @albomike, Facebook: Mike Albo.

ROSECRANS BALDWIN is the author of *Paris, I Love You but You're Bringing Me Down* and *You Lost Me There.*

BILL BARICH's books include *Crazy for Rivers, A Pint of Plain, Carson Valley,* and the racetrack classic *Laughing in the Hills*. He currently lives in Dublin, Ireland.

MADISON SMARTT BELL is a critically acclaimed writer of more than a dozen novels and story collections, as well as numerous essays and reviews for publications such as *Harper's* and *The New York Times Book Review*. His books have been finalists for both the National Book Award and the PEN/Faulkner Award, among other honors.

FRANK BILL has been published in *Granta, Playboy, The Oxford American, The New York Times, The Daily Beast, PANK,* FSG Work in Progress, *New Haven Review, Talking River Review, Plots With Guns, Thuglit, Beat to a Pulp* and many other outlets. His first book, *Crimes in Southern Indiana*, was released by Farrar, Straus & Giroux in September 2011 and his first novel, *Donnybrook*, hit March of 2013. He is currently at work on the follow up, *The Salvaged & The Savage,* and his reboot of James O'Barr's *The Crow* hit comic book stores in March 2014.

WILL BLYTHE is the author of *To Hate Like This Is to Be Happy Forever*. His work has appeared in *The New York Times, Esquire, Rolling Stone, The New Republic, Sports Illustrated, Elle,* and other publications. His fiction and sportswriting have been anthologized in *Best American Short Stories* and *Best American Sportswriting*. He lives on City Island in the Bronx.

SHANI BOIANJIU was born in Jerusalem in 1987. She served in the Israeli Defense Forces for two years. Her fiction has appeared in *The New Yorker, Vice,* and *Zoetrope: All Story*. She is the author of the novel *The People of Forever Are Not Afraid* and is the youngest recipient ever of the National Book Foundation's "5 Under 35" award. She lives in Israel.

JENNIFER FINNEY BOYLAN is the author of ten books, including her 2003 memoir *She's Not There*, one of the first bestselling works by a transgender American. Her nonfiction has appeared on the op-ed pages of *The New York Times* and in *GQ, Allure, Glamour,* and *Condé Nast Traveler*. A three-time guest of *The Oprah Winfrey Show*, she has twice appeared on *Larry King Live* as well as on the *Today* show. She has been the subject of a documentary on CBS News' *48 Hours*, and in the spring of 2007, she played herself on several episodes of ABC's *All My Children*. She has also been parodied with eerie accuracy by Will Forte on *Saturday Night Live*. Since 1988, she has been a professor of English at Colby College in Waterville, Maine.

KEVIN CANTY's seventh book, a novel called *Everything*, was published by Nan A. Talese/Doubleday in summer 2010. He is also the author of three previous collections of short stories (*Where the Money Went, Honeymoon,* and *A Stranger In This World*) and three novels (*Nine Below Zero, Into the Great Wide Open,* and *Winslow In Love*). His short stories have appeared in the *New Yorker, Esquire, Tin House, GQ, Glimmer Train, Story, The New England Review* and elsewhere; essays and articles in *Vogue, Details, Playboy, The New York Times* and *The Oxford American*, among many others. His work has been translated into French, Dutch, Spanish, German, Polish, Italian and English. He lives and writes in Missoula, Montana.

OSCAR CÁSARES is the author of the collection *Brownsville* and the novel *Amigoland*, which have earned him fellowships from the National Endowment for the Arts, the Copernicus Society of America, and the Texas Institute of Letters. His essays have appeared in *Texas Monthly, The New York Times*, and on National Public Radio. Since 2004, he has taught creative writing at the University of Texas at Austin, where he also currently directs The New Writers Project, the MFA program in the Department of English.

EMILY CHENOWETH is the author of the novel *Hello Goodbye*, which was a finalist for the Oregon Book Award and was named one of the top ten Northwest books of 2009 by *The Oregonian*. As a ghostwriter, she has penned seven young adult novels, one of which was a #1 *New York Times* bestseller. Her most recent novel is *First Love*, which she coauthored with James Patterson under the pen name Emily

Raymond. A former English teacher in Iowa and book reviews editor in New York City, Emily moved to Portland in 2005, where she has taught fiction workshops at Portland State University and Literary Arts.

SUSAN CHOI is the author of four novels. Her first novel, *The Foreign Student,* won the Asian-American Literary Award for fiction. Her second novel, *American Woman,* was a finalist for the 2004 Pulitzer Prize. Her third novel, *A Person of Interest,* was a finalist for the 2009 PEN/Faulkner Award. In 2010 she was named the inaugural recipient of the PEN/W.G. Sebald Award. Her most recent novel is *My Education.* She lives in Brooklyn, New York, with her husband, Pete Wells, and their sons.

KATE CHRISTENSEN is the author of six novels, including *The Epicure's Lament* and *The Great Man,* which won the 2008 PEN/Faulkner Award for Fiction. Her most recent book is *Blue Plate Special: An Autobiography of My Appetites.* Her essays and reviews have appeared in many publications, and her food-centric blog can be found at katechristensen.wordpress.com. She lives in Portland, Maine.

CRAIG DAVIDSON was born and grew up in St. Catharines, Ontario, near Niagara Falls. He has published four books of literary fiction: *Rust and Bone* (which was made into

an Oscar-nominated feature film of the same name), *The Fighter, Sarah Court,* and *Cataract City.* Davidson is a graduate of the Iowa Writers' Workshop, and his articles and journalism have been published in the *National Post, Esquire, GQ, The Walrus,* and *The Washington Post,* among other places. He lives in Toronto, Canada, with his partner and their child.

JANINE DI GIOVANNI is a contributing editor to *Vanity Fair,* where her work has received a National Magazine Award. She writes for the British, American, and French press, and has reported from Afghanistan, Iraq, Israel, Algeria, Gaza, the West Bank, Zimbabwe, Rwanda, Pakistan, East Timor, Ivory Coast, Bosnia, Kosovo, Liberia, Somalia, Nigeria, and Sierra Leone. She is the author of *Madness Visible, The Quick and the Dead, The Place at the End of the World, Ghosts by Daylight,* and of the introduction to the international bestseller *Zlata's Diary: A Child's Life in Sarajevo.* Two documentaries have been made about her life and work. In 2010, she was the president of the jury of the Prix Bayeux-Calvados for War Correspondents. She lives in Paris.

JOSH EMMONS has published two novels, *The Loss of Leon Meed* and *Prescription for a Superior Existence,* and is at work on a third. His fiction and nonfiction have appeared in *ZYZZYVA, Ecotone, The American Scholar,*

The New York Times Book Review, Esquire and elsewhere. He lives in Philadelphia with his wife, poet Katie Ford, and daughter, Maggie.

DAN FANTE is the author of the novels *Point Doom, 86'd, Chump Change,* and *Mooch;* the short story collection, *Short Dog;* two books of poetry; and the plays *The Boiler Room* and *Don Giovanni.* Born and raised in Los Angeles, he lives in Arizona with his wife and son.

CRAIG FINN is a songwriter and performer. He fronts the rock-and-roll band The Hold Steady and formerly sang for Lifter Puller. Originally from Minneapolis, he now lives in Brooklyn.

WILL FIRTH was born in 1965 in Newcastle, Australia. He studied German and Slavic languages in Canberra, Zagreb, and Moscow. Since 1991 he has been living in Berlin, Germany, where he works as a freelance translator of literature and the humanities. He translates from Russian, Macedonian, and all variants of Serbo-Croat.

TOM FRANKLIN wrote the story collection *Poachers,* the title novella of which won the Edgar Award and appeared in *Best American Mystery Stories of the Century* and *Best American Noir Stories of the Century.* He has written three novels: *Hell at the Breech, Smonk,* and *Crooked Letter, Crooked Letter,* which won the *Los Angeles Times* Book Award for Mystery/Thriller, UK's Golden Dagger Award for Best Novel and the Willie Morris Prize in Southern Fiction. Most recently Franklin has co-written a novel, *The Tilted World,* with his wife, poet Beth Ann Fennelly. They live in Oxford, Mississippi, with their three children, and both teach in the University of Mississippi MFA program.

DAVID HAJDU is the music critic for *The New Republic* and the author of four books of nonfiction and criticism, including *Lush Life* and *Positively 4th Street.* He is a professor at the Graduate School of Journalism at Columbia University, and he is working now on a history of popular music in America.

BENJAMIN HALE is the author of the novel *The Evolution of Bruno Littlemore* (Twelve, 2011) and the forthcoming story collection *The Minus World* (Simon & Schuster, 2015). He is the recipient of the Bard Fiction Prize, a Michener-Copernicus Award, and was nominated for the Dylan Thomas Prize and the New York Public Library's Young Lions Fiction Award. He has taught at the University of Iowa, Sarah Lawrence College, and the University of California at Berkeley. His fiction and nonfiction have appeared, among other places, in *Conjunctions, Harper's, The New York Times, The Washington Post, Dissent,* and *The Millions.* He is a contributing editor of *Conjunctions* and currently teaches writing and literature at Bard College.

PHIL HANRAHAN is the author of the football book *Life After Favre*. He has taught writing, worked for Oxford University Press and Zola Books, served as media aide to a former presidential candidate, and teamed with an Emmy-winning director on a documentary film about a journey through the Canadian Arctic's legendary Northwest Passage. Educated at Middlebury College, Oxford University, and Duke, he currently lives in New York City.

HEATHER HAVRILESKY (@hhavrilesky) is a columnist for *The Awl* and *Bookforum*, and is a regular contributor to *The New York Times Magazine*. She is the author of the memoir *Disaster Preparedness* (Riverhead, 2011).

JACK HITT writes for *The New York Times Magazine* and *The New Yorker*. His book, *Off the Road: A Modern-Day Walk Down the Pilgrim's Route into Spain,* was made into a 2012 motion picture, *The Way,* directed by Emilio Estévez and starring Martin Sheen. A radio piece for *This American Life* about the prison in Guantanamo, entitled "Habeas Schmabeas," earned a Peabody Award. He has won the Livingston and Pope Awards, and most recently, his *Harper's* report on American anthropology was selected for a collection of the best science writing of the past 25 years, *The Best of the Best of American Science Writing.* His work also appears in *Rolling Stone, Wired* and *Garden & Gun*. His one-man show, *Making Up the Truth*, ran at the Public Theater in New York in November 2012, and his latest book, *Bunch of Amateurs: A Search for the American Character,* was recently released in paperback.

LAURA LIPPMAN is an award-winning crime writer who has published 19 novels, a novella and a book of short stories. Her latest novel, *After I'm Gone,* was published in February 2014. She lives in Baltimore and New Orleans.

SEAN MANNING is the author of the memoir *The Things That Need Doing* and the editor of four nonfiction anthologies: *The Show I'll Never Forget: 50 Writers Relive Their Most Memorable Concertgoing Experience; Rock and Roll Cage Match: Music's Greatest Rivalries, Decided; Top of the Order: 25 Writers Pick Their Favorite Baseball Player of All Time;* and *Bound to Last: 30 Writers on Their Most Cherished Book.* He has written for *Playboy, Esquire.com, The Village Voice, USA Today, Deadspin, The Awl,* and United Airlines' *Rhapsody,* where he works as executive editor. He lives in Brooklyn, New York.

MALACHY McCOURT has written several books, including the best-selling *A Monk Swimming,*

Singing Him My Song, Danny Boy, Voices of Ireland, and *The Claddagh Ring*. Complementing his literary work, McCourt is also a skilled actor. He appeared in the television series *Oz* and in feature films such as *The Bonfire of the Vanities*. He lives in New York City.

DUFF McKAGAN played bass for Guns N' Roses for twelve years and co-wrote many of their most iconic songs. He formed Velvet Revolver with his former bandmate Slash and fronts his own band, Loaded. He has written weekly columns for Seattleweekly.com and ESPN.com, and his 2011 memoir *It's So Easy (And Other Lies)* was a *New York Times* bestseller. He lives in Seattle with his wife, supermodel Susan Holmes McKagan, and their two daughters.

JOE MENO is a fiction writer and playwright who lives in Chicago. A winner of the Nelson Algren Award, a Pushcart Prize, and a finalist for the Story Prize, he is the author of six novels and two short story collections including *The Great Perhaps, The Boy Detective Fails,* and *Hairstyles of the Damned*. His latest is *Office Girl.*

AZADEH MOAVENI is a former Middle East correspondent for *Time* who spent over a decade covering political conflict, youth movements, and war from Egypt to Afghanistan. She is the author of *Lipstick Jihad* and *Honeymoon in Tehran*, and co-author, with Nobel Peace Laureate Shirin Ebadi, of *Iran Awakening.*

MITCH MOXLEY has written for *The Atlantic, The New York Times, The Wall Street Journal, Time* and elsewhere. He is the author of *Apologies of My Censor: The High and Low Adventures of a Foreigner in China,* about the six years he lived in Beijing. He is currently based in New York.

ALISSA NUTTING is author of the novel *Tampa* (Ecco/HarperCollins, 2013) and the short story collection *Unclean Jobs for Women and Girls* (Starcherone/Dzanc, 2010), which won the Starcherone Prize for Innovative Fiction judged by Ben Marcus. Her fiction has appeared in publications such as *The Norton Introduction to Literature, Tin House, BOMB,* and *Conduit.* Her essays have appeared in *Fence, The New York Times, O: The Oprah Magazine,* and other venues.

KAREN OLSSON's second novel will be published by Farrar, Straus and Giroux in 2015. Her journalism has appeared in *The New York Times Magazine, Texas Monthly,* and other magazines. She lives in Austin, Texas, with her family.

JACK PENDARVIS lives in Oxford, Mississippi. He is the staff writer for the TV show *Adventure Time.*

ROBERT PERISIĆ is a bestselling author in his home country of Croatia. He came to prominence during the 1990s, writing with a clear anti-war sentiment. Today, he is considered one of the most important writers and journalists in the country. He has published award-winning nonfiction, fiction, poetry, and criticism in his native language. *Our Man In Iraq*, the first of his novels to be translated in English, was published in 2013 by Black Balloon Publishing. He currently lives in Zagreb, Croatia.

NEAL POLLACK is the author of eight books of fiction and nonfiction, including the best-selling memoirs *Alternadad* and *Stretch*, the cult classic *The Neal Pollack Anthology of American Literature,* and the novels *Jewball* and *Downward-Facing Death*. He's contributed to every English-language publication except for *The New Yorker*. Pollack lives in Austin, Texas, with his wife and son.

BUZZ POOLE has written about books, design, art, and culture for numerous outlets, including *Print, The Village Voice, The Believer, Los Angeles Review of Books*, and *The Millions*. He is the author of the story collection *I Like to Keep My Troubles on the Windy Side of Things;* the *New Statesman* named his examination of unexpected iconography, *Madonna of the Toast,* one of 2007's Best Underground Books.

SCOTT RAAB is a graduate of Cleveland State University and the University of Iowa's Writers' Workshop. An *Esquire* magazine Writer-at-Large since 1997, he's also the author of *The Whore of Akron: One Man's Search for the Soul of LeBron James.*

ISHMAEL REED is an essayist, novelist, poet, and playwright whose numerous honors include a MacArthur Fellowship and nominations for the Pulitzer Prize and National Book Award. His works include *Mumbo Jumbo, Flight to Canada, Airing Dirty Laundry, Barack Obama and the Jim Crow Media,* and *Juice*. A former professor at the University of California at Berkeley as well as at Harvard, Yale, and Dartmouth, he lives in Oakland, California.

ADAM ROSS lives in Nashville with his wife and two daughters. His debut novel, *Mr. Peanut*, a 2010 *New York Times* Notable Book, was also named one of the best books of the year by *The New Yorker, The Philadelphia Inquirer, The New Republic,* and *The Economist.* It has been published in 16 countries. *Ladies and Gentlemen*, his short story collection, was included in Kirkus Reviews Best Books of 2011 and included "In the Basement," a finalist for the BBC's 2012 International Story Award. His nonfiction has been published in *The New York Times Book Review, The Daily Beast, The Wall Street Journal*, and *The Nashville Scene.*

His fiction has appeared in *The Carolina Quarterly* and *FiveChapters*. A 2013-2014 Hodder Fellow at Princeton University, he is currently working on a novel.

DAVY ROTHBART is the author of the essay collection *My Heart Is an Idiot*—named a Best Book of the Year by *Vanity Fair, Chicago Tribune, The Huffington Post,* and NPR—and the story collection *The Lone Surfer of Montana, Kansas*. He is also the author of the national bestseller *Found* and creator of the magazine of the same name. A contributor to public radio's *This American Life*, he lives in Ann Arbor, Michigan.

JAMES SALLIS has published fifteen novels including the Lew Griffin series, *Drive*, and *The Killer Is Dying*, plus multiple collections of stories, poems and essays; the standard biography of Chester Himes; three books of musicology; and a translation of Raymond Queneau's novel *Saint Glinglin*. He has received a lifetime achievement award from Bouchercon, the Hammett Award for literary excellence in crime writing, and the Grand Prix de Littérature policière. His latest novel is *Others of My Kind*. A retrospective, *Black Night's Gonna Catch Me Here: Selected Poems 1968-2012,* is due this year.

ROSIE SCHAAP writes the "Drink" column for *The New York Times Magazine*, and is the author of *Drinking With Men: A Memoir.* She has also been a bartender, a fortuneteller, a librarian at a paranormal society, an English teacher, an editor, a preacher, a community organizer, and a manager of homeless shelters. A contributor to *This American Life,* she is currently working on a book about whiskey.

ELISSA SCHAPPELL is the author of two books of fiction, most recently *Blueprints for Building Better Girls,* which was chosen as one of the Best Books of the Year by *The San Francisco Chronicle, The Boston Globe, The Wall Street Journal, Newsweek/Daily Beast and O Magazine*, and *Use Me*, a *Los Angeles Times* Best Book of the Year, a *New York Times* Notable Book, and runner-up for the PEN/Hemingway award. She is co-editor of two anthologies, *The Friend Who Got Away* and *Money Changes Everything*. Her fiction, nonfiction and criticism have appeared in many publications including *The Paris Review, The New York Times Book Review, SPIN, BOMB, One Story*, and anthologies such as *The Mrs. Dalloway Reader, Bound to Last, The Future Dictionary of America, Cooking and Stealing* and *The KGB Reader*. A former Senior Editor at *The Paris Review* and a Founding editor, now Editor-at-Large of *Tin House* magazine, she teaches in the MFA program at Columbia and in the low-residency program at Queens in North Carolina. She lives in Brooklyn.

JIM SHEPARD is the author of six novels, including *Project X*, and four story collections, including *You Think That's Bad*. His third collection, *Like You'd Understand, Anyway*, was a finalist for the National Book Award and won The Story Prize. *Project X* won the 2005 Library of Congress/Massachusetts Book Award for Fiction, as well as the ALEX Award from the American Library Association. His short fiction has appeared in, among other magazines, *Harper's, McSweeney's, The Paris Review, The Atlantic Monthly, Esquire, DoubleTake, The New Yorker, Granta, Zoetrope: All-Story,* and *Playboy*, and he was a columnist on film for *The Believer*. Four of his stories have been chosen for the *Best American Short Stories* and one for a Pushcart Prize. He's won an Artists' Grant from the Massachusetts Cultural Council and a Guggenheim Fellowship. He teaches at Williams College and lives in Williamstown with his wife Karen, his three children, and two beagles.

PAUL SHIRLEY wrote *Can I Keep My Jersey?: 11 Teams, 5 Countries, and 4 Years in My Life as a Basketball Vagabond*. He is at work on his second book, whose title, he promises, will not be so long.

DARIN STRAUSS is the internationally-bestselling author of the novels *Chang & Eng, The Real McCoy,* and *More Than It Hurts You* as well as the National Book Critics Circle Award-winning memoir *Half a Life*. A recipient of the Guggenheim Fellowship, the American Library Association Award, and numerous other prizes, he has recently been named an opinion columnist at Al-Jazeera America and is the Clinical Associate Professor of Fiction at NYU's creative writing program. His work has been translated into fourteen languages and published in nineteen countries.

HUNTER R. SLATON is a magazine editor and writer who hopes one day to make it back to Antarctica. He lives in Brooklyn.

KATY ST. CLAIR writes the TV column "Kill Your Television" for the *SF Weekly*, where previously she wrote the nightlife column "Bouncer" for ten years.

DAVID TREUER is an Ojibwe Indian from Leech Lake Reservation in northern Minnesota. He is the author of three novels and a book of criticism. Most recently he published *Rez Life: An Indian's Journey Through the Land of His People* with Grove/Atlantic. His essays and stories have appeared in *Esquire, TriQuarterly, The Washington Post, The New York Times*, the *Los Angeles Times*, and *Slate*.

J. MAARTEN TROOST is the author of *The Sex Lives of Cannibals, Getting Stoned with Savages, Lost On Planet China,* and *Headhunters On My*

Doorstep. He lives with his wife and two sons in Washington, D.C.

ANDREW W.K. is the KING OF PARTYING—infamous for his bloody nose, famous for his high-life attitude, beloved for his extremely energetic rock-and-roll music, he is currently at work on a book titled *The Party Bible*, which will be published by Simon & Schuster.

EDITH ZIMMERMAN is the founding editor of *The Hairpin.* She's written for *The New York Times Magazine, GQ, Elle, The Awl,* and *This American Life.*

ACKNOWLEDGMENTS

The editor thanks the following people for their help and encouragement. They are listed here with their favorite bars:

Jami Supsic
Walter Foods
Brooklyn, New York

James Rickman
The Rush Inn
Santa Cruz, California

James Manning
The Diamond Grille
Akron, Ohio

Judith Ley
Papa Joe's
Akron, Ohio

Elizabeth Koch
The Why Not
Wichita, Kansas

Barbara Cleveland Bourland
The Barbary
Philadelphia, Pennsylvania

Janna Rademacher
Colorado Boy
Ridgway, Colorado

Lori Shine
Bodegas Castaneda
Granada, Spain

Leigh Newman
Club Paris
Anchorage, Alaska

Arvind Dilawar
Cain's Tavern
Brooklyn, New York

Freddie Moore
Mission Dolores
Brooklyn, New York

Ryan DeShon
The Violet Hour
Chicago, Illinois

Michelle King
Sweetwater Tavern
Boston, Massachusetts

Adina Applebaum
The Woods
Brooklyn, New York